night raphy

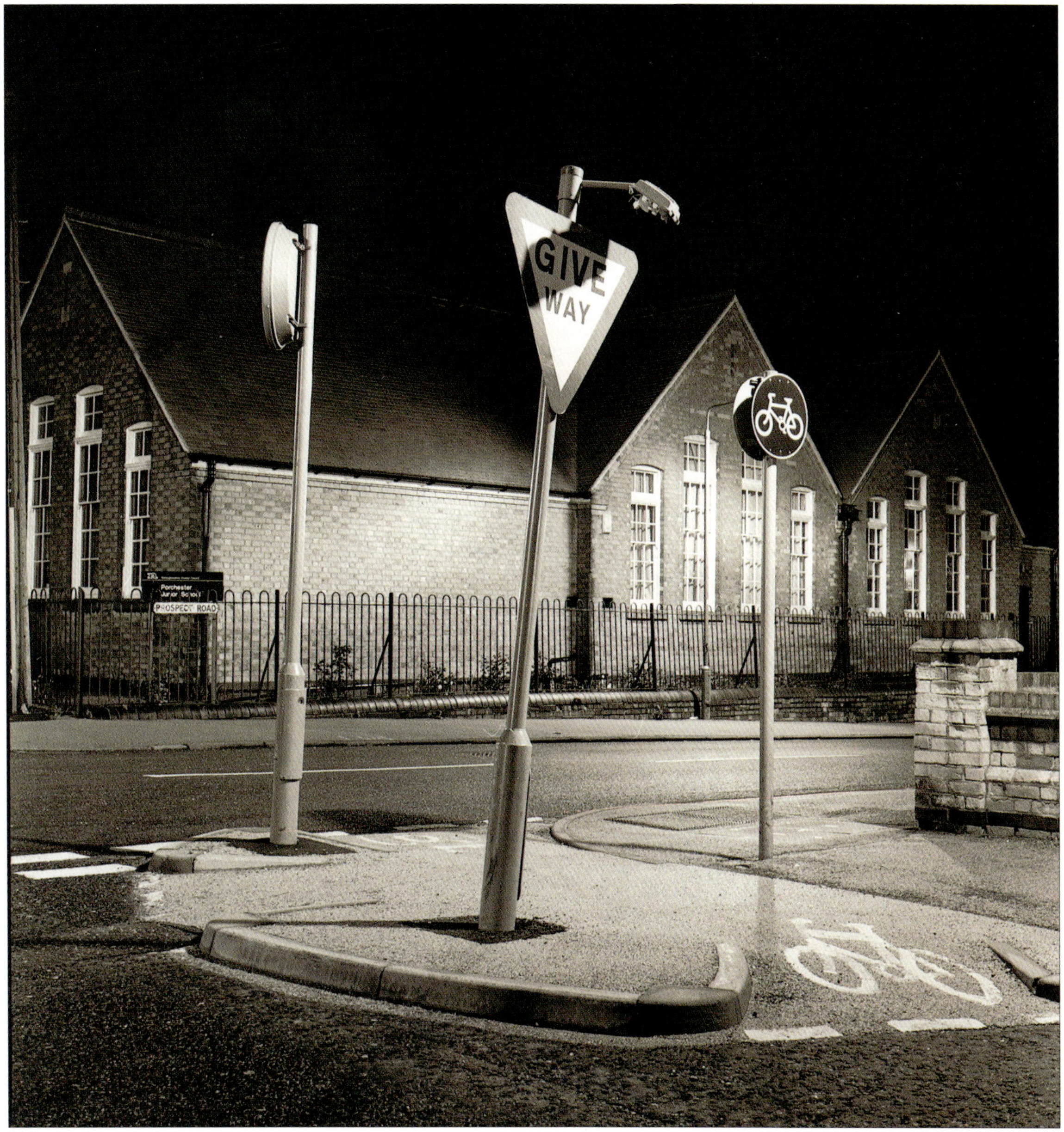

ANDREW SANDERSON

argentum

First published 2001 by Argentum, an imprint of
Aurum Press Ltd, 25 Bedford Avenue, London, WC1B 3AT.

A catalogue record for this book is available from the British Library.

ISBN 1 902538 12 9

Origination – Graphic Ideas, London, N1.
Printed in Singapore by Imago.

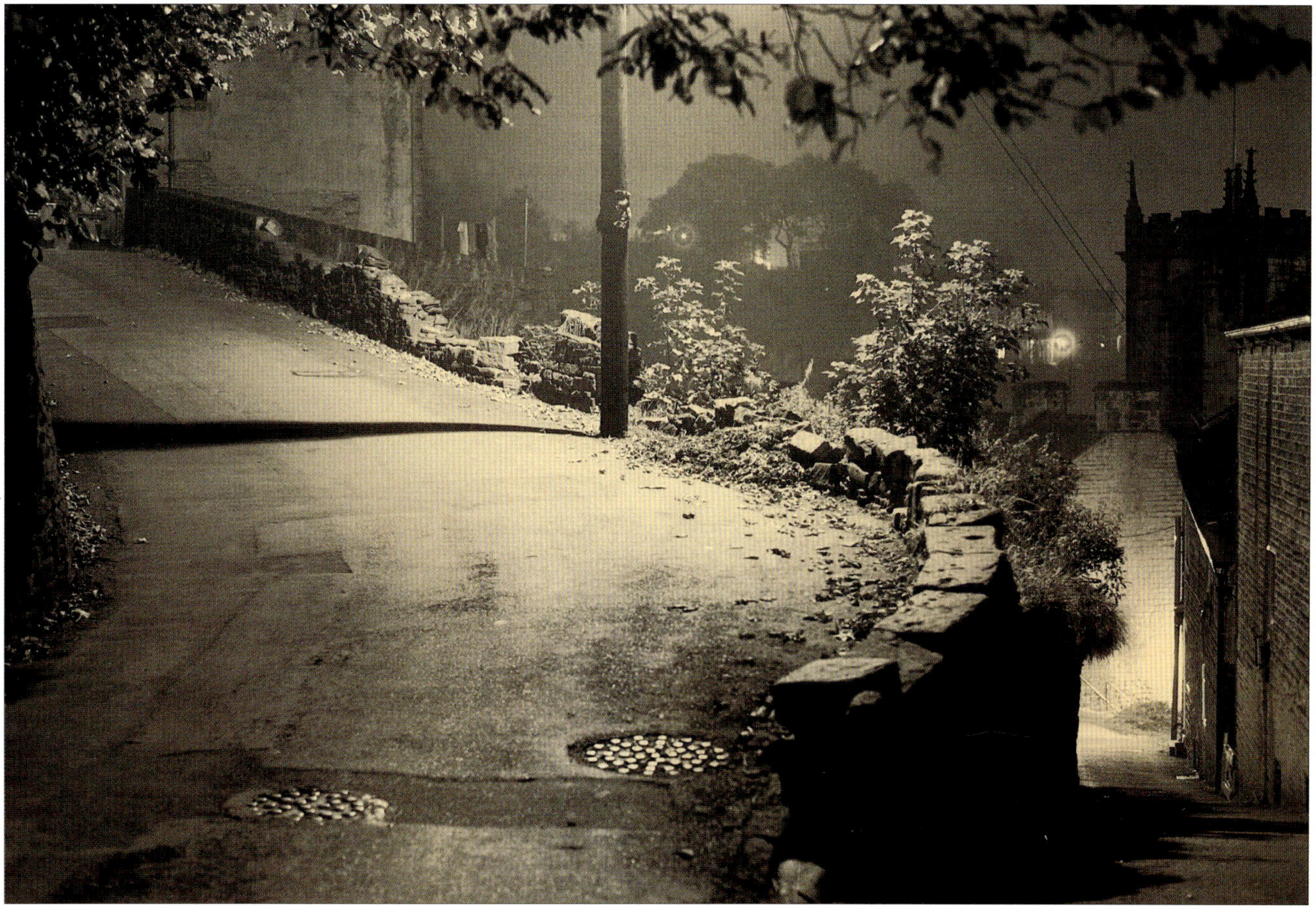

For; Debbie, Alice, Will, and Lily.

With thanks and appreciation to;
Mum and Dad, Ian, Thrin, Pam, Vid,
Derek, Sarah and Christine.

Special thanks to Eddie Ephraums,
Chris Dickie and Tony Worobiec for permission to
reproduce formulae and tables, and much appreciation to
Gordon Hutchings for his research into pyro.

I would also like to thank Ilford Imaging, Kentmere and
Polaroid UK for their kind support.

contents

Introduction 6

The basics 8
Where should I go? 11
Ideal conditions 13
What makes a great night photograph? 13
Equipment 14

The technical stuff 20
Street lighting types 20
Film speed and its relation to exposure 20
Film types 24
Reciprocity failure 25
Choice of format 27
Metering light levels at night 29
Bracketing 30
Flare/Halation 34
Bracketing 35

The fancy stuff 40
Supplementary lighting 40
Using fill in flash 40
Painting with light 42
Shooting in snow/fog 42
Shooting in colour 58
Other possibilities 61
Handheld night photographs 63
Exposing by moonlight 64
Deciding on an exposure 69

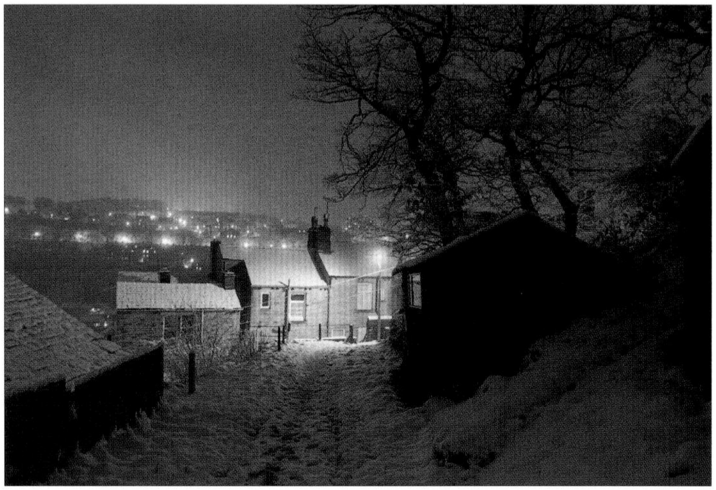

Snow

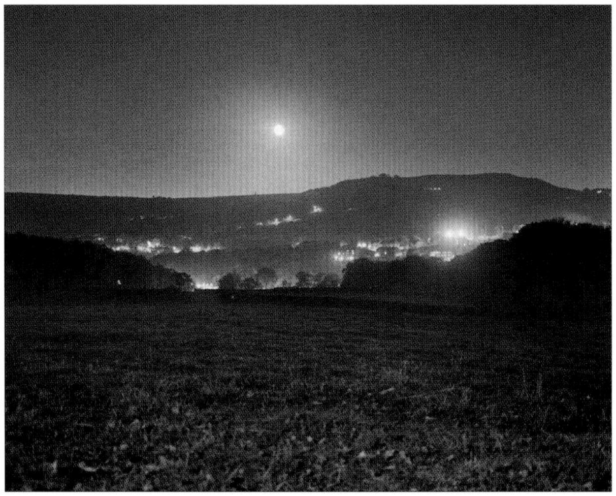

Moonlight

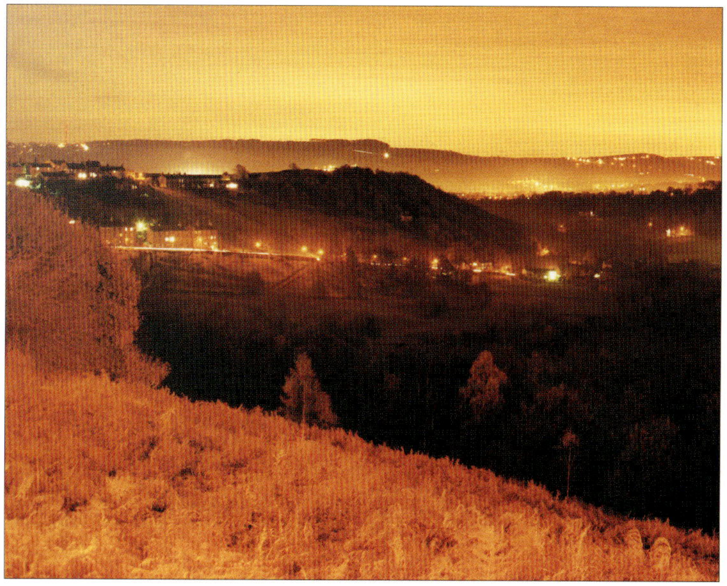

Colour

Processing and printing 76

Coping with contrast 76

Contrast control during processing 76

Dilute/static development, Two bath development, Pyro development 79

Contrast control during printing 82

Split grade printing, Pre-flashing, Making and using Lith masks, Lith printing 82

Printing examples 97

Improving the print 101

Toning, staining, etc. 101

Examples of night photography and how they were made 109

Traffic problems / unwanted attentions 114

Formulae and calculations 116

Ten key steps to good night photography 120

Glossary 122

introduction

Everyone has experience of street lighting, but have you ever noticed its wonderful, magical quality? Or do you only see it as a necessity? If you have only used it as an aid to getting around at night, then I suggest that you go out tonight and have another look.

Small pools of light, deep areas of black and gunmetal grey, back lighting, side lighting, spot-lit details, how much more dramatic could it be? I often find it so enthralling that it can be unreal, especially in the fog and, even more so, in the snow.

On occasion the wonder and beauty of it has made me lose track of time, and caused an overexposed frame, necessitating another shot.

Photography in this kind of light would appear to be a daunting and technically demanding prospect, but I believe night photography is one of the easiest areas of photography to master. For instance, visualising what would make a good black and white photograph at night is not difficult, the scene viewed under ordinary sodium (orange) street lighting can be said to be monochrome already. Under this vivid orange light it is difficult to identify colours, the scene is restricted to just two – black and orange.

Theoretically, it should be easy to imagine the final black and white image, by mentally converting from black and orange to black and white.

As for the exposure, remember that, unlike pictures taken by daylight with its ever changing light intensity and direction, photography by street lighting is consistent in its illumination and dramatic effect, night after night.

Therefore, when experimenting with night photography, mistaken frames can be shot and re-shot until the correct exposure has been arrived at.

Incorrect exposures are no longer 'lost' photographs, any unsuccessful photograph can be repeated on another occasion, until the desired result is obtained.

Copley's Bakery

Ilford XP2 Super.

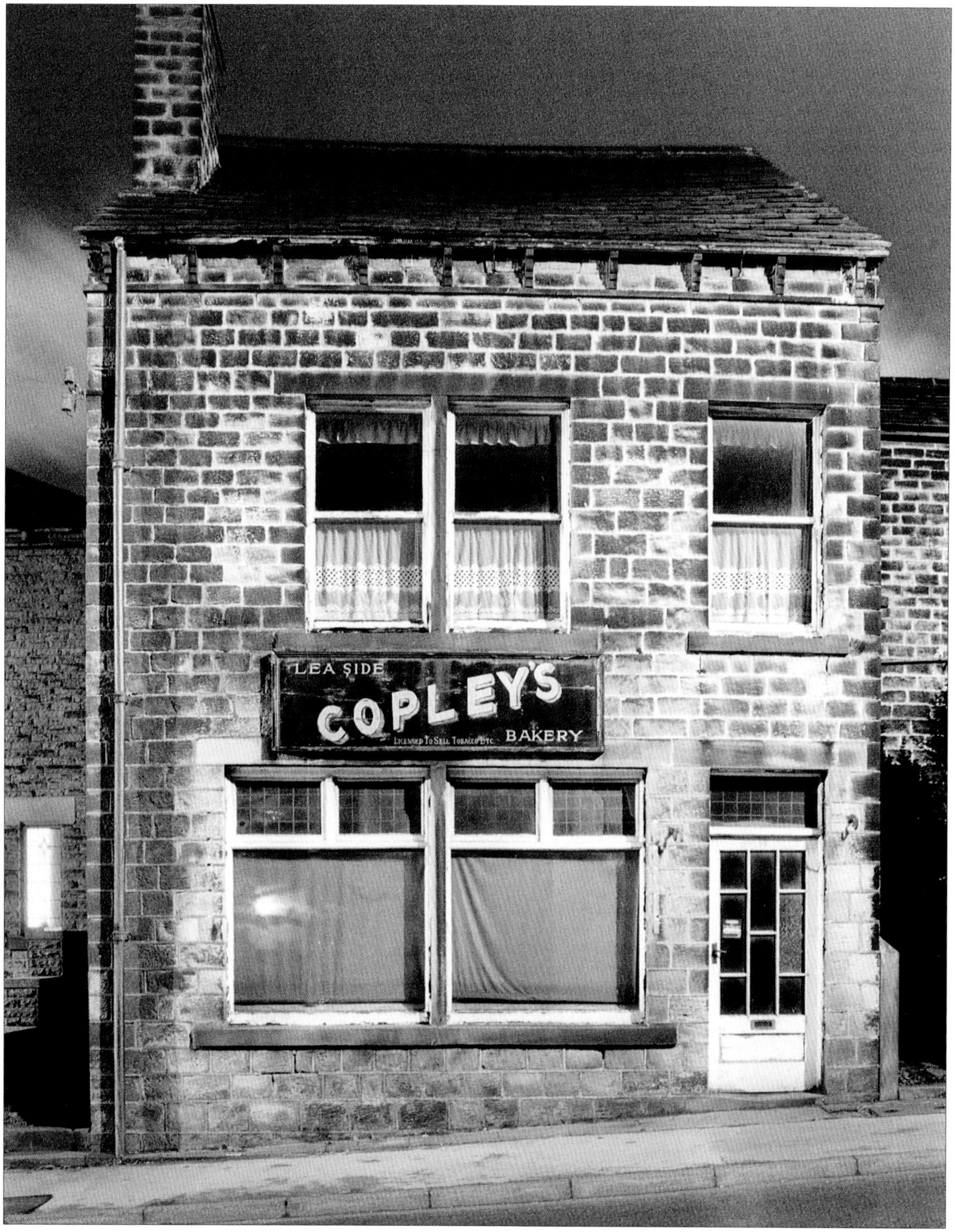

the basics

Welcome to the magical world of night photography, an area of the craft which has, sadly, never been one of the favoured 'genres'.

Many photographers work in the usual disciplines, and claim to be landscape/portrait/still-life workers, but how many have you met who described themselves as night photographers?

Perhaps it has been considered an area only for the expert or the foolhardy?

I experimented with night images in my early years as a photographic novice, before anyone had convinced me that it was too difficult or complicated to attempt. In my innocence I just went out and 'did it'. I took six pictures one evening near to where I lived (I can still remember the date, 16 September 1978) and all were printable – one of those images is still amongst my favourite photographs, and appears on the title page of this book.

Since that date (twenty-two years to press) I have not met one other night photographer. Why should that be? Do all photographers consider it a no-go area?

Throughout photography's short history, various workers have taken a detour into night photography, though it seems to be a technique that photographers dabble in occasionally, rather than pursue with a passion.

Some names I can recall who have worked in night photography at one time or another (and this is by no means a comprehensive list) are; Robert Adams, Brassai, Alvin Langdon Coburn, Paul Diamond, William A Fraser, O.Winston Link, Richard Misrach, Alfred Stieglitz, Karl Struss, and Margaret Bourke White.

Readers may wish to investigate some of these works and marvel at the quality that was achieved before the advent of fast films.

I would like to suggest that the reader adopt the attitude that these days night photography is neither complicated nor difficult, unless you wish to make it so. This book will attempt to point out simple methods of determining exposure, what equipment to use, highlight possible problems, and give explanations and examples in an easily understood way.

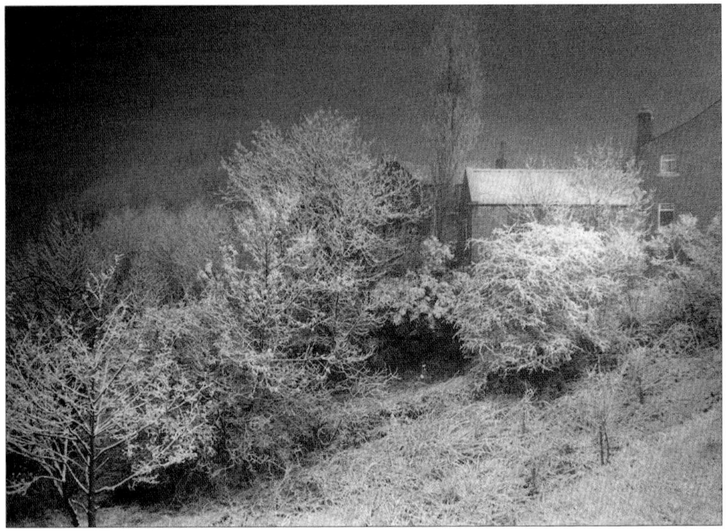

Snow covered garage and garden

Ilford HP5.

It is not my intention to overwhelm the reader with technique, the more technical sections are included for the experienced worker.

If you are inspired by the contents of this book to attempt shooting after dark, you may discover for yourselves the beauty of night photography.

As you begin to see the multitude of new photographic possibilities in familiar places, a whole new area of photography will open up for you. Your own locality will suddenly be seen in a totally new light (no pun intended).

You may also discover with night photography, as I have, how peaceful and relaxing it can be. Akin, I think, to fishing (a subject about which I know absolutely nothing), but which also involves long periods of waiting.

Standing around during long exposures and taking things slowly can be very therapeutic, and I find it a good way to lose the stresses of everyday living.

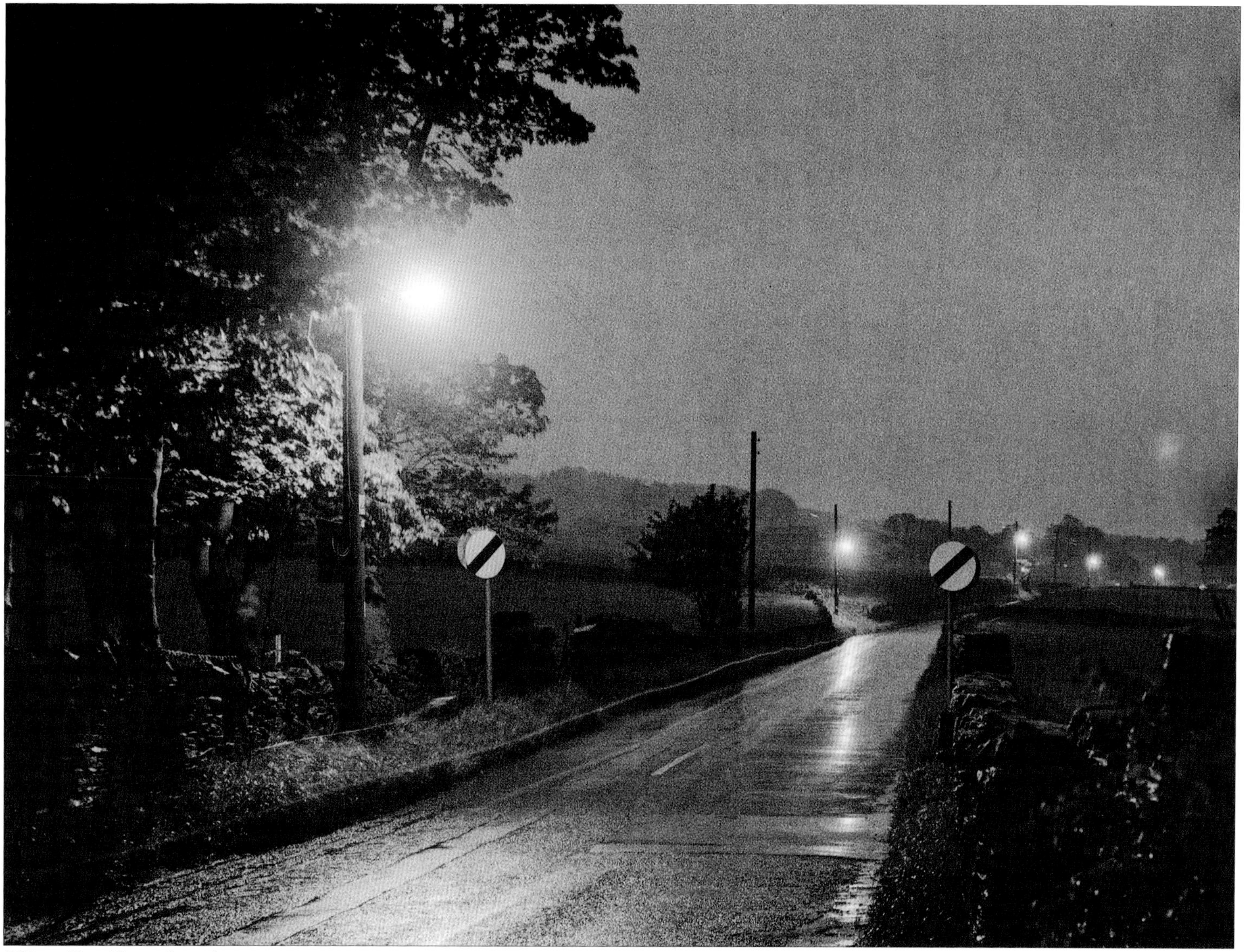

After the thunderstorm

Ilford HP5.

This picture was taken on an old wooden plate camera and involved setting up, focussing, loading the darkslide and giving a long exposure (9 minutes) whilst holding an umbrella in one hand!

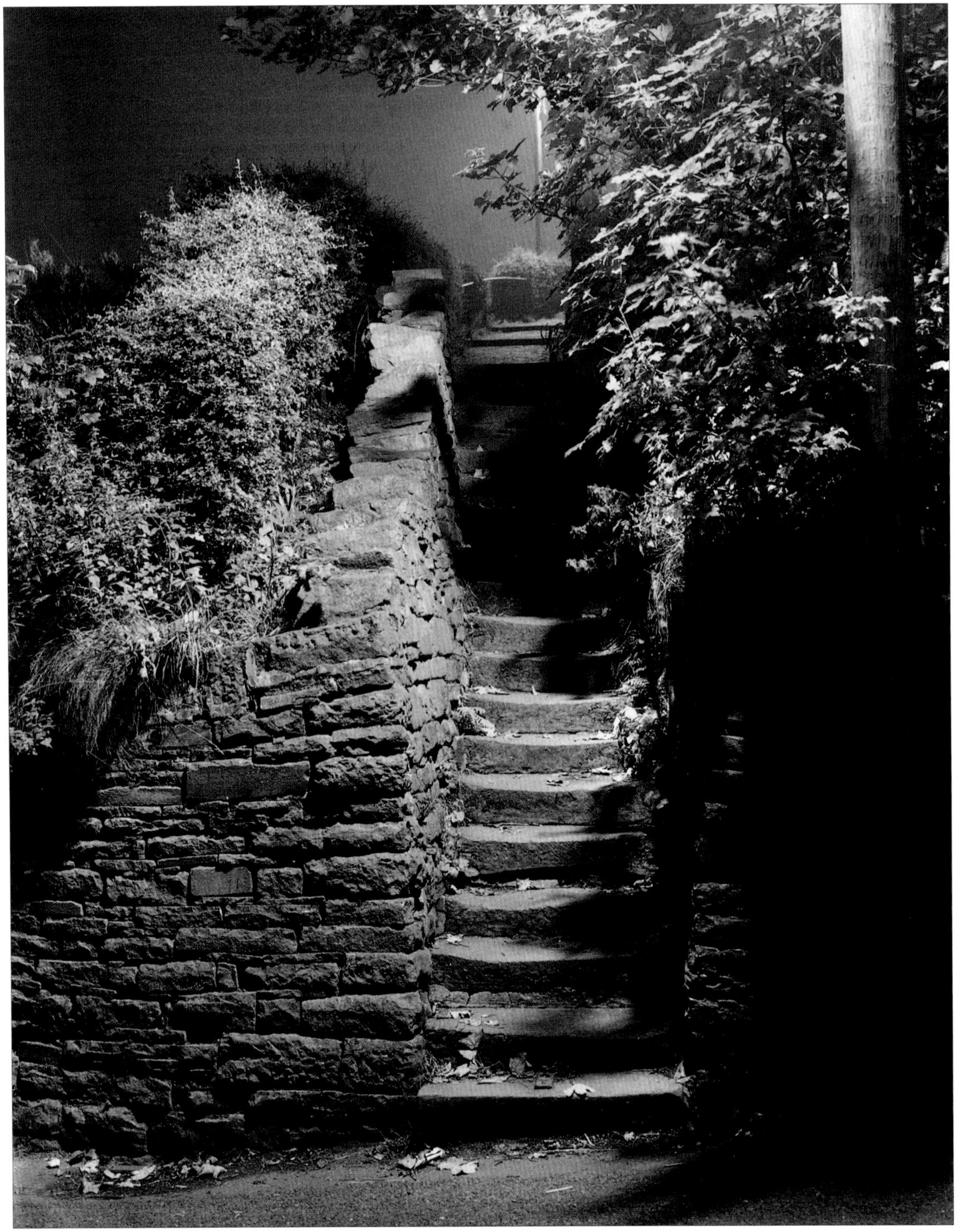

Shortcut to Deanhouse

Ilford HP5 6x7cm negative film rated at 400 ISO and processed in Paterson Acutol.

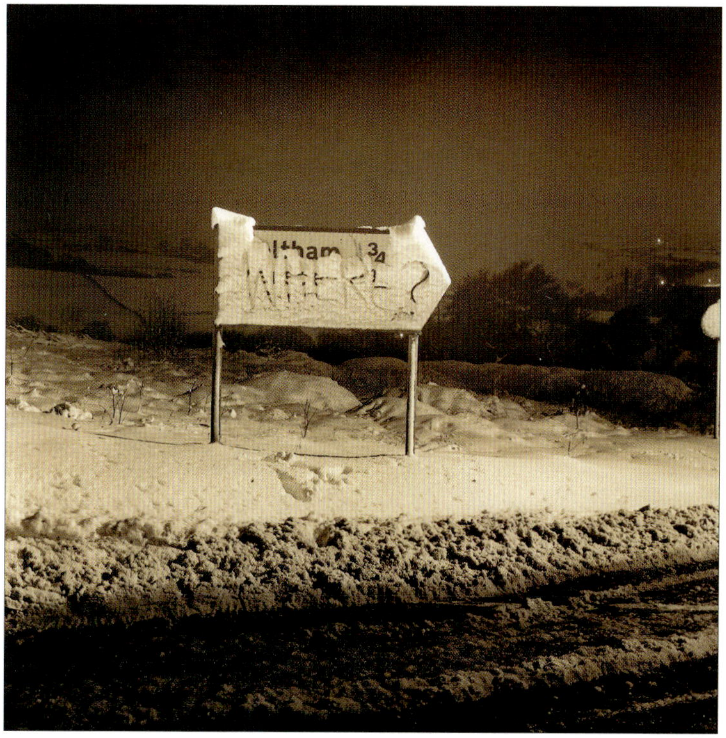

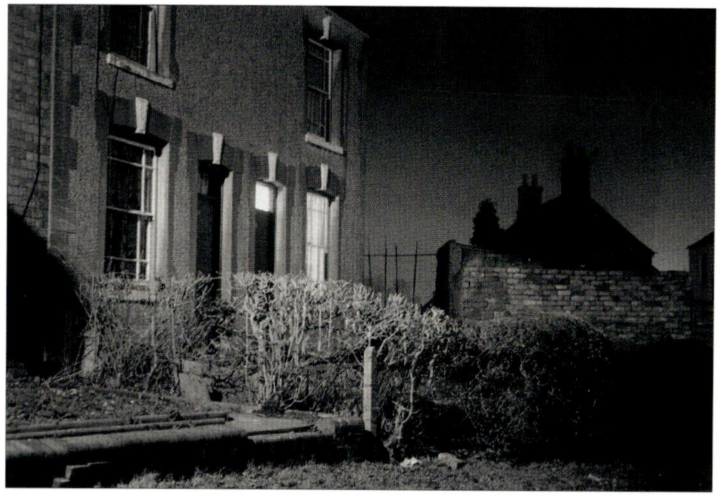

Coalville, Leicester
Ilford HP5.

For this book I have selected images that I hope will evoke these therapeutic feelings to inspire the reader in the way that night photography inspires me. At the same time, I have tried to choose pictures that are illustrative of different forms, styles, or techniques of this type of work.

Technical information is provided for those who wish to take it to a more advanced level, but please understand that it is not necessary to understand all the information in this book to take night photographs. My first successful pictures were done when my 'learning curve' was still just a flat line.

Where should I go to take night photographs?

This depends on where you live, and what kind of images you wish to take. There are many types of artificial light and the level of illumination varies tremendously.

If you live in a small village on one of the Scottish islands you may only have the odd street lamp. If you live in a city the lighting can be so intense in places that it's almost like daytime.

Bear this range of lighting in mind if you try taking pictures after dark. Get used to working with the light that you have available locally, then, with a little experience, travel further afield and begin to experiment with other lighting types.

All that is required for good results is a minimal amount of equipment and a fair amount of patience (and a note book).

For your first forays into night work I suggest that you find a location close to home. Choose an average scene and, using the exposure chart on page 23, shoot a few frames at various exposures and take notes.

When your film is processed choose the negative that best suits your own style of printing. Achieving printable results from your first film can make the difference between frustration and excitement, and whether to take it further with more challenging lighting, locations or exposures. So don't be frightened to use a bit of film.

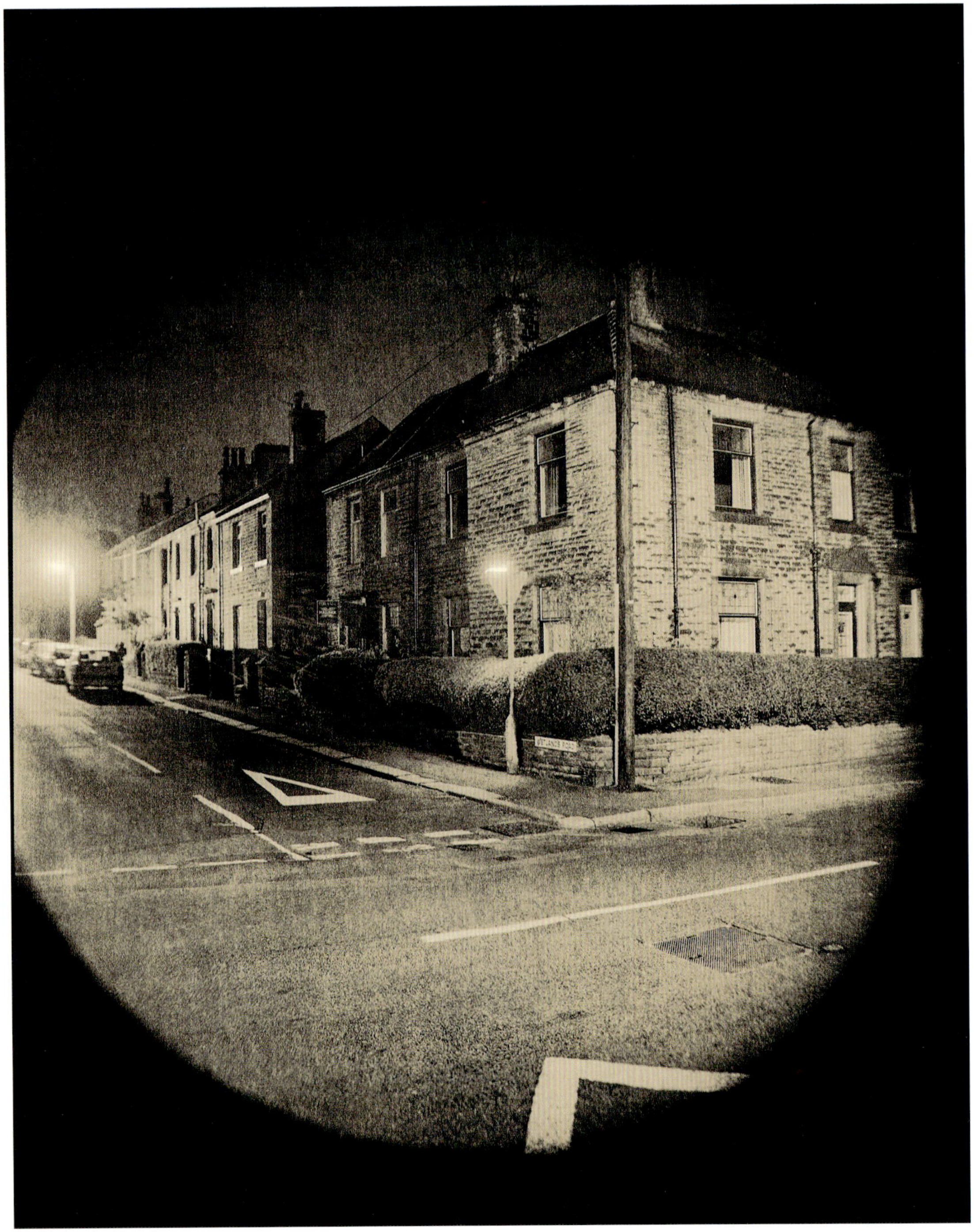

Corner of Wetlands Road

Ilford HP5 5x4in processed in Ilford ID11. This was taken using a lens which could not cover the full area of the negative, giving an interesting circular image.

Autumn trees

Autumn trees with orange foliage reflect more light and can stand out quite strikingly. Here the print has been sepia toned to simulate the original colour.
Ilford HP5 processed in Ilford ID11.

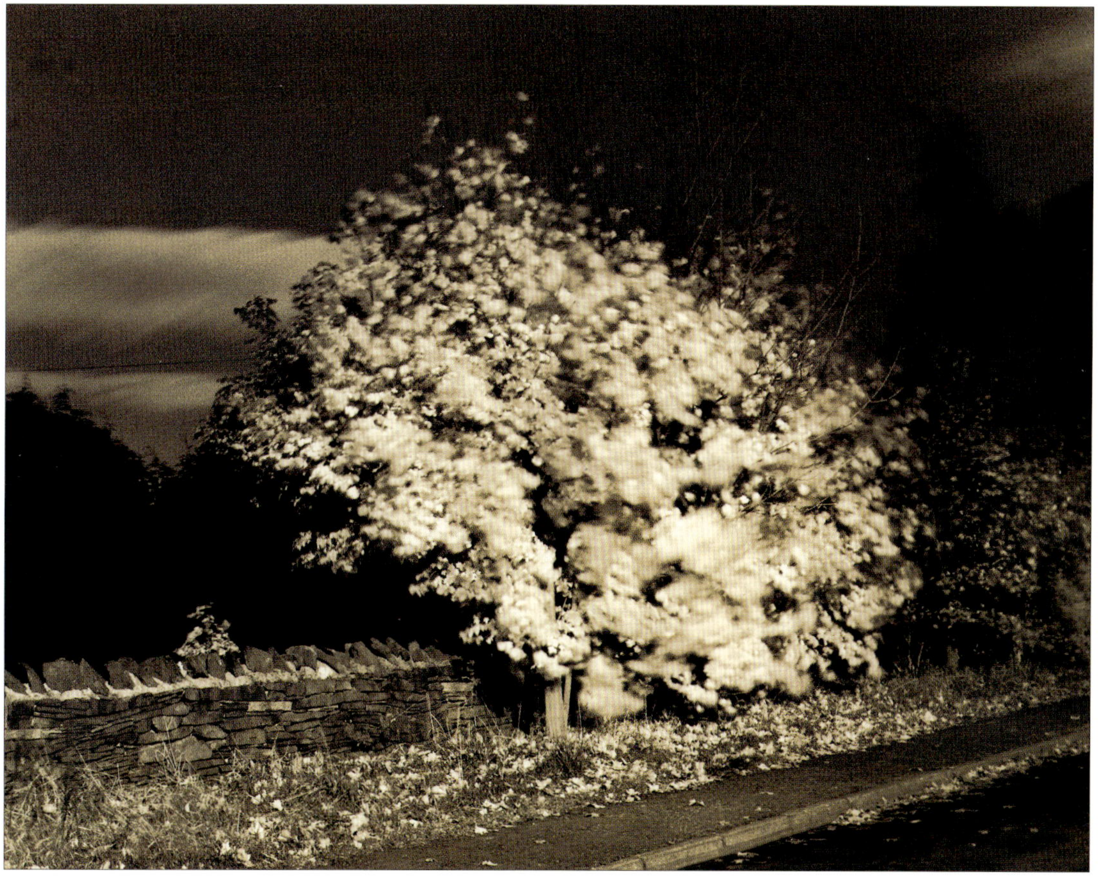

Ideal conditions

Personally, I prefer to do my night photography during the autumn. Summer is too humid and the evenings are so light that I can't start shooting until nearly midnight whereas in autumn I can start sooner and feel cooler.

There are two other reasons why I prefer the autumn:

1. The leaves on the trees have turned orange and light brown. This means that foliage records on the film, even when it is some distance from the light source, and because the leaves reflect more light, the whole feel of the shot is different.

2. The air usually has a little mistiness to it, and sometimes fog, which reduces the glare of the lamps and provides a nice separation of tones into the distance. This is when the scene starts to become atmospheric and the location becomes much more photogenic.

Snow might not be everyone's idea of an ideal condition for night photography, but photographically it is superb. With a good heavy snowfall there are pictures everywhere you look. Snow is an excellent reflector and the increased brightness everywhere reduces the exposure time by approximately one stop.

What makes a great night photograph?

This might seem, at first, to be a difficult question to resolve. But the answer is really quite obvious, it has to be the quality of light.

Good light can transform a familiar, mundane place into something tremendous whereas some great locations can have

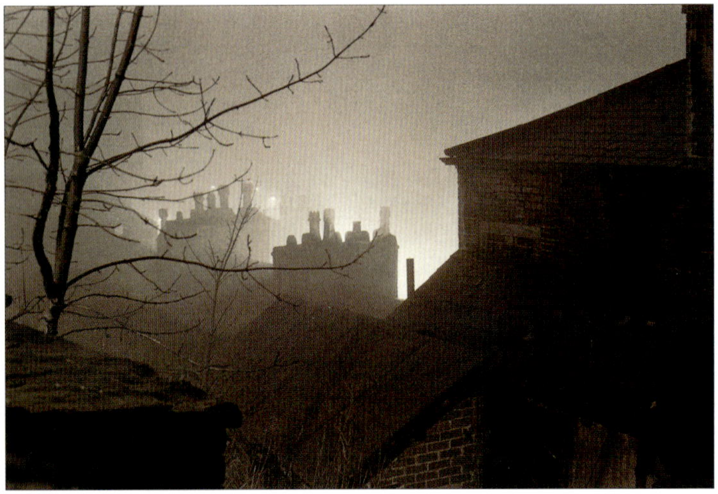

Misty chimneys
Ilford HP5.

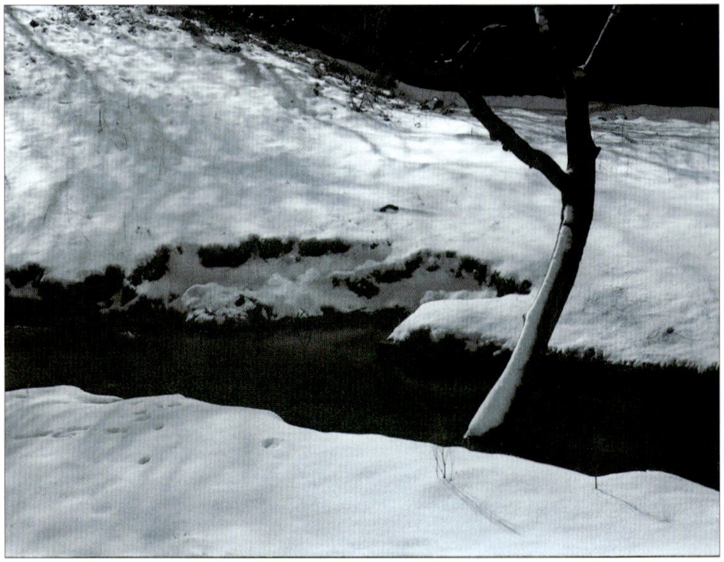

Stream and sapling in the snow
Ilford XP2.

very poor lighting at night, and some have none at all. A good night photograph is one in which there are enough lights or light sources to give the impression of night, but not too many as this can be distracting.

A good balance is needed. The streetlights must have detail but appear bright. The sky should be dark but have enough tone to separate the branches of trees or buildings.

Night photography needn't be all about street scenes and street lighting. Be open to all types of light. Anything can be used for the exposure; security lights, bonfires, torches, the moon, even car headlights! All have their own magical quality.

Fog and snow can also introduce a theatrical, magical quality if utilised properly, enhancing certain features or creating different lighting effects. I have expanded further on this later in the book.

As I mentioned in the introduction, places seen by street lighting can give the impression of being 'other worldly' and this cannot be anticipated by scouting for locations in daylight. There is no substitute for just walking the streets and being inspired. It is not even necessary to carry a camera when discovering the best situations. Come back some other night, the lighting will most likely be identical.

The equipment

Night photography can be undertaken with the minimum of equipment; a camera, a tripod and a stopwatch. I work on the principle that the less you carry, the less there is to lose in the dark.

Cameras and lenses

For my own way of working I use a fully manual camera fitted with a standard lens. I prefer a manual camera because it can be set with little effort and, in very dark conditions, the controls can be adjusted by feel alone. Automatic cameras may be used if the metering system can be trusted in very low light, but the liquid crystal displays in some are difficult to read, and long exposures are a drain on the batteries.

My decision to restrict myself to a standard lens is an aesthetic one and also a practical one. I find that using one lens simplifies composition. I prefer the optical supremacy that prime lenses provide, the lack of distortion inherent in a standard, and last but not least, it lessens the load I have to carry.

These are not the only reasons for preferring to use a standard lens. Wide angle lenses are more likely to take in unwanted street

Under the trees

Exposures can be made with any available light. This was illuminated by car headlights alone. Ilford XP2.

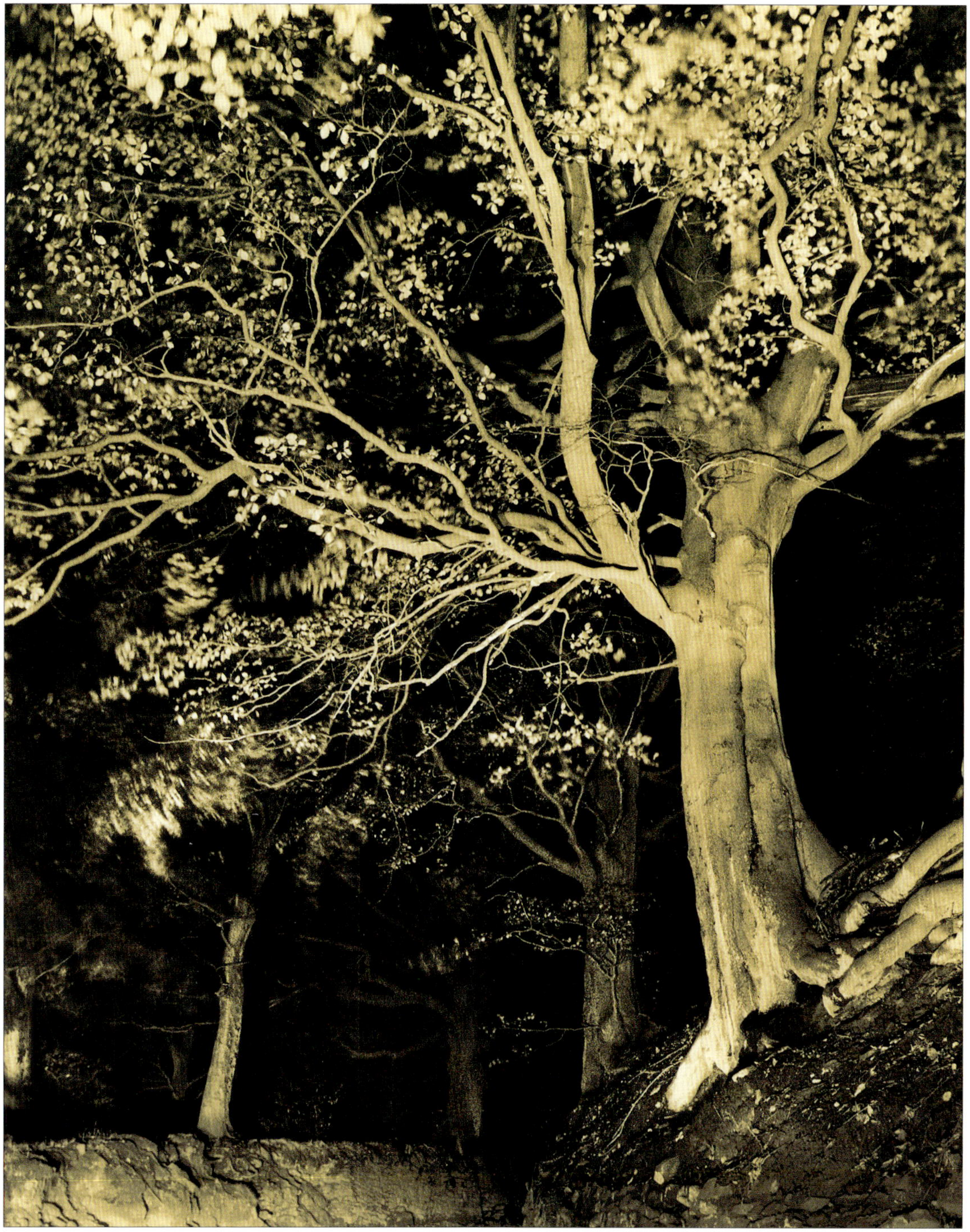

lights and other light pollution as well as the scene to be photographed. Trying to exclude the lights to lessen flare becomes more and more difficult as the angle of view increases, and becomes virtually impossible with super-wide lenses.

Longer lenses have different problems, most obviously camera shake. You may think your tripod is rigid but try a two minute exposure using a 200mm lens and you may be surprised.

Each small vibration caused by the wind or traffic will be magnified, the longer the lens the greater the magnification and susceptibility to vibration.

Also with longer, heavier lenses, the weight of the lens may pull the camera down during the exposure leaving your image streaking from top to bottom. This is a very real possibility with cheap flimsy tripods.

Tripods

Many photographers spend a great deal of money on good quality cameras and lenses but have quite a different policy when purchasing a tripod, and are often prepared to get the cheapest, lightest one in the shop.

Before buying a tripod consider the main reason for having one – to keep your camera steady, fixed and rigid.

The first consideration for most is weight. Many buy the lightest tripod they can find and, of course, waste their money because the legs are so flimsy that it is useless in the slightest breeze. Apply this simple rule; the tripod must be as heavy as the camera to begin to be steady.

Invest in a decent tripod and it will serve you for the rest of your life, and maybe someone else's after that! Bear in mind that a golfer carries a heavy bag of clubs around the golf course because they are the necessary tools to play the game. A golfer would never consider using something much lighter if it compromised on performance.

If the prospect of carrying a camera and your tripod daunts you then perhaps serious night photography is not for you (see section on hand-held pictures).

I believe the combined weight of a decent sturdy tripod and a 35mm camera is not really that great but, to reduce the strain, you could drive between locations or ask a friend along to help with the gear, and keep you company.

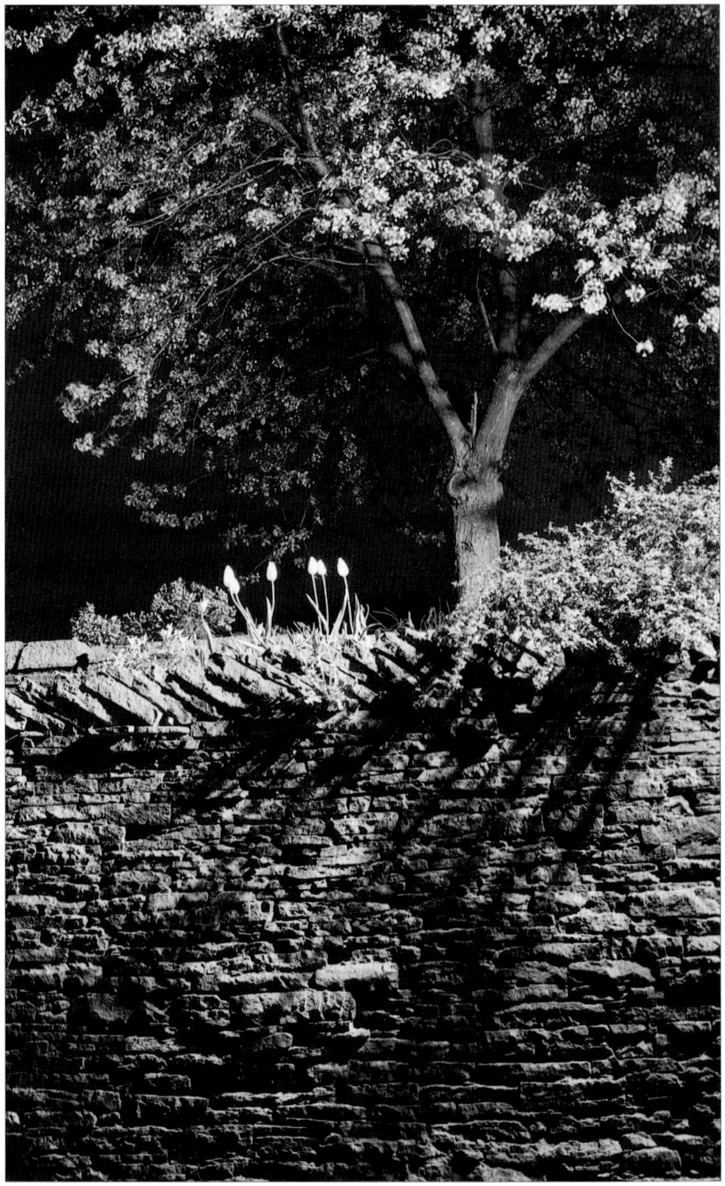

Six tulips

Ilford HP5 processed in Ilford ID11.

The result of using a poor quality tripod on a windy night. Ilford HP5.

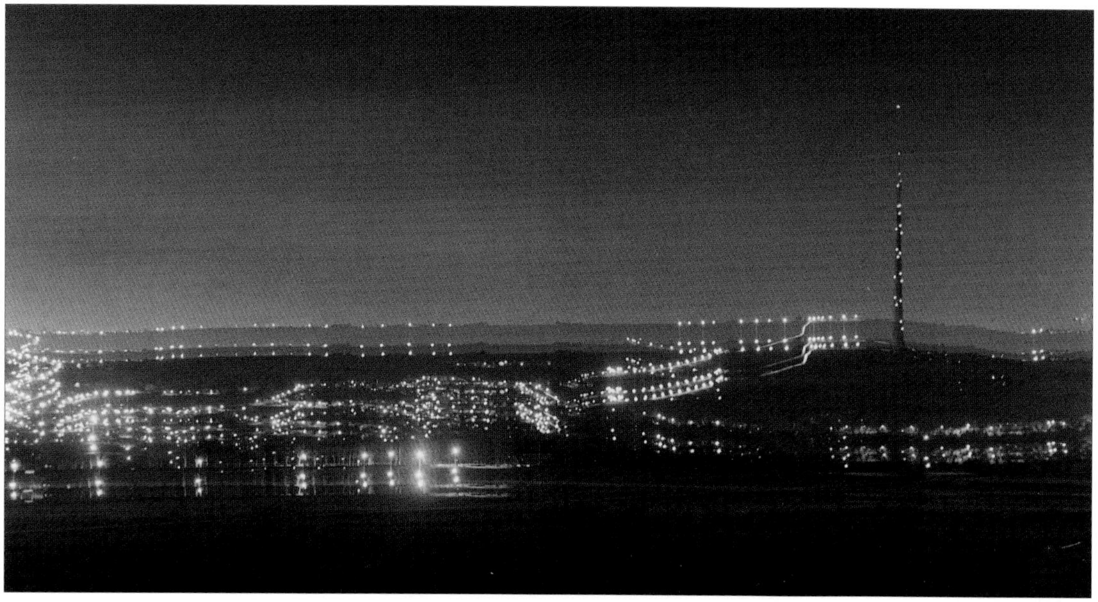

Using a telephoto lens on a poor quality tripod can result in the lens sagging down during the exposure leaving vertical streaks. Ilford HP5.

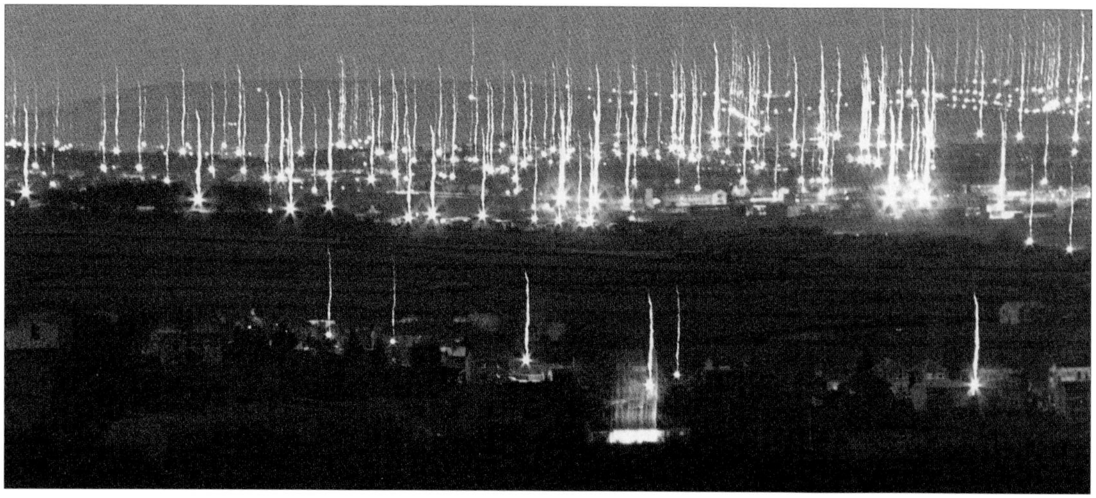

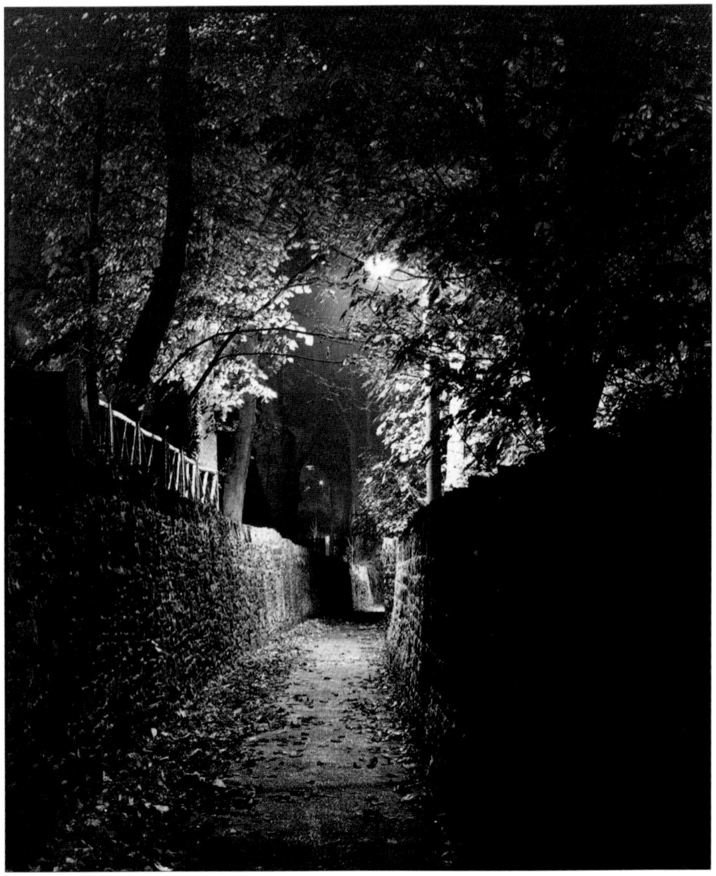

Alleyway

I find a standard lens is adequate for 95% of pictures.

Ilford HP5 processed in Paterson Acutol.

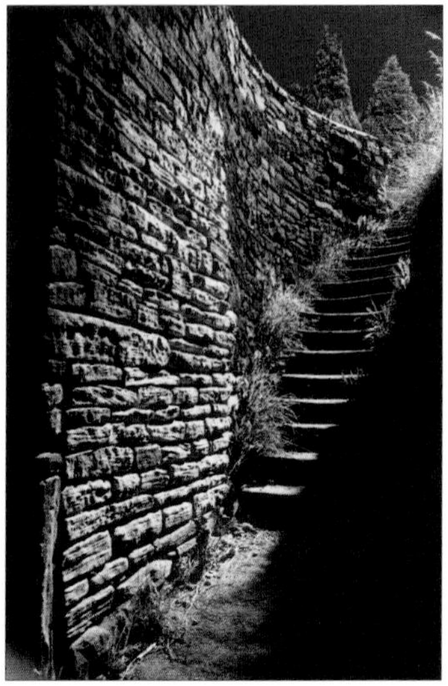

Steps down to Goose Green

Wide angle lenses may be used in situations where no bright lights appear in the view. Make sure that the lens is well stepped down to keep the corners sharp.

Ilford XP2.

8 min 49 sec at f32.

Stopwatch

I would recommend that all photographers intent on night photography should seriously consider buying a digital stopwatch. One which has a large, easy to read display is the most practical for timing exposures in the dark. A useful feature of some is the facility to count down with an audible signal at the end. This can be useful for very long exposures.

The previously mentioned items are obviously the minimum requirement for practising night photography. Other items you may care to take along are:

1. Small torch – for checking apertures, looking in your camera bag or finding dropped items.

2. Notebook and pen – to keep a record of your exposure times and aperture settings.

3. Cable release – an essential item really. Once you have used one you'll never want to be without one. Make sure it's of the locking type.

4. Small flash gun – for brightening-up totally black shadow areas and creating another light source.

5. Photographs – previous examples of your (or someone

else's) night photography. Someone is bound to ask you what you are doing.

6. Radio or walkman – the longer exposures can seem to take forever, music helps to relieve this.

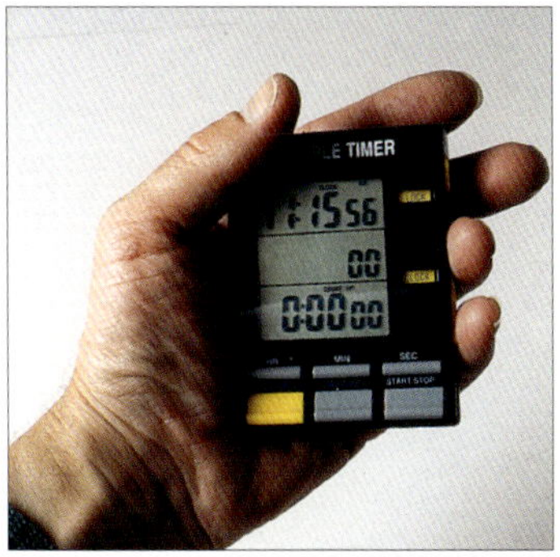

A digital stopwatch with large display

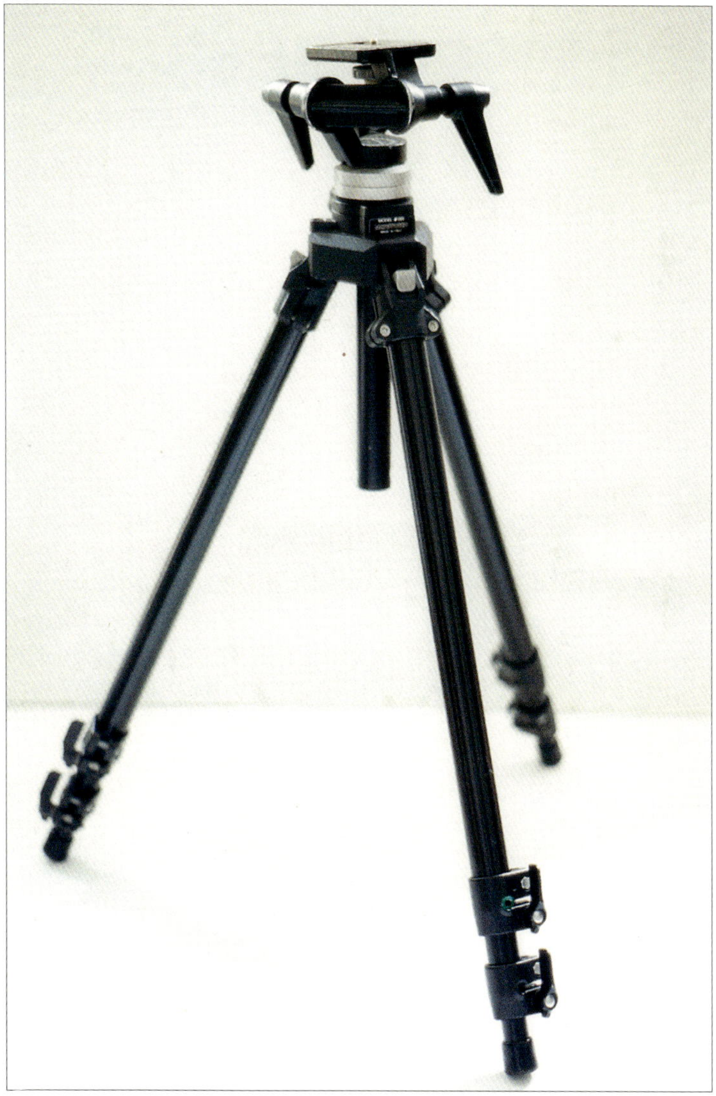

Choose a sturdy tripod

7. Thermos flask – an item you won't want to be without when shooting in winter.

8. Gloves – essential for night scenes in the snow.

the technical stuff

Street lighting types

Street lighting may be considered to be a constant, repeatable source of lighting, but don't mistakenly think that this is the same as consistency. Lighting can vary tremendously in intensity with a move to another location. What proves to be the correct exposure close to home may not work in another town or city.

The intensity (and colour) can range from small fluorescent tubes attached to road signs, through white mercury vapour and the common orange sodium type, right up to high pressure sodium, not to mention neon displays and halogen floodlighting.

This obviously means that the correct exposure for night photography depends very much on where you are, and what type of lighting you are working with. It is not enough to just find good locations. Attention must be paid to the light source.

Most of my photographs have been taken under orange sodium light because, where I prefer to shoot, at one time it was nearly impossible to find any other type of lighting. In the last few years though, the high pressure sodium lamp has gradually been introduced. This gives an extra stop of light which is always an advantage, although I prefer the appearance of the shorter sodium type if it is to be included in the frame.

Photographers who prefer to shoot city scapes and motorways are going to have considerably shorter exposures than those that I generally use. Most motorways have high pressure lamps of a higher wattage than those found in street scenes and are generally sited closer together, providing a very bright situation for photographs. The three most commonly found lighting types are:

1. Mercury vapour

A cold, white light with a hint of green which becomes a much stronger green cast when recorded on colour film. White streetlights don't provide much in the way of lighting. They seem to have a lot of glare and yet illuminate the scene poorly. Mercury vapour lighting requires longer exposures than all other types. Not very common now.

2. Sodium

The ever present orange streetlight with a very narrow spectral bandwidth. This is the most monochrome of all lighting types and makes previsualising extremely simple. These are the most efficient type of light giving more lumens per watt. All exposure guides, unless stated otherwise are based on this type of lighting.

3. High pressure sodium

This type is becoming more common nowadays. The pale orange/white light produced by these lights is twice the brightness of ordinary sodium lamps and has a wider spectral bandwidth. Because of this it is easier to identify colours under this light.

Due to the increased visibility and better colour recognition under high pressure sodium lighting, this type is being introduced more and more because of the obvious advantages in crime detection and identification.

Exposures under high pressure sodium light are amongst the shortest encountered and produce colour images with very little cast.

Film speed and its relation to exposures at night

Practically speaking, very slow films should be avoided for night photography. For instance, a 50 ISO film in average orange sodium light will require an exposure of 2 hours and 15 minutes using an aperture of f22. For most people this is too long.

At the other end of the scale, a 3200 ISO film would only require 36 seconds at f22 which would seem more preferable. This speed advantage is, however, offset by a higher granularity and loss of detail.

To take account of different photographic preferences I have compiled a chart of guide exposures for a range of films between 100-3200 ISO. This chart gives the sort of negative density that I prefer, but I realise that printing styles and preferences can vary enormously. So, please test the exposures with your film/ developer combination and adjust to your own needs. The chart

Old lamp post

Ilford HP5 5x4 in processed in Ilford ID11. Another shot taken with the lens that gives a circular image.

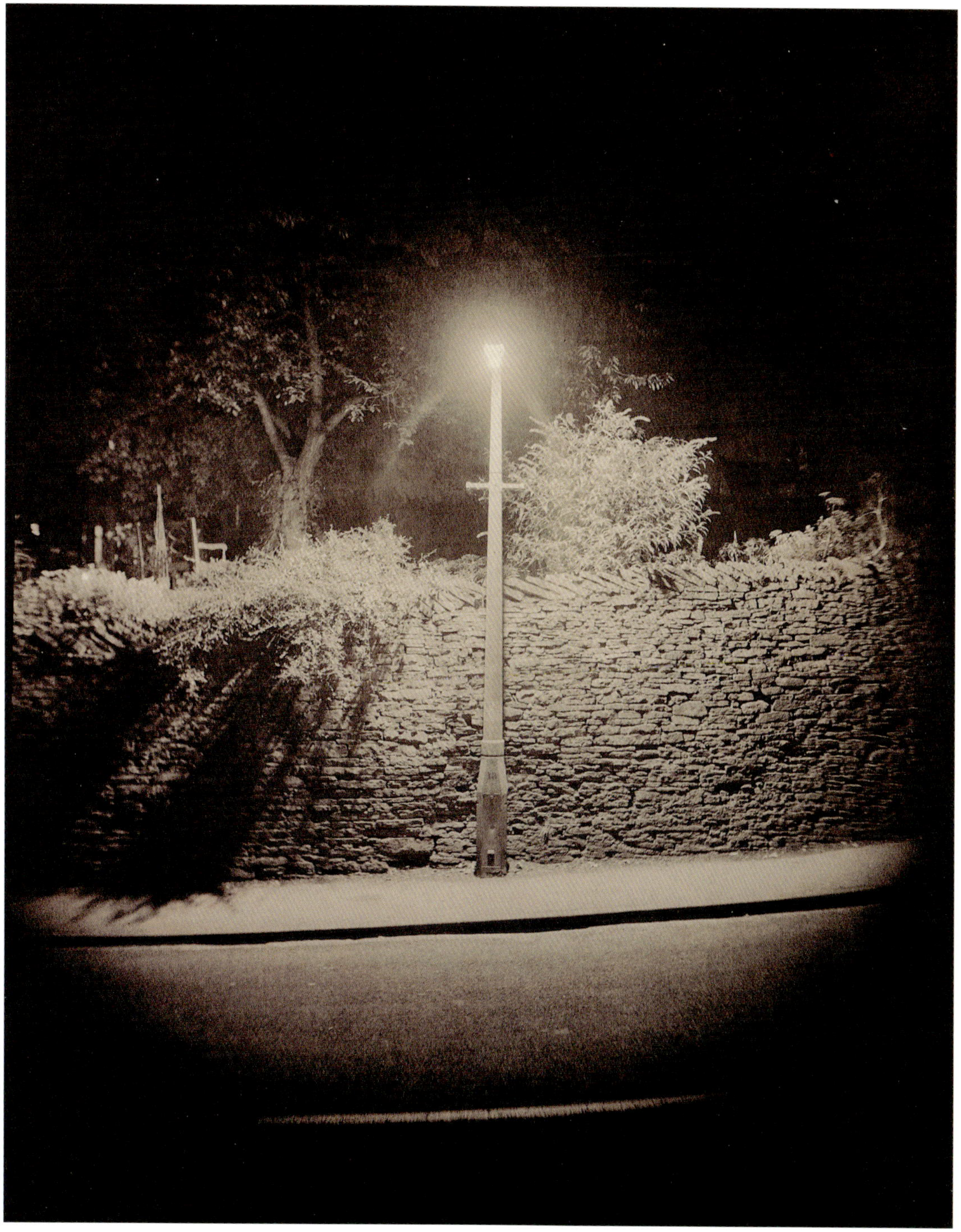

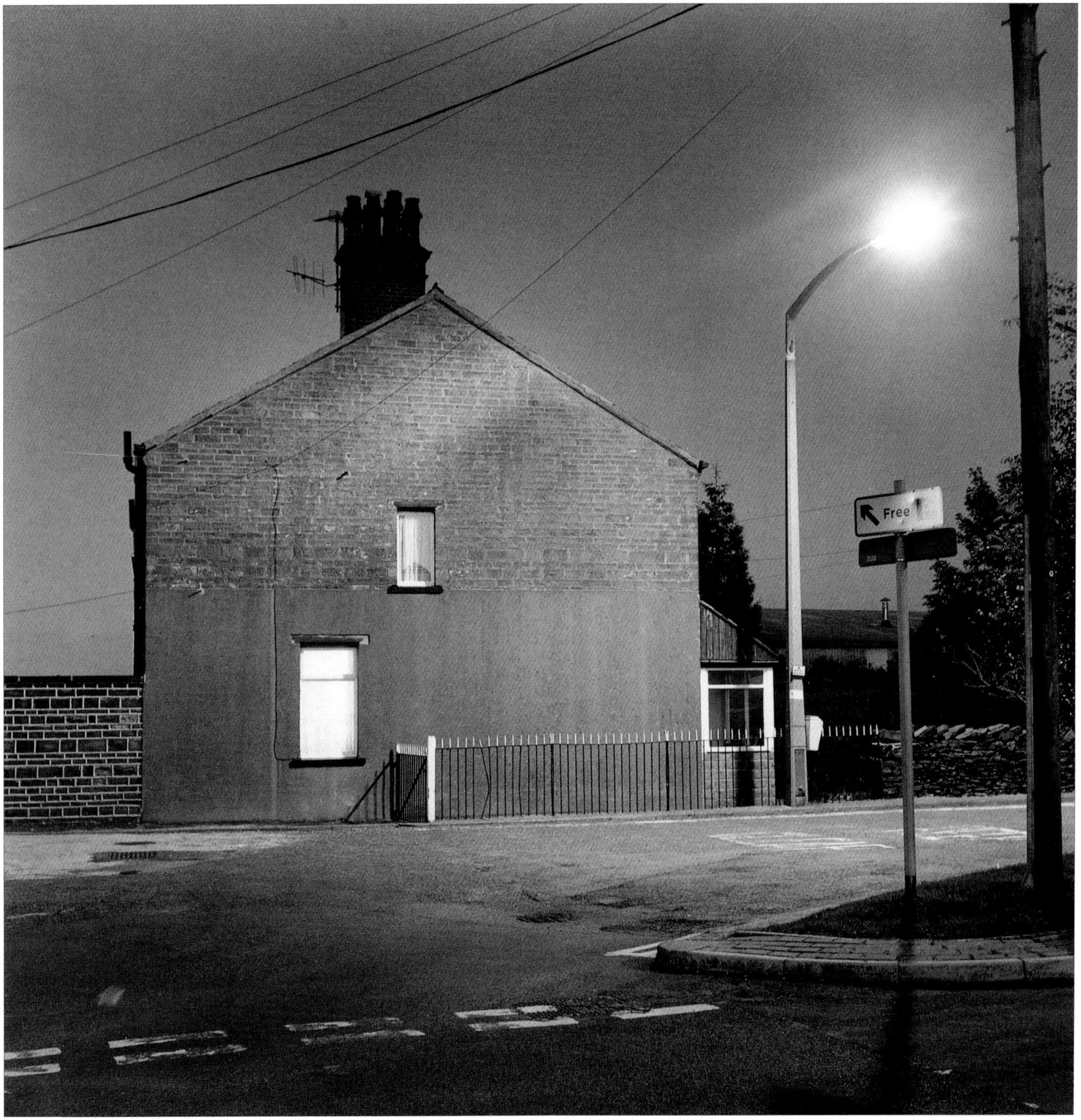

House end and white tipped railings

Ilford HP5 6x6cm negative processed in ID11.

CHART OF RELATIVE EXPOSURE TIMES FOR A RANGE OF FILM SPEEDS BETWEEN 100-3200 ISO (IN AVERAGE SODIUM LIGHTING)

Film speed	f2	f2.8	f4	f5.6	f8	f11	f16	f22
100	6 s	14.7 s	36 s	1 m 28 s	3 m 36 s	8 m 49 s	21 m 40 s	52 m 50 s
200	2.45 s	6 s	14.7 s	36 s	1 m 28 s	3 m 36 s	8 m 49 s	21 m 40 s
400	1 s	2.45 s	6 s	14.7 s	36 s	1 m 28 s	3 m 36 s	8 m 49 s
800	½ s	1 s	2.45 s	6 s	14.7 s	36 s	1 m 28 s	3 m 36 s
1600	¼ s	½ s	1 s	2.45 s	6 s	14.7 s	36 s	1 m 28 s
3200	⅛ s	¼ s	½ s	1 s	2.45 s	6 s	14.7 s	36 s

only applies to exposures under the common orange sodium light, but giving an extra stop under white light and one stop less under high pressure sodium lamps will make the chart accurate for other lighting situations.

All exposure times given include extra exposure calculation to deal with reciprocity failure (see next section).

A quick glance at the bottom left and top right of the chart reveals the enormous range of possible exposure times, from ⅛ of a second for an extremely grainy picture with no depth of field, right through to almost 53 minutes for a fine grained picture with maximum depth of field (only for the committed photographer with endless patience).

My own personal preference is for 400 ISO film. This gives quality negatives that have good grain, especially on roll film, combined with workable exposure times that permit a number of variations within one evenings shooting.

In average sodium light conditions an exposure of 1 minute 28 seconds at f11 on a 400 ISO film will give a good negative and this is probably an ideal – depth of field/long exposure/grain size compromise.

Some might question my choice of a fast film if quality is important. 400 ISO films have had a reputation for being very grainy. But I feel this is an outdated opinion. Fast films of today are now far better than they were 20 years ago, especially the chromogenic films (Ilford XP2 super and Kodak T400 C.N.). For print sizes of 10x8 inches from a 35mm negative, the quality is superb.

I realise that photographers can be peculiarly pedantic at times and may have one particular film/developer combination that is used for everything. I like to try out different films occasionally,

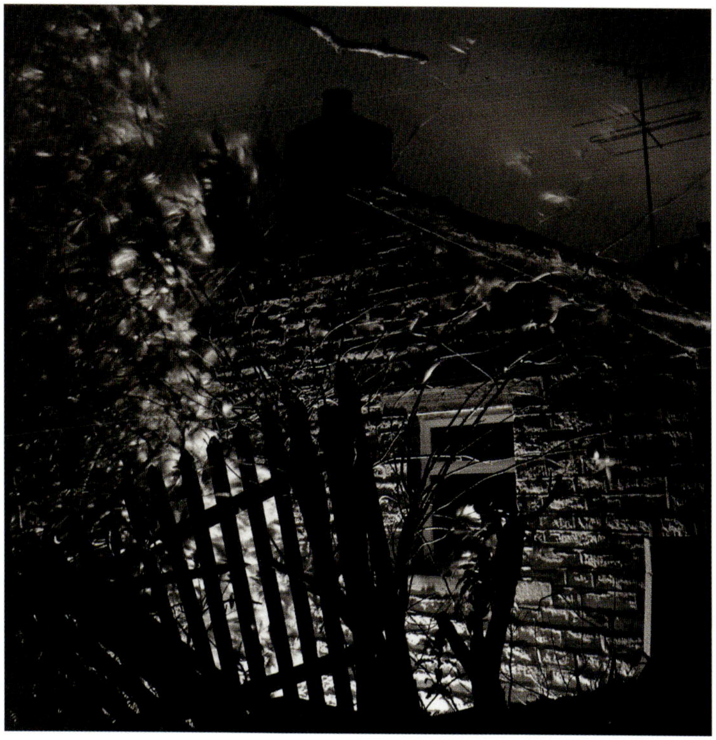

Security light

Ilford HP5 6x6 negative processed in ID11.

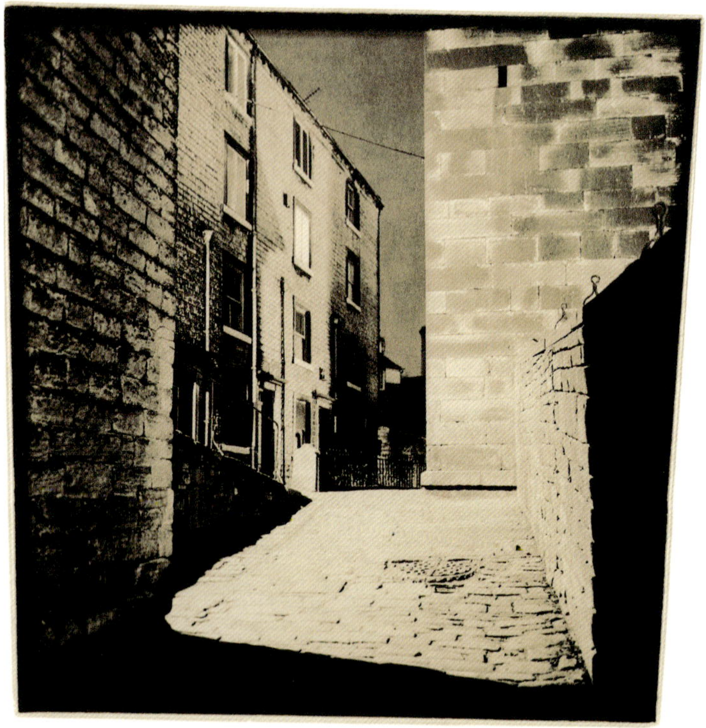

Behind the church

The camera was tilted up slightly for framing and the converging verticals were corrected in printing by tilting the masking frame. Distorted borders included for effect.

Polaroid negative type 665.

and I have used a few types for night work, but for ease of explanation I will refer to 400 ISO films throughout the book. If your way of working is different to this, then please bear with me.

Film types

Having decided on 400 ISO as the preferred speed, the photographer is faced with more decisions – what make and what type? Here follows a list of currently available black and white films in 35mm format: Ilford HP5, Ilford Delta 400, Ilford XP2 Super, Kodak TRI-X, Kodak T.MAX 400, Kodak T400 C.N., Agfapan 400 and Fuji Neopan 400.

There are a couple of films in this list that I personally do not like to use for night photography, but I think it would be unkind for me to reveal which they are, since they may produce results that are perfect for another photographer.

I suggest that you choose one film to start with, and use it exclusively for at least two years to get used to its particular qualities and limitations. Changing film types too frequently will make each shot you take a matter of luck and accident. Sticking to one film and one developer will allow you to predict your print quality before you fire the shutter.

The difference between the quality of your night photographs, compared to those of other photographers, is more likely to be determined by your vision and your choice of location rather than your film/developer combination.

I have recommended 400 ISO films for general use in night photography after trying a variety of speeds. If your preference is for grainy images then please go ahead and use the very fast films. Your exposures on a 3200 ISO film are going to be comparatively short at only 15 seconds at f16 in average sodium light.

Be prepared for contrast problems when shooting on 3200 ISO films. They are, strictly speaking, only 1000 ISO films which have been provided with development times that effectively 'uprate' them to 3200 ISO.

I prefer to rate these films at 1600 ISO, an exposure difference of one stop, and reduce the development time by 15-20%. (The development times for this rating are usually provided with the films.)

Rated at 1600 ISO, these films perform very well, better, I think, than 400 ASA (as they were then) films of 20 or 30 years ago (does anyone remember HP4?). I think that the grain structure and size on 3200 ISO films rated at 1600 ISO is very similar to the lovely quality that used to be produced with the long since discontinued HP4, certainly in 35mm, but with the advantage of two stops extra speed.

Chromogenic films

As I mentioned briefly above, chromogenic films such as Ilford XP2 Super and Kodak T400 C.N. are very good for night photography. They are fast and fine grained and, perhaps more importantly, very forgiving of overexposure.

The image layer of a chromogenic film is made up of dye layers rather than clumps of silver and this gives a lower contrast in areas of heavier exposure.

Polaroid films

Polaroid produce a number of interesting films, and I have experimented with some of them for night photography. Being slower they tend to need quite long exposures, especially if the lens needs to be stopped down at all. This would seem a necessity with a 5x4 camera, but this is not too important if the images are small 5x4 Polaroid prints.

When using the exceedingly nice Polaroid type 55/665 films, which produce a negative for enlargement, then depth of field becomes important as the images will be enlarged.

Unfortunately these films are rather slow. Polaroid claim 50 ISO, but I usually give half a stop more exposure bringing the speed down to 32. An ISO of 32 is rather a handicap with night photography, needing exposures in the region of twenty minutes at f8 taking into account reciprocity failure, and more than four hours if the lens is fully stopped down to f32.

So, despite these being wonderful films, they are not really practical for this kind of work.

I have tried colour Polaroid for night pictures but find it responds poorly and has a very strong green cast under orange sodium light. The sepia print film that they produce is better. It has a faster speed (200 ISO) which allows shorter times and it also displays a very nice shade of brown which is well suited to night images.

Please note that, because Polaroid films have lower speeds and need a different calculation for reciprocity, they cannot be used to check exposures for conventional films at night.

Infra red

Some readers may have considered the possibility of shooting night photos on infra red film for an unusual effect. Let me give you a little tip that may prevent wasted film – don't do it!

Infra red film does not respond to the light from sodium lamps in the same way as conventional black and white films (Ilford S.F.X. is sensitive to visible light as well as I.R. and will respond if used without filtration, but this removes the infra red effect). Unless you are willing to put up with excessively long exposure times for no aesthetic advantage (sodium lamps emit no infra red) steer clear of infra red film for this type of work.

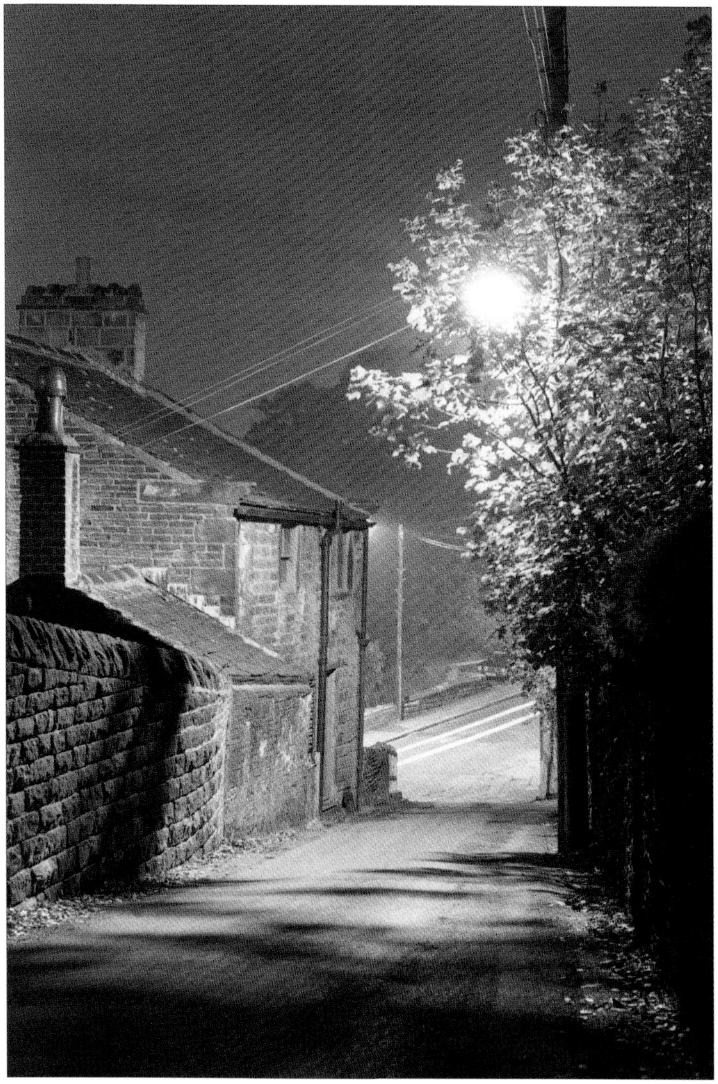

Junction of Back Lane and Station Road
Ilford HP5 processed in Microphen.

Reciprocity failure

For those photographers who shoot in daylight or with flash, reciprocity failure may be something you have heard of but never had any need to investigate. However, if you are intending to produce night photographs, I recommend that you study this chapter, otherwise you may find your exposures will be inaccurate.

Reciprocity is the logical relationship between shutter speeds and apertures. Perhaps best summed up as a 'give and take' relationship.

EXAMPLE

If three frames were exposed in succession as indicated:

Exposure 1	1/1000 at f2
Exposure 2	1/500 at f2.8
Exposure 3	1/250 at f4

the resulting negatives would all be the same density.

Note how the apertures get smaller as the exposures get longer.

Moving down from 1/1000 second shutter speed to 1/500 second would allow one stop extra light to reach the film. But a smaller aperture of f2.8 rather than f2 would reduce the amount of light reaching the film by one stop. Moving down from 1/000 second shutter speed to 1/250 second would allow two stops of extra light to reach the film. A smaller aperture of f4 would reduce the amount of light reaching the film by two stops also, thereby balancing the change made by altering the shutter speed. This balance is known as reciprocity and the relationship works for a range of shutter speeds covering normal use.

Once indicated exposures become longer than one second this relationship no longer holds true, and the film must be given an extra amount of exposure to achieve the correct density. This change in the reciprocal arrangement between shutter duration and exposure is referred to as reciprocity failure. The amount of extra exposure needed increases exponentially and can be arrived at by reference to the chart for determining exposure increase due to reciprocity failure.

Before exposing any film at night your metered exposures need to be adjusted for reciprocity failure, so you will need to refer to this chart for every exposure you make that is longer than 1 second. Write it out and keep it in your camera bag.

I can vouch for the accuracy of this chart. I have a small copy of it stuck to the back of my light meter and have used it for years, and I have to say that it has been priceless. In many situations the adjusted exposure has proved to be much longer than my intuition and instinct suggested.

There are as many different printing styles as there are photographers. Because of this I can't claim to have a chart of 'correct' exposures. The information, if used properly, will give you negative densities that are easy to print. Don't be afraid to adapt the information to suit your own way of working. This information is a guide, not a gospel.

Once you have a degree of confidence about judging exposure, then photographing further afield where re-shooting is not possible should not be a daunting prospect.

Polaroid type 55/type 665 films

As previously stated, these films are interesting in that they produce a negative as well as a print. The quality is superb though at 50 ISO (32 ISO produces better negatives, however this makes them a little slow for night photography.

I found that the normal calculations for reciprocity failure do not apply to these materials (Polaroid give very little information about this). So, a few years ago, I did some rudimentary experiments to establish a reference chart. The results were a little surprising. When I put the figures into graph form it didn't have a smooth curve as would be expected. I redid some of my tests and came up with the same results, so I stuck with it.

I offer it to you here with the disclaimer that this was not a scientific test. I experimented out in the field where the results would be applied. If anyone has the time to fine tune these results I would be interested to see their findings.

One thing I noticed with type 55/665 was that the negative needed different calculations for reciprocity depending on whether highlight, mid or shadow detail was important so I have given times for each.

When using Polaroid films at night you may find conditions too cold to be able to process them without getting patchy results. My own method is to remove the film without processing it and take it home to warm it for a few hours before pulling it through the rollers (5x4 film only).

RECIPROCITY CORRECTION CHART FOR POLAROID TYPE 55/665

Indicated exposure	Corrected exposure		
	high	mid	shad
15 seconds	20 s	30 s	45 s
30 seconds	40 s	1 min	1 min 30
1 minute	1 mins 30	2 mins 30	3 mins
2 minutes	2 mins 45	4 mins 30	5 mins 45
3 minutes	4 mins 30	7 mins	9 mins 30
4 minutes	6 mins	10 mins	14 mins
6 minutes	8 mins 30	13 mins 30	20 mins
8 minutes	11 mins	17 mins	26 mins

Polaroid used in this way is obviously no advantage over conventional film, especially when you consider the low speed.

Choice of format

Although I have tried night photography on many formats from 35mm to 10x8, and pinhole cameras, (don't bother trying), the three sizes I will concentrate on here are 35mm, roll film and 5x4 format. This will cover most applications.

35mm

35mm film cameras are the most popular format, and for good reason. They combine lightness in weight, versatility, eye-level operation, through the lens focusing and metering, and good quality, with low cost and ease of operation. (However, these last two reasons are increasingly being proved not to be the case.)

Many photographers who use large format or roll film started out with 35mm, and most likely still use it for some types of work.

In the early days of photography, 35mm was referred to as 'miniature' because most photographers used much larger formats. The quality of the negatives from these 'miniature' cameras was not considered worthy of 'serious work'. Nowadays the quality that can be achieved from a 35mm camera with a good lens and a fine grain film would astound photographers from 50 years ago.

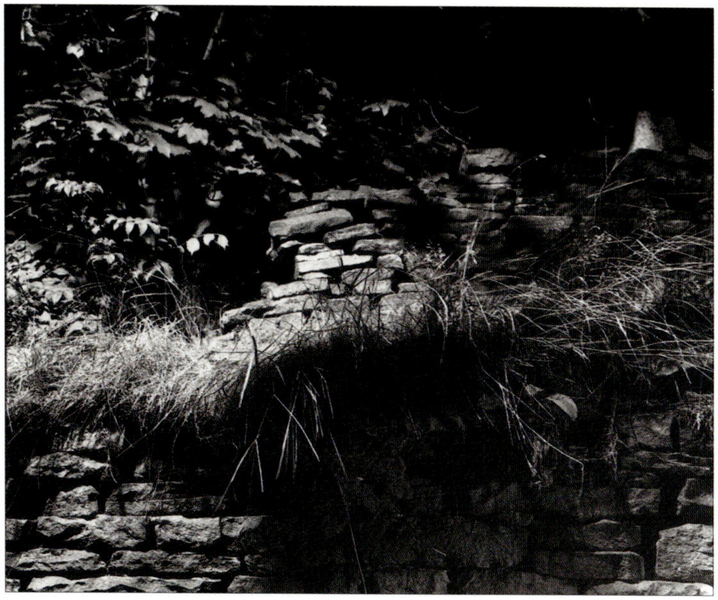

Grassy wall

Ilford HP5.

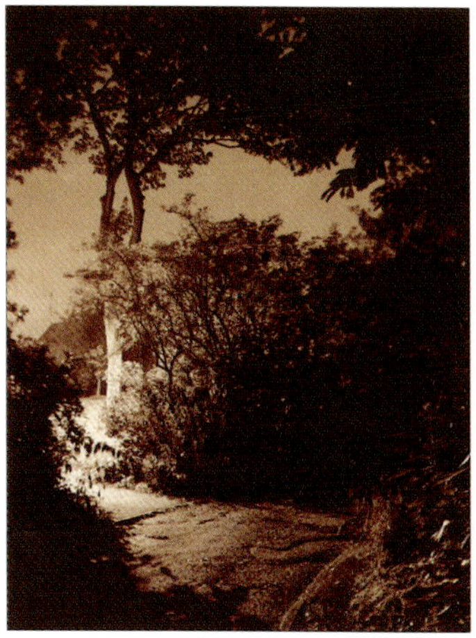

Yorkshire night scene, October 1996

Polaroid sepia print film. Exposed for 20 mins at f8.

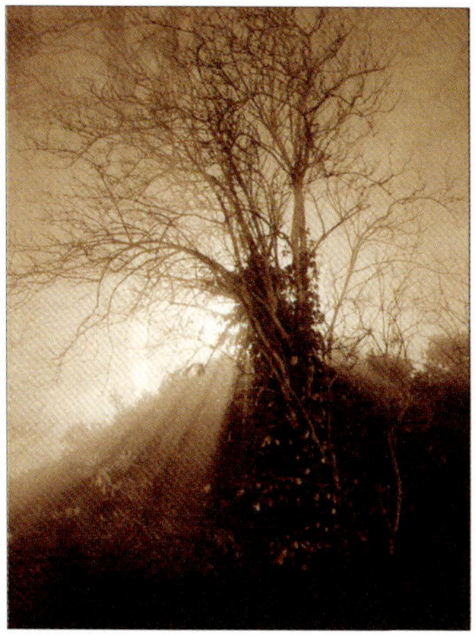

Misty night scene, Yorkshire, Nov. 1996

Polaroid sepia print film. Exposed for 20 mins at f8.

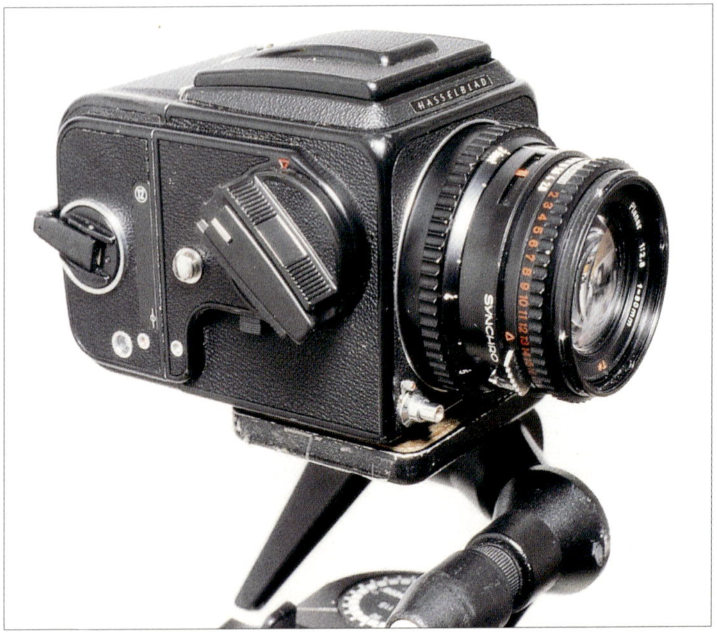

A medium format Hasselblad camera

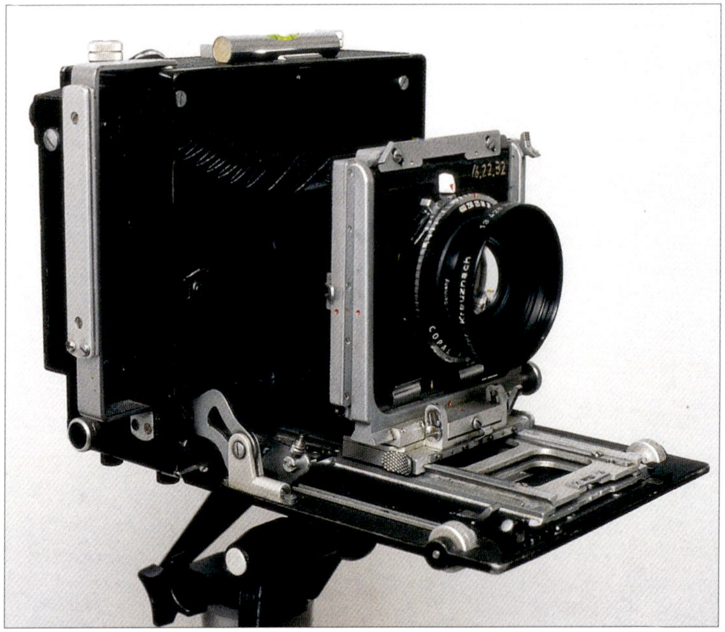

An MPP Mk VII field camera

Roll film/medium format

Moving up from 35mm to roll film will give an immediate increase in quality with a decrease in ease of operation and number of frames per film. Do not worry about these two apparently negative aspects of roll film, because the increase in quality is so dramatic, and the standard of your work will improve so much, that you will overlook the inconvenience.

Working with roll film/medium format is a slower way of working, and this will dictate the kind of photography that can be undertaken (with practice these cameras can be used quite quickly but can never fully compete with 35mm for speed of operation).

I personally think that out of all the film sizes I have used, from 35mm to 10x8, roll film is my favourite. This format is an ideal compromise between quality and ease of use. I especially like the 6x6 square format which has a unique quality that separates it from all other formats. I can't quantify what that is, the square format alters the rules of composition in a subtle way, and I think this causes me to work differently.

One thing to consider when moving from 35mm to roll film is that depth of field is lessened as focal length is increased (assuming a fixed aperture) so that if depth of detail in your night photographs is important, you will need a smaller aperture than that needed to achieve the same result on 35mm, and this will necessitate longer exposures.

Put simply, depth of field on 6x6cm camera set at f8 is less than the depth of field from a 35mm camera at f8 (standard lenses on both).

5x4

Another leap in quality comes with a move from roll film to 5x4. However, the increase in quality is offset by the extra weight, slower method of working and increased cost per shot.

The oft quoted advantage that sheet film has over all smaller formats is the facility for controlling verticals with rising front, and perspective control utilising tilt, swing and shift. With the exception of rising front, these operations are rather difficult to set accurately in the dark, although it can be done,

It is usual practice to stop the lens right down to f32 or f45 when using camera movements such as tilt or swing, but this is not really practical for night photography due to the excessively long exposures this would cause, although I am sure that there are photographers out there, with far more patience than me, who would be willing to try.

Perhaps the second most important feature of sheet film is the facility for shooting and processing single exposures. This can be a great advantage when shooting test exposures or determining development times.

Because of the long exposures inherent in night photography, a flat bed field camera is advised over a monorail design, the latter being far more susceptible to vibrations and movement due to wind.

Metering light levels at night

Reading exposure using the camera meter

The difficulty for most workers in night photography is how much exposure to give?

Determining the correct exposure for after dark images can pose a few problems for the unwary. Firstly, the low levels of illumination are often too dim to influence the light meter (especially in some older cameras), and secondly, the exposure indicated, if longer than one second, will be inaccurate.This is due to reciprocity failure (see the chart opposite).

Don't let this put you off. I have devised a handy chart for finding the correct exposure using the meter in your camera which includes an allowance for reciprocity failure (see page 30).

Firstly, take a reading of the scene with the aperture set at f2 (pointing the camera down to exclude bright lights from the viewfinder). If the meter reading indicates an exposure of one second, and you wish to take your picture with an aperture of f11, read along from one second and down from f11. Where they meet, read off your final exposure i.e. 11 minutes 20 seconds.

Those of you who use 28-80mm zoom lenses should refer to the chart for metering at f4.

This chart has been compiled from experience. I have used it many times and can recommend its accuracy. If, after using the chart you find your exposures are incorrect, then this is probably due to inaccurate metering. Some older cameras are not very good at metering in low light situations. Consider buying a hand

CHART FOR DETERMINING EXPOSURE INCREASE DUE TO RECIPROCITY FAILURE

Indicated exposure (seconds)	**Actual exposure after calculation for reciprocity failure (seconds)**
¼	¼
½	½
1	1
2	2.5
3	4
4	6
5	8
6	10
7	12.5
8	14.7
9	17.2
10	20
11	22.5
12	25
13	27.5
14	30
15	32.8
16	36
32	1 minute 28 seconds
1 minute 4 seconds	3 minutes 36 seconds
2 minutes 8 seconds	8 minutes 49 seconds
4 minutes 16 seconds	21 minutes 40 seconds
8 minutes 32 seconds	52 minutes 50 seconds
17 minutes 4 seconds	2 hours 15 minutes

I would like to thank the British Journal of Photography for permission to reproduce this information.

TIP

When metering, consider that the degree to which the lamps are overexposed depends on how far from the lamp your metering position is.

If you are photographing something near to the lamp your exposure will be shorter. When the point of interest is some distance from the lamp your meter will indicate a longer exposure, which will mean that any lamps included in the scene will be more heavily exposed.

QUICK REFERENCE CHART FOR DETERMINING NIGHT EXPOSURES WHEN METERING WITH THE CAMERA (f2 LENS)

Indicated exposure lens at f2	FINAL APERTURE f4	f5.6	f8	f11	f16	f22	f32
1/8	1/2	1	2.5	6	15	32	1 min
1/4	1	2.5	6	15	32	1 min 20	3 mins 20
1/2	2.5	6	15	32	1 min 20	3 mins 20	8 mins 40
1	6	15	32	1 min 20	3 mins 20	8 mins 40	21 mins
2	15	32	1 min 20	3 mins 20	8 mins 40	21 mins 20	50 mins
4	32	1 min 20	3 mins 20	8 mins 40	21 mins 20	50 mins	2 hours
8	1 min 20	3 mins 20	8 mins 40	21 mins 20	50 mins	2 hours	4 hrs 25 mins

CHART FOR f4 LENSES

Indicated exposure lens at f4	FINAL APERTURE f5.6	f8	f11	f16	f22
1/8	1/4	1/2	1	2.5	6
1/4	1/2	1	2.5	6	15
1/2	1	2.5	6	15	32
1 s	2.5	6	15	32	1m20s
2 s	6	15	32	1m20s	3m20s
4 s	15	32	1m20s	3m20s	8m40s
8 s	32	1m20s	3m20s	8m40s	21m20s

meter. From the beginning though I strongly recommend some form of note taking, a note pad or scrap of paper, or even better, a small hand held recorder (these can be used one-handed, and in total darkness).

Reading exposure using a hand meter

Taking a light reading using a separate hand held light meter is a more versatile and accurate method of determining exposure.

Two methods can be applied. Firstly, pointing the meter at the scene to be measured. This is known as a reflected exposure reading. Metering in this way can sometimes be influenced by bright lights or large areas of white such as snow, or in situations where there is an excess of very dark tones. These are very real possibilities in night photography.

Secondly, standing in the scene, pointing the meter back at the camera, and taking an incident reading. (This can only be done if the meter has an opaque light baffle which can be placed over the light cell.) An incident reading measures the light falling on the meter and is not unduly influenced by large areas of white or black. This is the most accurate method, but cannot be undertaken with a cheap light meter. Only meters capable of reading below E.V. 2.5 (400 ISO) should be used. I have no hesitation in recommending the Gossen Lunasix or Profisix light meters for this type of photography. I have used mine for more than eighteen years and they have given me excellent service.

Bracketing

When experimenting with night exposures for the first time, it is advisable to bracket your exposures. (Afterwards the need for bracketing is largely unnecessary when referring to the exposure charts in this book.) Bracketing is normally understood to mean exposing three frames, the first at one stop less than the indicated exposure, the second at the indicated exposure, and another frame at one stop more than the indicated exposure.

This is intended to provide you with a usable negative in situations that are difficult to meter.

When photographing at night it is unlikely that the exposure is

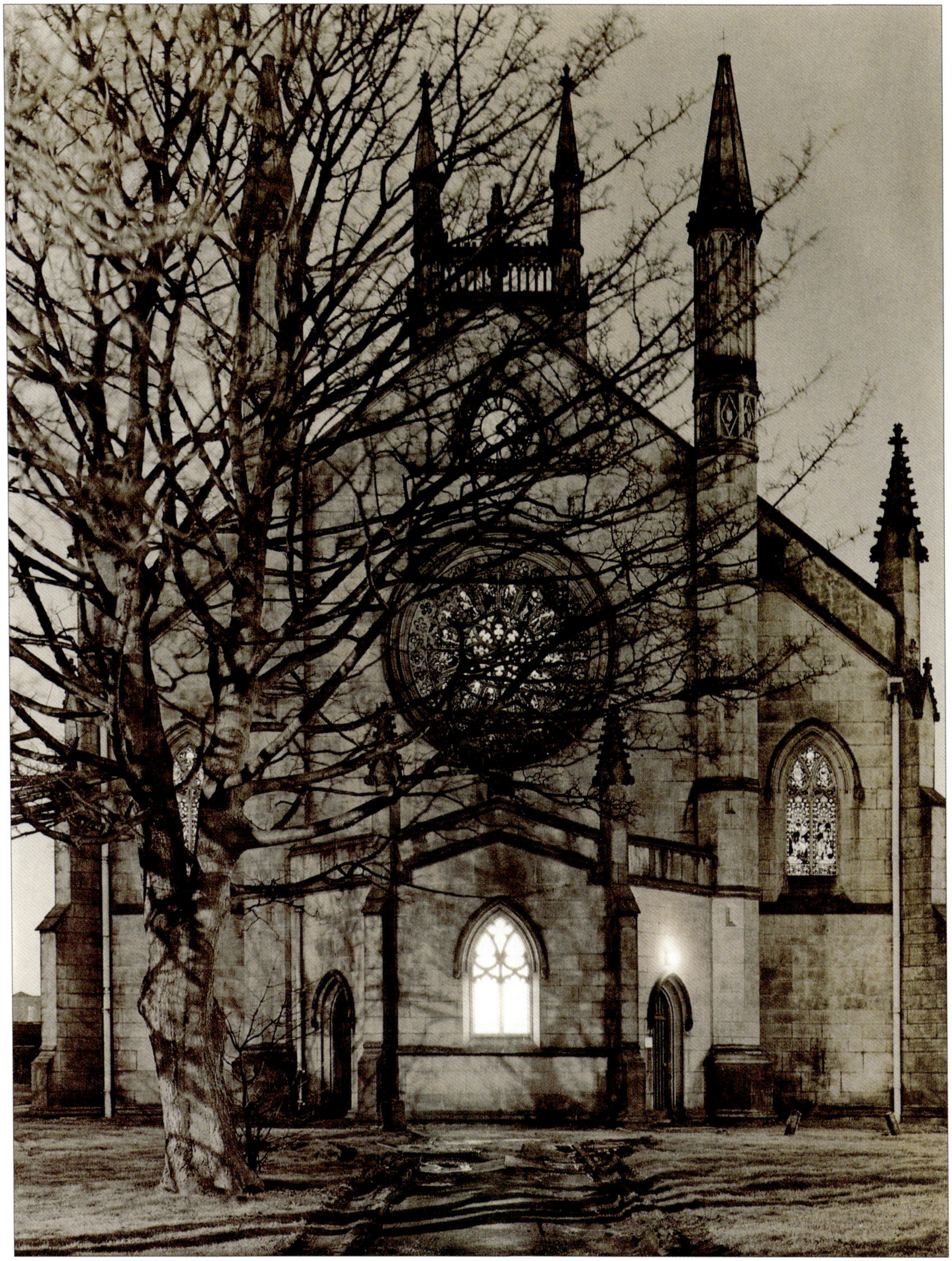

Near Audenshaw, Manchester

One of the most useful aspects of 5x4 is the facility for rising front to keep verticals parallel when photographing above eye level. Ilford HP5 processed in Ildford ID11.

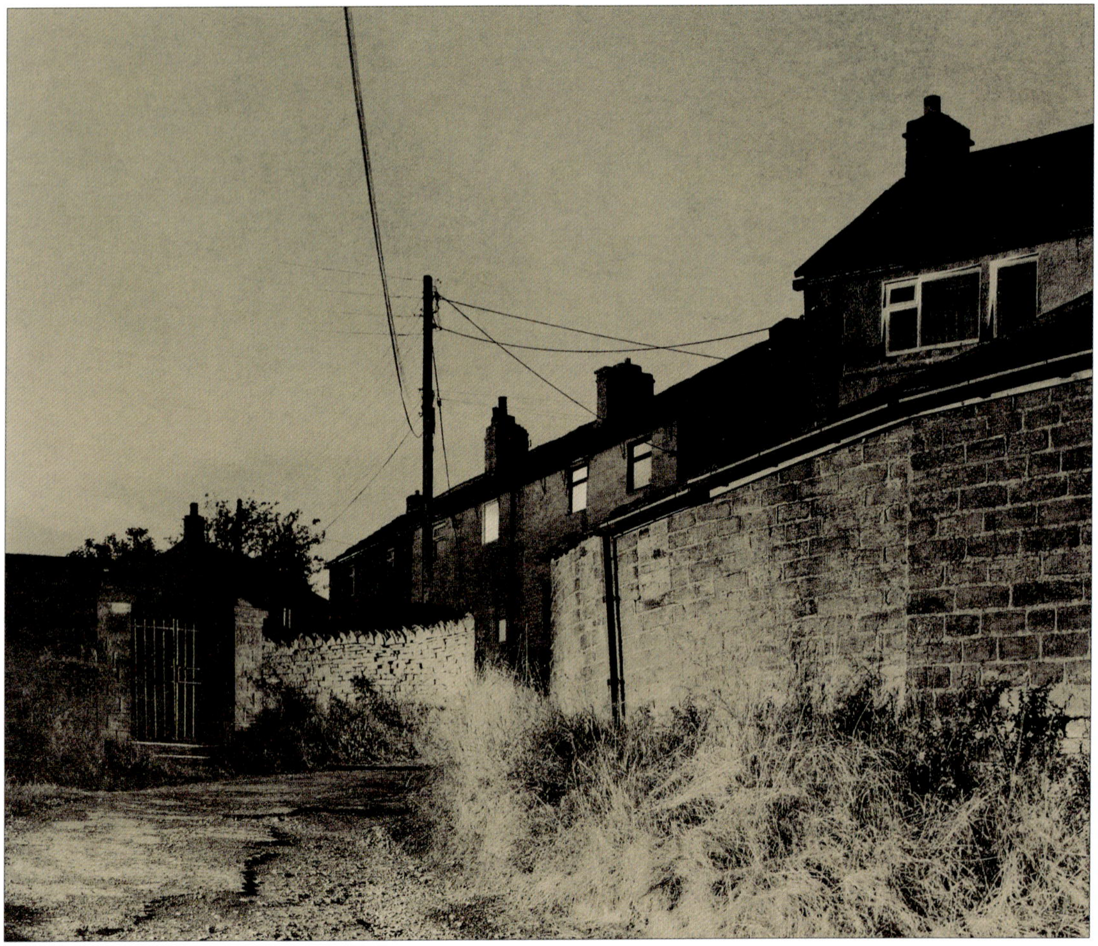

Houses at Snowgate Head

Lith print from 5x4 negative showing use of rising front to view scenes above eye level. The telegraph pole and drainpipe in the centre were actually tilted away from vertical, and are not as a result of the camera being tilted. The vertical lines in the window frames at top right, and the gate in the lower left, show correct positioning. Ilford HP5 processed in Ilford ID11.

going to be less than that indicated by the meter so the sequence of three exposures should begin with the indicated time and increase with each exposure.

This method is certainly recommended for the beginner, even though it would appear to be a wasteful way to take pictures, but venturing into night photography without any clue about what you are doing, (whether right or wrong) is going to prove more wasteful in the long run.

Bracketing will ensure that at least one of your negatives is printable. It is important to remember not to alter the exposure time, only the aperture. Altering the exposure time would entail another calculation for reciprocity failure which will over complicate the situation, and in some cases indicate excessively long exposures.

EXAMPLE

Metered exposure – 2 sec at f2.

Exposure after calculation for reciprocity – 8m.49s for f16.

Bracketing by exposure time, including calculation for reciprocity – 8m.49s/21m.40s/52m.50s at f16.

Bracketing by aperture – 8m.49s at f/16, f/8 and f/56.

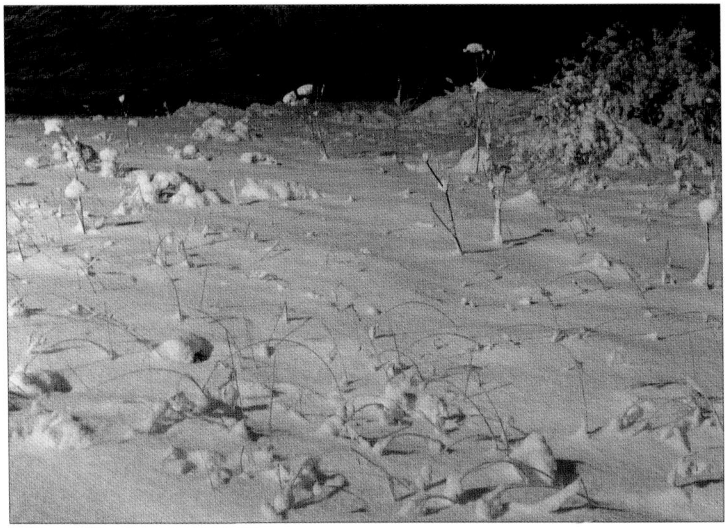

Metering in snow using the reflected method causes the whites to record as a mid grey.

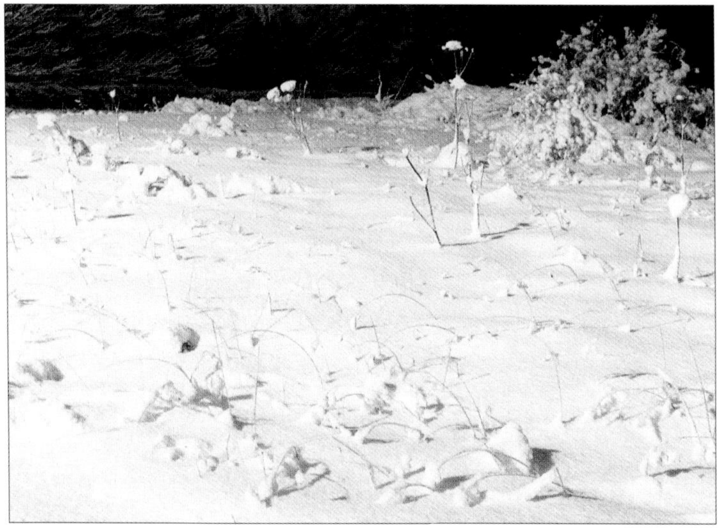

The more accurate method of reading the incident light gives clean whites.

Adding the exposures for the first sequence gives a total of 83 minutes 19 seconds, but the total for the second sequence is only 26 minutes. From this it can be seen that bracketing with apertures is the better option.

To fully exploit the results of your bracketing take notes of every variation. These notes will then become an invaluable reference for future exposures in similar situations.

The zone system and its limited application to night photography

Many photographers will be familiar with the concept of the zone system, and may even practice it with their own photography.

The zone system is an excellent exposure and processing system, which allows very fine control of density and contrast. It would seem an ideal tool for night photography, as it would appear that the facility for fine contrast control, and the production of near perfect negatives, would make printing this kind of work extremely simple.

In practice the method is only half useful, as the negative contraction (contrast increasing) part, has no application for naturally contrast-high situations. The night negative needs a normal or contrast reducing process in virtually every situation. The facility for reducing contrast is the other side of the zone system 'coin', and this aspect is potentially very useful.

To utilise the zone system properly, a reliable and accurate system of exposure readings needs to be established, and this is usually done with a spot meter.

Reading an exposure from deep shadows at night is not possible with a spotmeter, and almost impossible with a good quality handmeter. Similarly, taking a reading from the brightest point on a streetlight for the highlight measurement, can prove problematic with a handmeter (unless you have a ladder), although this can be done with a spotmeter., but these are not the main reasons why this technique is only partially useful.

Another problem arises with the contrast in relation to reciprocity, because contrast is increased as exposures become longer.

A shot taken at 1 second at f 2 will display a different contrast to one given the equivalent exposure for f22. This variation makes accurate zone measurement impossible, resulting in nothing but an approximation of the zone system.

The suggested methods for contrast reduction do come in very handy for night work, but unless the problems stated above are overcome, these methods are nothing more than downrating.

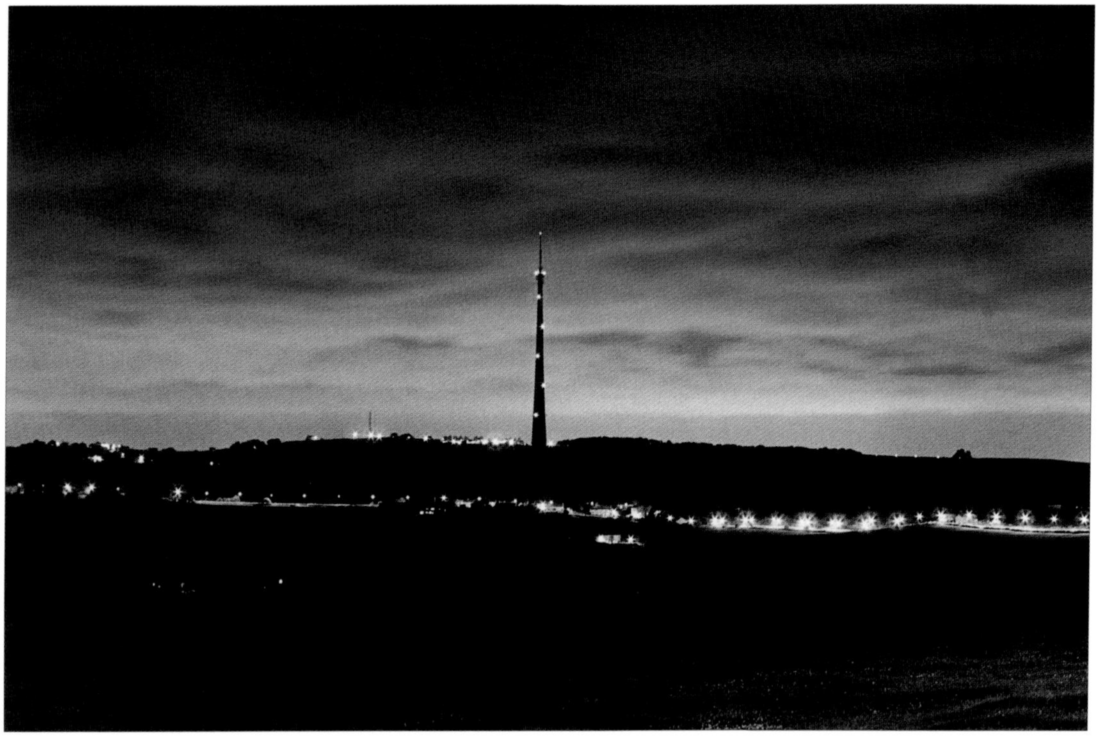

TV mast

Taking a meter reading off the foreground is not always possible. For a scene such as this the lights do not unduly influence the meter because they are so distant and a reading can be taken of the scene or the sky.

Ilford HP5 processed in Ilford ID11.

Flare and halation

Flare

One aspect of night photography which is rarely discussed, is the ever present threat of flare.

Flare can ruin a perfectly good night photograph, and often with no indication in the viewfinder beforehand.

Flare is caused by stray light 'bouncing around' inside the lens, reflecting off the numerous glass surfaces, leaving areas of brightness that degrade the shadows. This can range from a slight fogging, to areas of intense brightness, sometimes dominating the picture.

This can often happen, even when the view through the lens looks perfectly unaffected.

As the lens aperture closes down at the moment of exposure, the intensity and shape of the offending light changes, introducing bright shapes, banding, or as is often seen in landscapes shot into the sun, a series of hexagons running diagonally across the frame.

In some situations, generally I think with older lenses which are not super multi coated, a kind of circular banding, like the grooves of a record, is noticed.

This can range from very fine lines only noticeable on prints above 20x16in, to broad bands which are even visible on a contact sheet. I have only ever encountered this problem under sodium light which I believe is due to the narrow spectral bandwidth of this type of light, setting up an interference with the coatings on older lenses.

I have not been able to find any information about this particular effect, though, as I say, It seems to be restricted to sodium light and old lenses so it may not be a problem for the vast majority of photographers, To be on the safe side, make a habit of shielding the lens from nearby lights if they are forward of the camera position, but out of the viewfinder.

Examples of bracketing

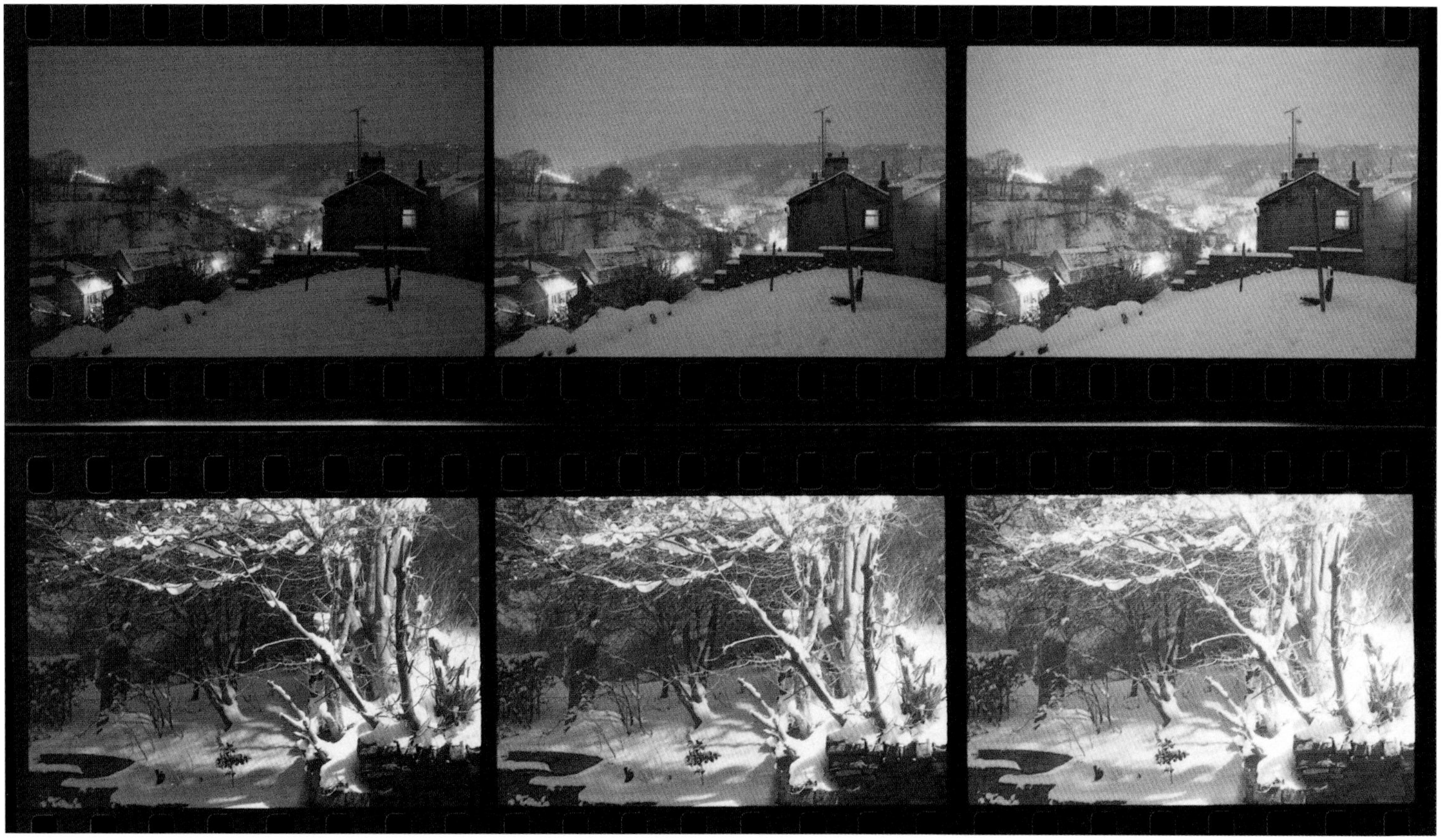

These frames show how slight differences in exposure can dramatically change the picture, the longer exposures revealing much more shadow detail, but at the expense of the highlights. These can sometimes be 'rescued' by clever printing (see section on split grade printing).

To shield the lens, stand to one side of the camera with the offending light source behind you, hold up your hand or piece of card until you see it cast a shadow onto the lens, and open up the shutter. Keep your hand/card there until the exposure is finished; this is known as flagging. This way you may look a bit odd to passers by, but you will not be troubled with flare.

Halation

With light sources that are part of the composition and consequently within the frame, flagging is not a possibility. In this case, flare can be minimised by taking care not to over develop the film, this is because flare and halation (halos of brightness around the lamps) are not caused by just the light that reaches the film, they are also due to a chemical effect known as infectious development, where silver halides are affected by strong developer activity nearby.

When an intense point of light reaches the film it scatters light around, affecting adjacent areas. These heavily exposed points, and the secondary exposed areas, gather a momentum in processing that rapidly builds up density, creating a large area of

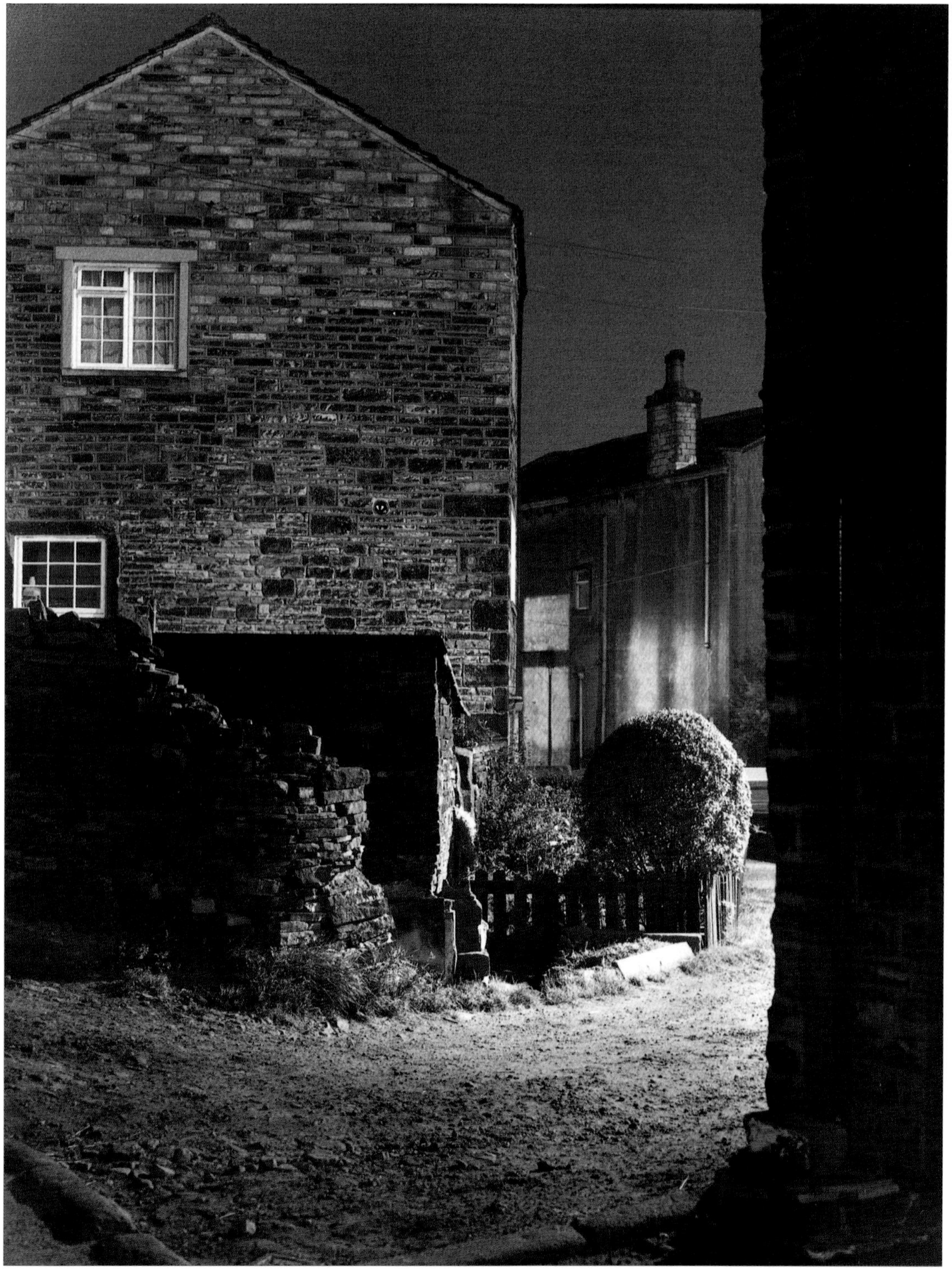

Netherthong, Yorkshire

Ilford HP5 from a 6x7cm negative processed in Paterson Acutol.

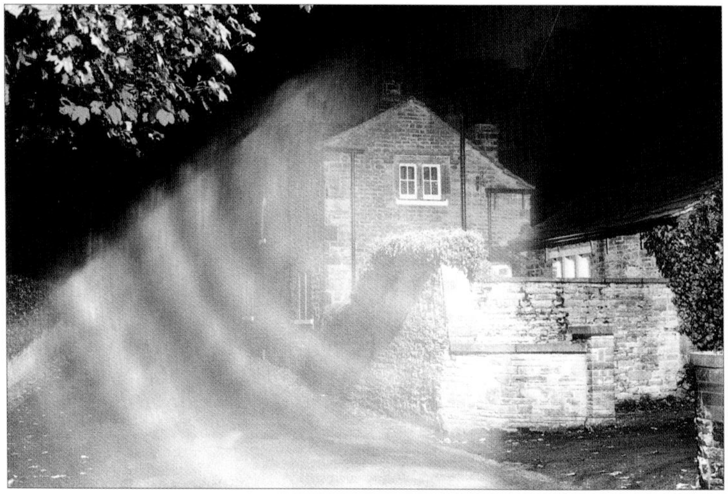

An extreme example of flare. Picture A

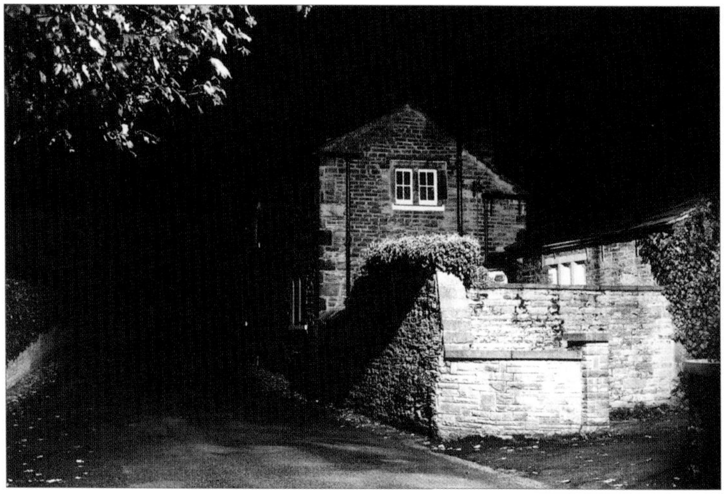

Flagging the lens. Picture B.

Shielding the lens with the hand or a piece of card during the exposure will prevent stray light from reflecting around within the lens. Picture A shows the scene obscured by flare and picture B shows how shielding the lens can prevent it.

near black on the negative, which is all but impossible to print-in.

To keep halo and flare to a minimum, I would recommend firstly, flagging the light, and secondly, careful processing. The important point about processing for night photography is to not over develop.

Keeping the development below the critical point could be achieved by reducing the development time for your film, with a corresponding reduction in film speed – in effect, downrating. Half a stop would be enough to keep the maximum density from reaching black, whilst still giving a full negative. This would not be too great a sacrifice for improved image quality – would it?

Refer to the formulary and processing section at the end of the book for downrating procedure.

The contrast reducing processes described elsewhere are ideal for reducing flare and halo, especially pyro.

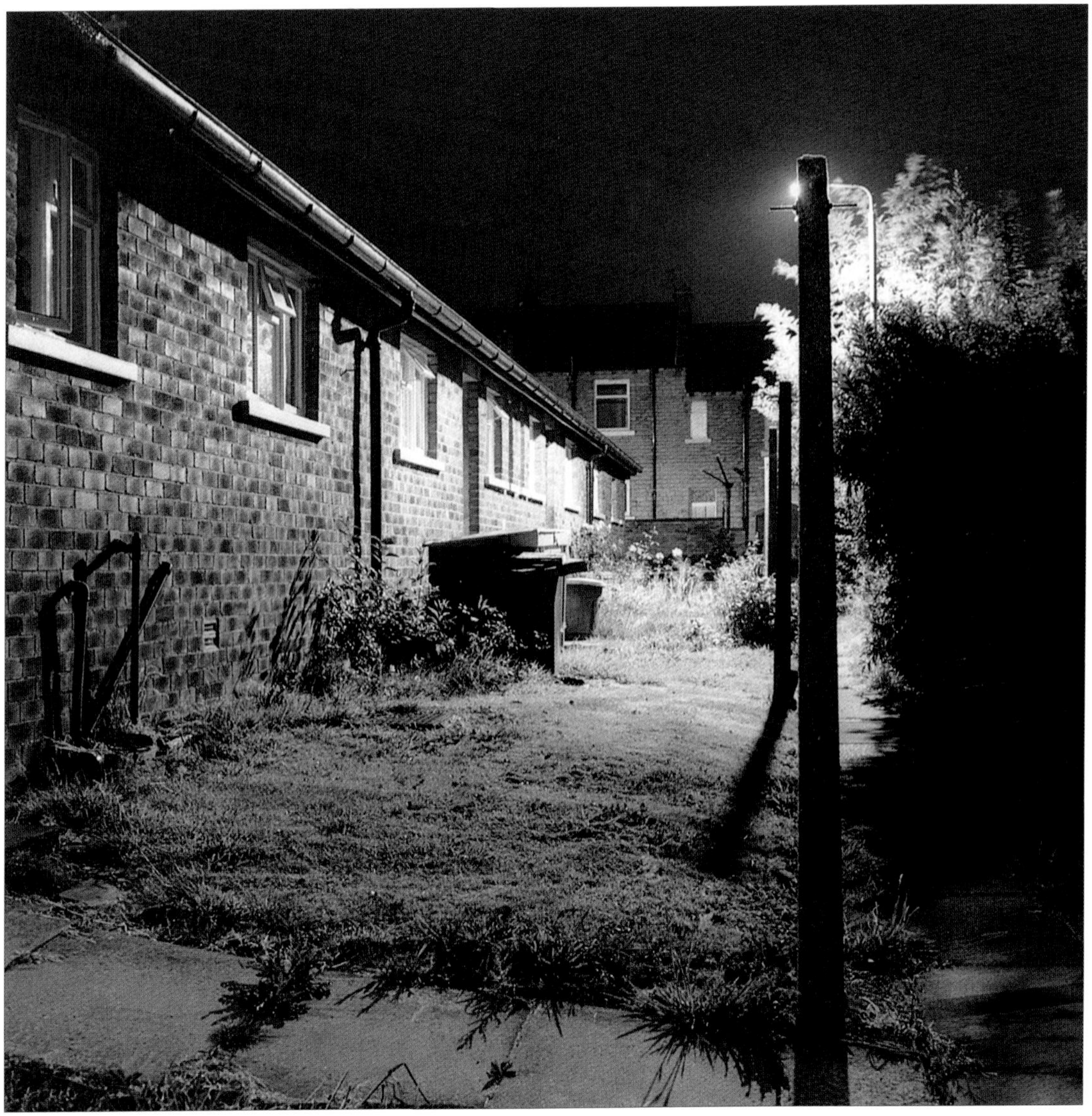

Back gardens

To reduce the effects of flare, use posts or tree branches to obscure the bright lights.

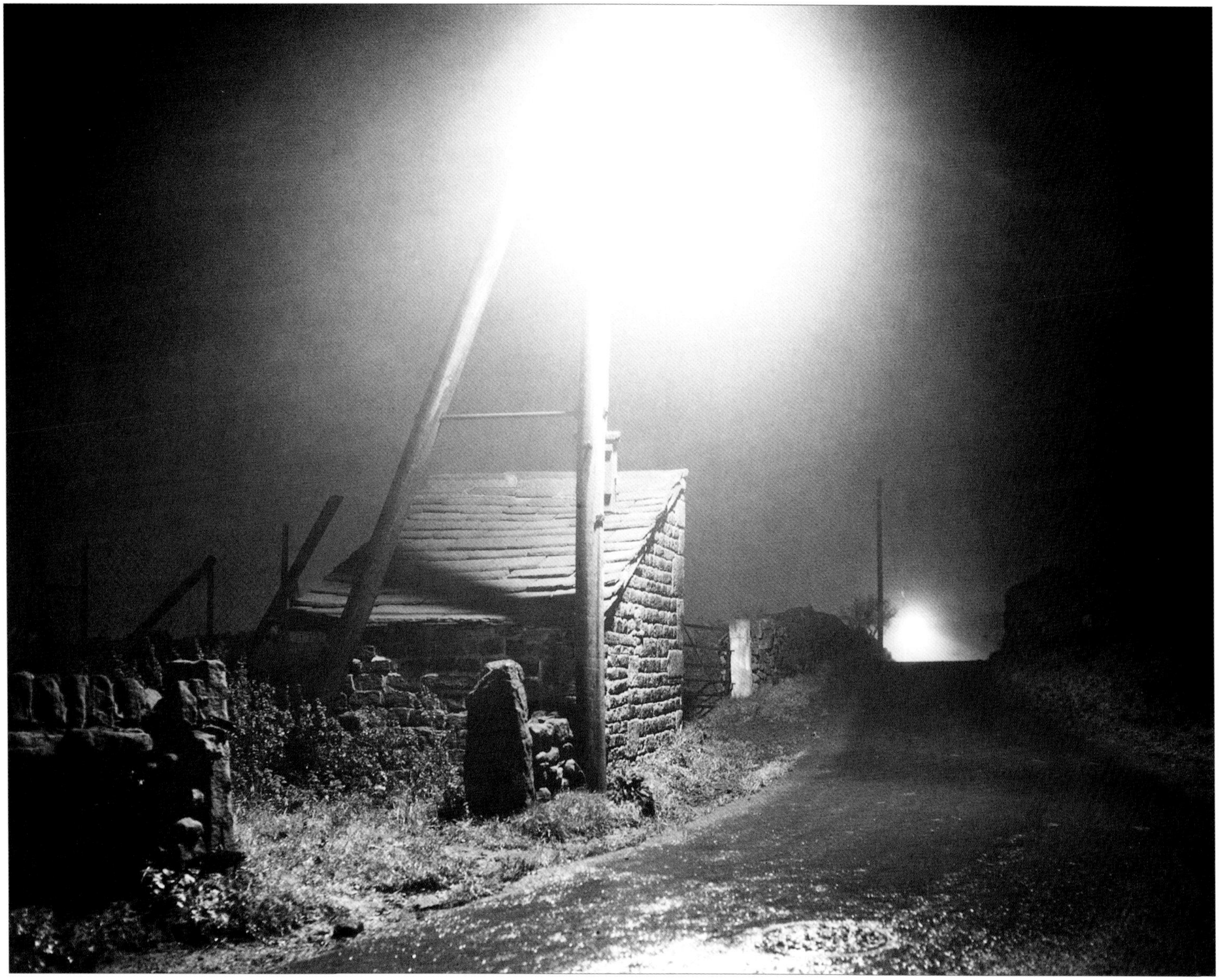

Small cowshed

A hot spot of flare that is difficult, or impossible, to burn in is a result of over developing the film.

the fancy stuff

Supplementary lighting

Photographing by street light alone, you will often find that large areas of the scene are completely black. Compositionally this can sometimes be an advantage, but this is not always the case. It may be desirable to bring out some detail in the dark areas, and this can be achieved quite easily by adding light from a flash gun or a torch. With long exposures there will be plenty of time to fire off the flashgun at least once, and it may be necessary to fire it a number of times in certain situations.

Similarly, using torch light to fill in, can lift shadows very well, although this is harder to quantify. A flash would be used in a situation when a broad area of light was needed, whereas a torch can be applied selectively, to bring out small details or give a little extra to parts of the scene which are not in full light.

Using fill-in flash

Some cameras, as you are probably aware, have built-in flash guns, which are fired automatically whenever the camera is used in low light. This type of fill-in flash is not useful in night photography, and would result in a flat, uninteresting picture, even if it were bright enough to illuminate the scene. Most built in flashguns are not powerful enough to fully illuminate a scene which is perhaps only twenty feet away.

Subjects need more flash when photographed out of doors. This is because, when used inside they rely on a large amount of reflected flash from walls and ceilings to make up the exposure, this is obviously not available out in the field, and results in subjects looking underexposed, even when the correct flash to subject setting has been applied

Flash is not without its uses however, if used intelligently, When taking night photographs using a locking cable release, you are free to walk away from the tripod during the exposure. You therefore have the option of 'filling in' from the side which will look more natural and pleasing, this can give the impression of another street light at some distance.

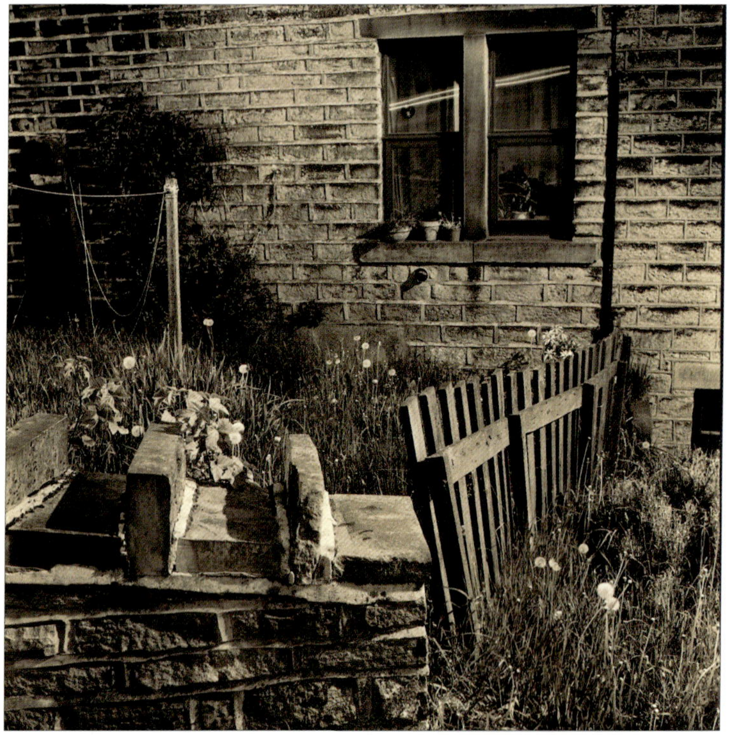

In some situations a night photograph appears to have been taken in daylight. This often happens when the scene has only one light source and no sky to indicate the time of day.
Ilford HP5 6x6cm negative processed in Ilford ID11.

Theoretically, your flash exposure should be less than the streetlight exposure. The 'correct exposure' should refer to that lit by the street light, and the flash gun is used to lighten the shadows just enough to give you printable detail. In practice, as I have mentioned above, you may find that more is needed.

In some situations the lighting is fine, but the night scene appears on the print to look as if it were taken in broad daylight, this often happens when the scene has only one light source, and

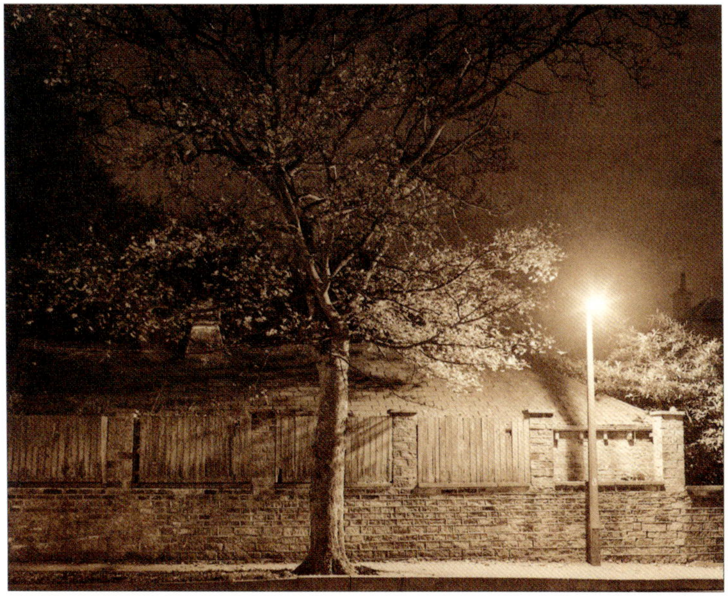

No fill in flash.
Ilford HP5 6x7 negative processed in Ilford ID11.

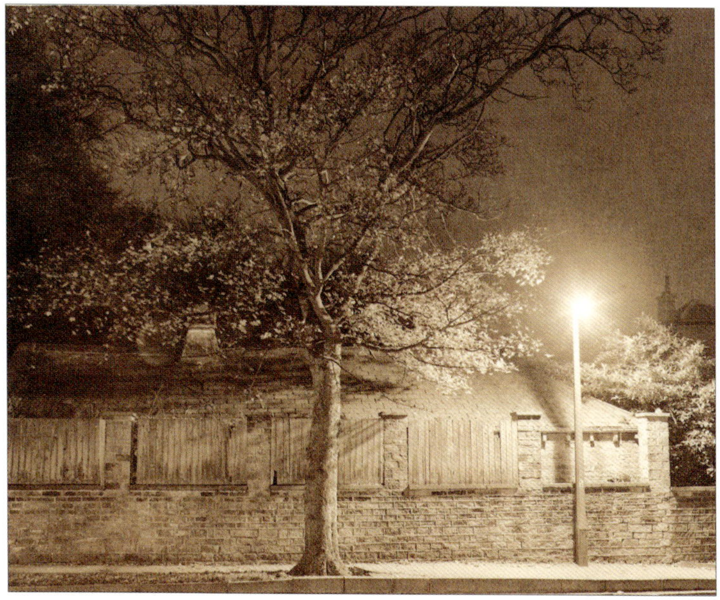

With fill in flash from right to lighten shadows.
Ilford HP5.

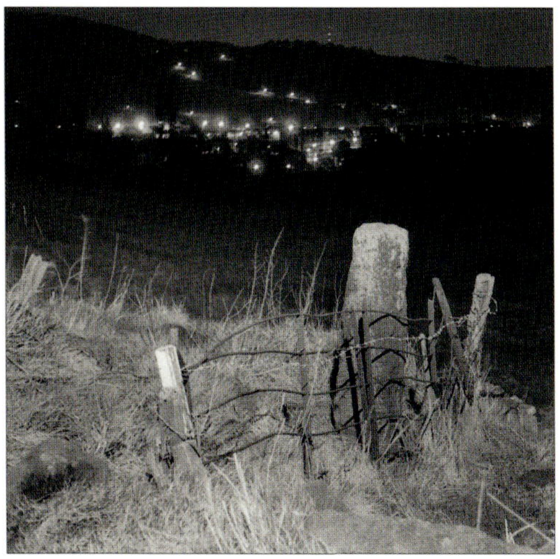

Distant lights

A flash fired to illuminate the foreground can sometimes reveal unexpected detail. Ilford HP5 cropped from a 35mm negative processed in Ilford Microphen.

no sky to indicate the time of day. This is an ideal situation where fill in can be utilised in a subtle way, the unwanted daylight effect is easily remedied by the use of a little flash from one side, giving the impression of more than one streetlight.

Technique

When filling in with flash I recommend that you: set your flash to 'manual' rather than the 'auto' setting; check the aperture on the camera, (say f11); read off the correct distance for that aperture on the flash gun, (say 12 feet); and fire the flash from that distance, then expose a second frame, firing the flash from 24 feet, (double the indicated distance), and one more frame, firing the flash from half the distance – 6 feet. The degree of fill in will depend on your subject or scene.

Try this again, firing twice for each picture taken, this will ensure at least one shot with the correct amount of fill in.

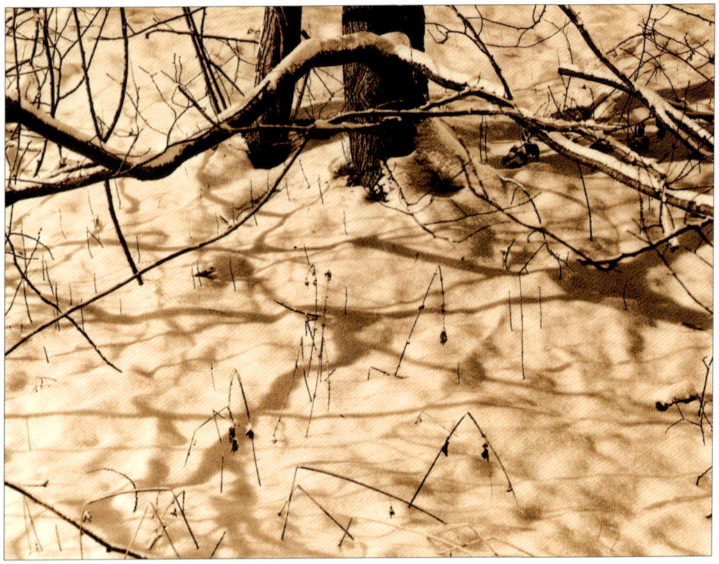

Branch shadows on snow

Another image that looks as though it were taken in daylight although this was exposed entirely streetlight.

Ilford HP5

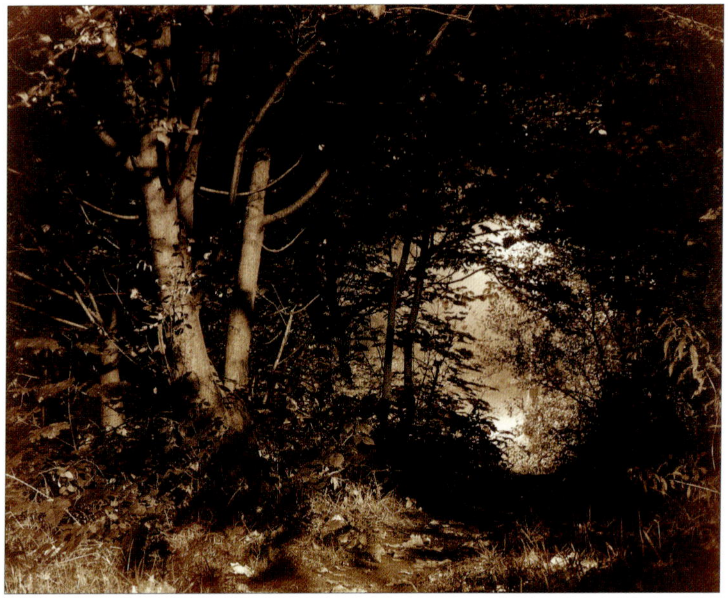

Night, Meltham, West Yorkshire

With more than one light source, an immediate impression of night is given. This can be created with a flashgun.

Ilford HP5

'Painting with light' (using a torch)

Another option for 'filling-in' is to use a powerful torch. This can give an unusual effect which can be an advantage, but is difficult to meter or quantify.

As with flash, the effective brightness of your torch light depends on the distance between you and your photographic subject, the exposure is also affected by how long the torch is applied, or 'shone'.

The effect is of course, cumulative, and waggling a torch beam around in your shadow areas can easily give you bright 'hot spots' in areas that you have gone over a few times.

If you are unfamiliar with this method, then it is probably wise to shoot a few frames, varying the amount of torch light in each to give you a choice of fill-in effects to choose from when printing.

Remember of course, that if you print your own negatives, a bit too much torch in the shadows does not mean a wasted shot, the density can be corrected in the darkroom by burning in the offending area on the print.

Shooting in snow

A heavy snowfall can provide an excellent opportunity for creative night photography, and is one of my favourite conditions for taking pictures.

At first glance, weather like this would prompt many to curl up in front of the fire and watch the t.v., and most do, but they miss out on a magical world of possible night photography, when everything is extremely photogenic.

With a fresh fall of heavy snow there are pictures everywhere you look. The right kind of snowfall can provide an amazing array of pictorial possibilities.

The experience of walking around at night when the snow is clinging to everything, changing the shapes of familiar things, is something that gives me an enormous amount of pleasure. I love to observe the play of light, the rounded shapes, and the way that everything looks completely different.

Obviously, getting around is a little difficult, but apart from that, I believe that photography in the snow is actually easier.

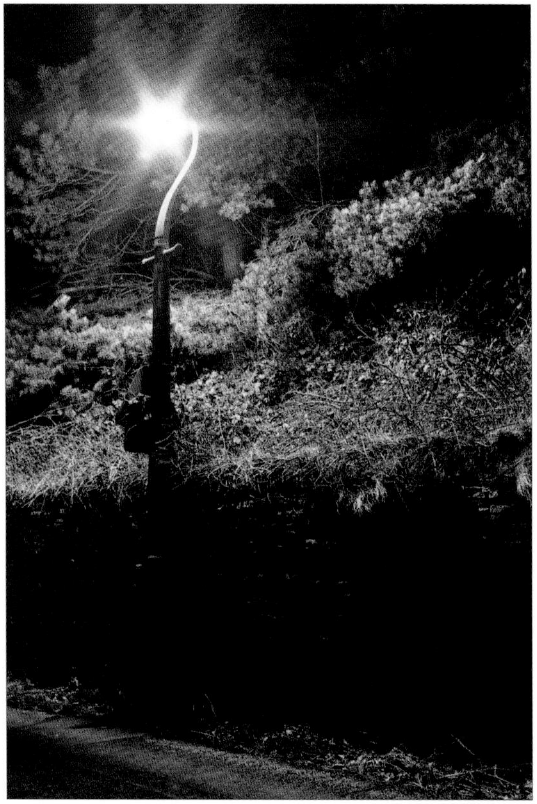

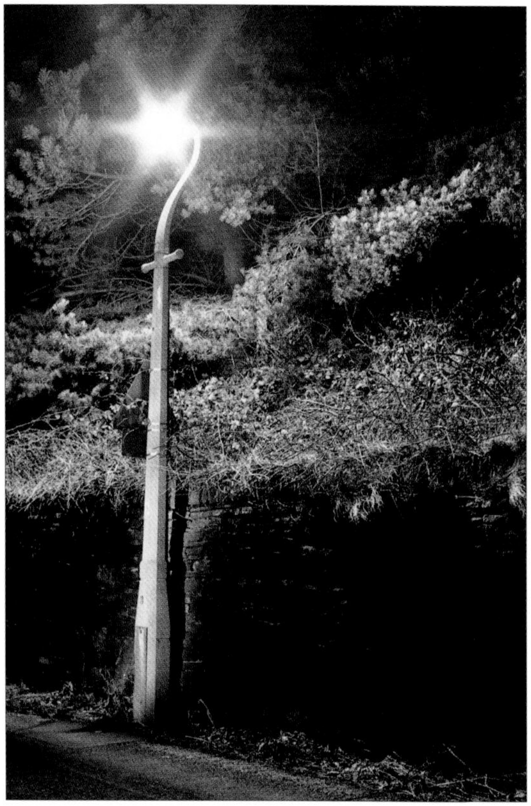

A torch can be used selectively to reveal detail or to hilight elements within the picture.

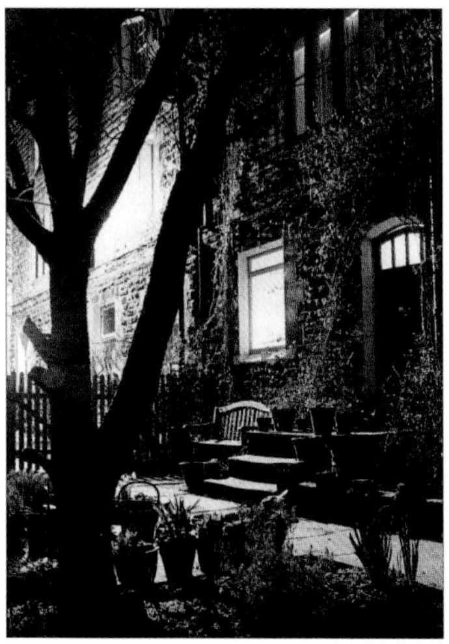

No fill in.

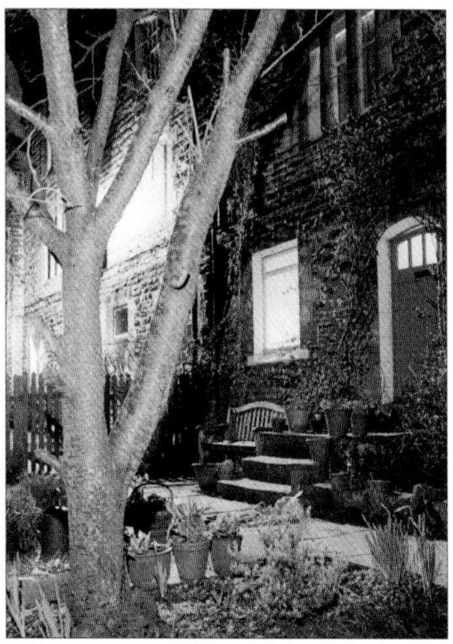

Direct flash fill in.

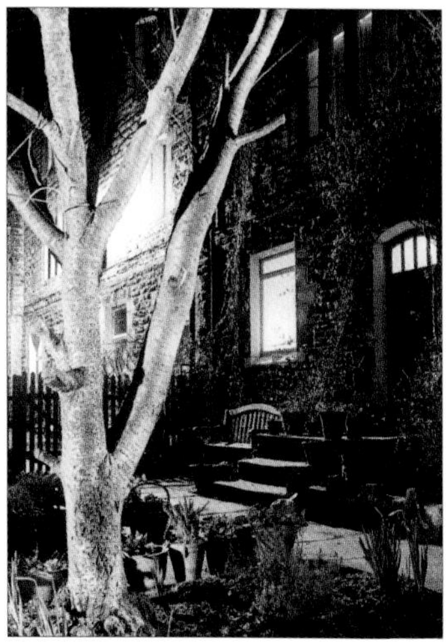

Torch fill in.

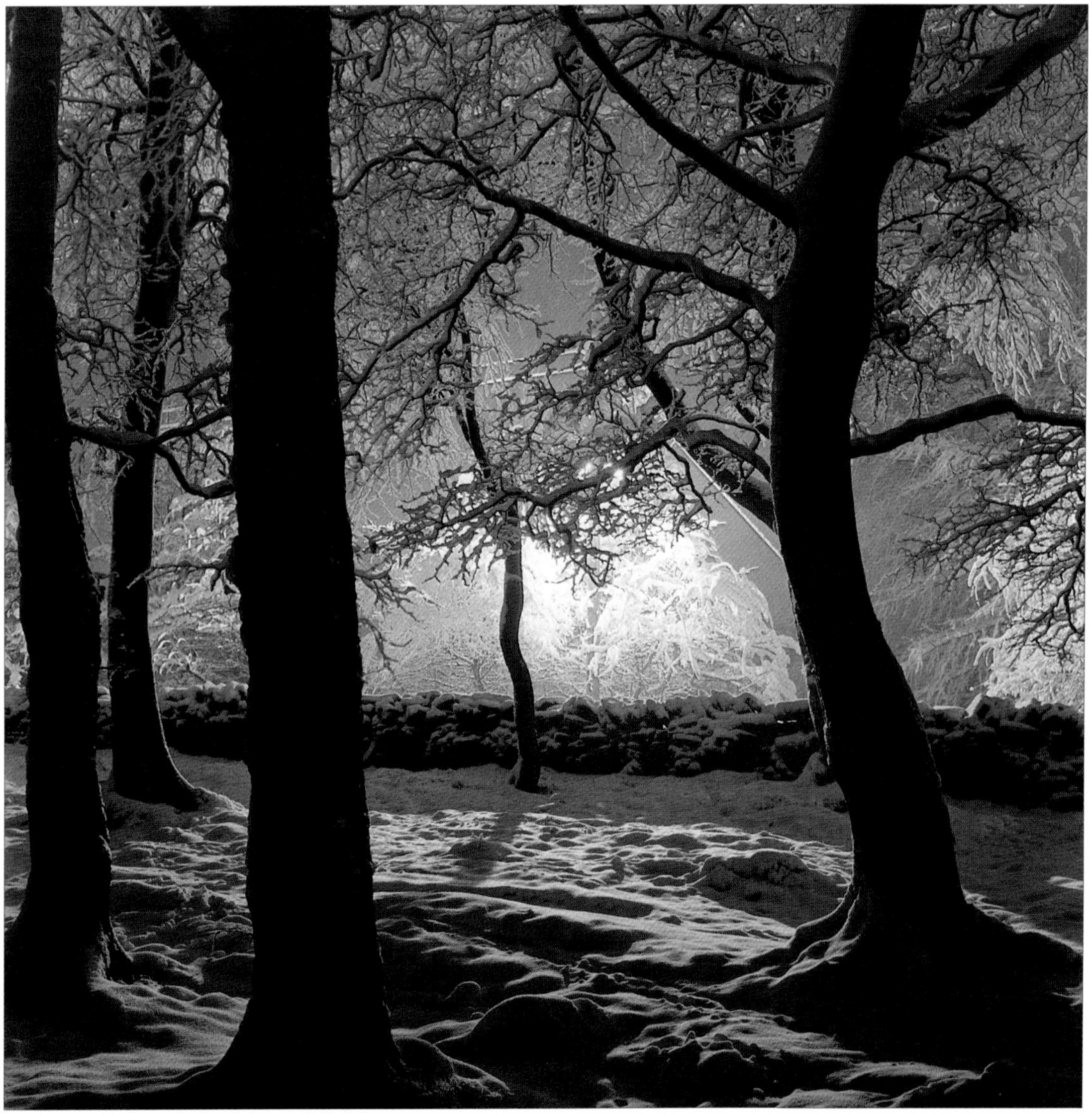

Looking out of the trees

Ilford HP5 6x6cm negative processed in Ilford ID11.

Consider that exposures are shortened by about a stop, shadows are filled in by the reflective properties of snow, and details in the distance, well away from streetlights, are bright enough to record on the film with good separation, giving depth to landscapes.

It doesn't last long though, and should be photographed immediately. Within a few hours, traffic, snow ploughs, people, – all will have a detrimental effect on the conditions. Pretty soon the snow becomes wet and begins to drop off the branches and wires, so it is essential that you go out as soon as possible for the best shots.

If you think; 'it's a bit cold just now, I'll go after I've watched 'Last of the summer wine', then the best will have passed.

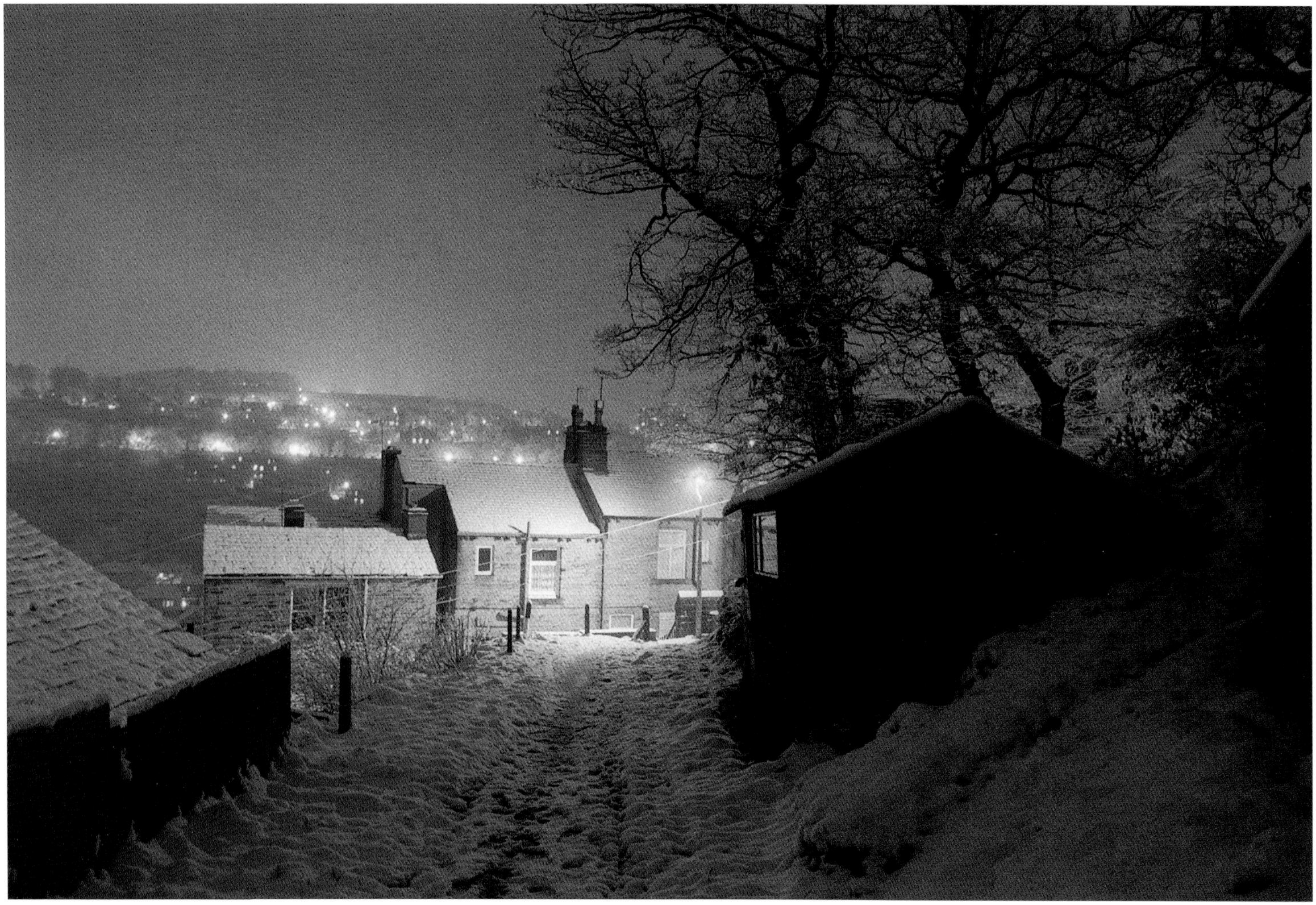

Armitage Bridge, West Yorkshire
Ilford XP2.

Even though snow poses extra difficulties for photography, I would recommend all creative photographers to experience this kind of light/weather combination at least once. Careful, it's addictive!

Shooting in fog

Another wonderful weather condition as regards night photography.

Fog is really good for providing strong shapes and dramatic lighting, and excellent for reducing flare where lights appear in the scene, it separates the foreground and background making it easy to produce good night photographs.

Fog pictures also seem more suited to toning, this is probably due to the way the tones are separated into larger areas and often have a larger proportion of mid tones distributed throughout the picture.

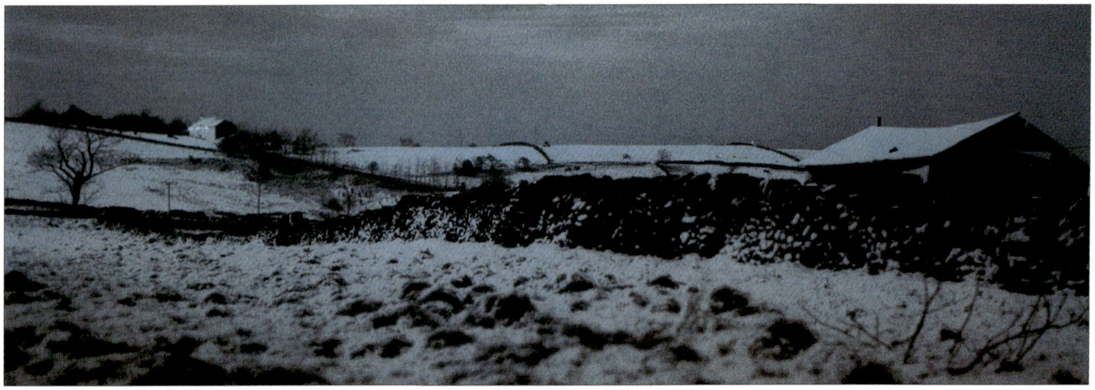

Looking towards Wolfstone

Ilford HP5 from a 35mm negative processed in Ilford Microphen.

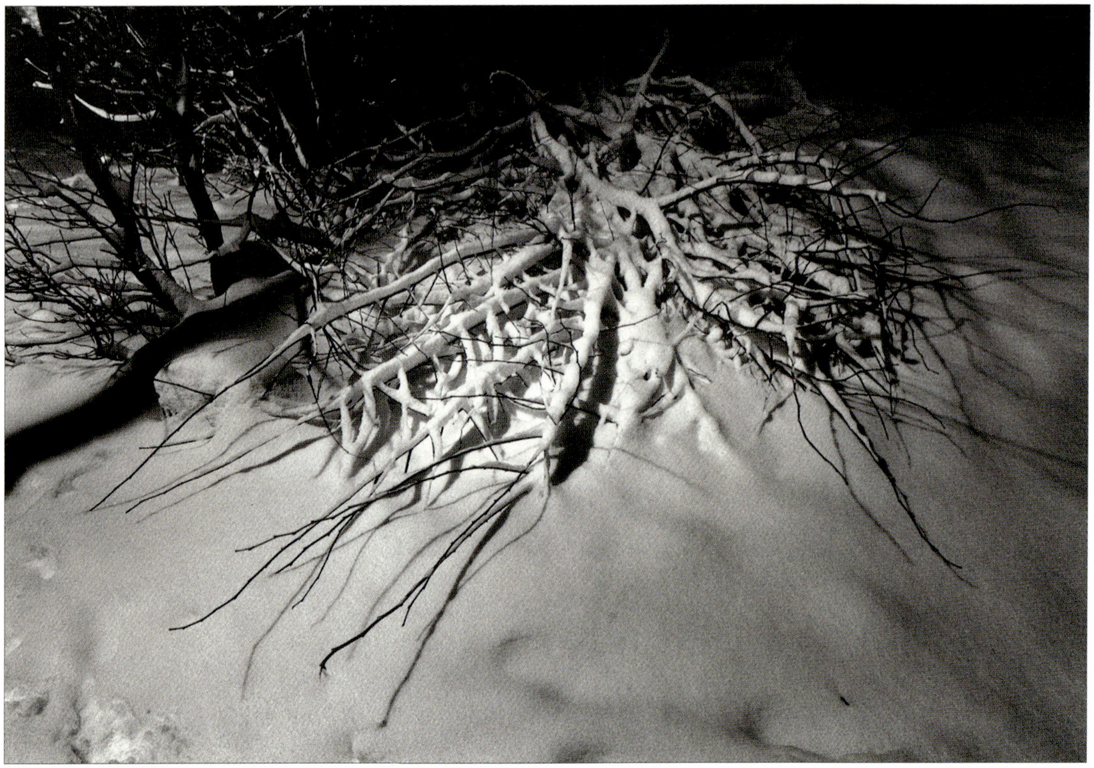

Fallen branches under snow

Look out for small details within the landscape too. These can say as much about the weather conditions as a wider view. Ilford HP5 6x7cm negative processed in Agfa Rodinal.

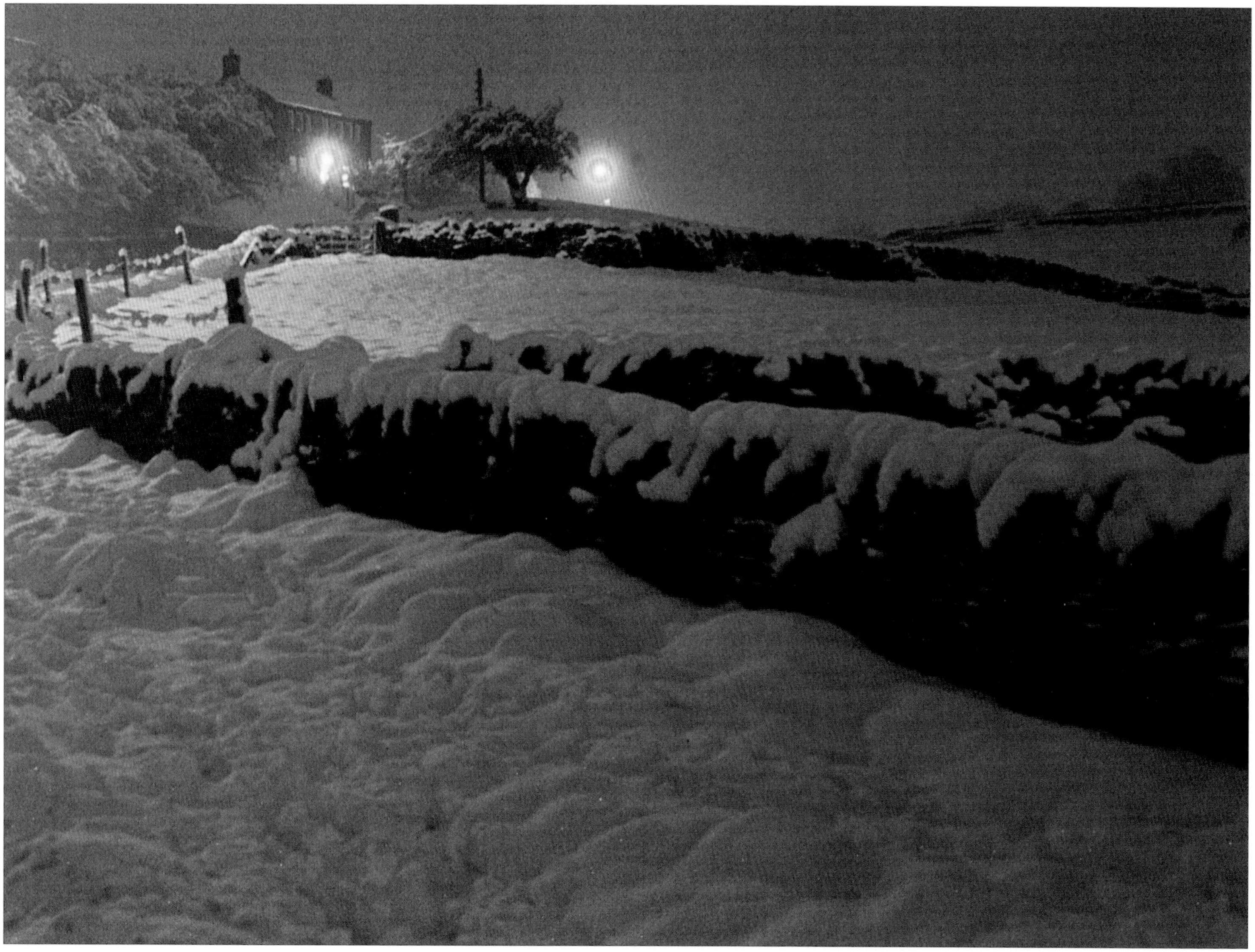

Cinderhills

A very heavy fall of snow does make it difficult to get around, but produces a more picturesque result.
Ilford HP3 processed in Agfa Rodinal.

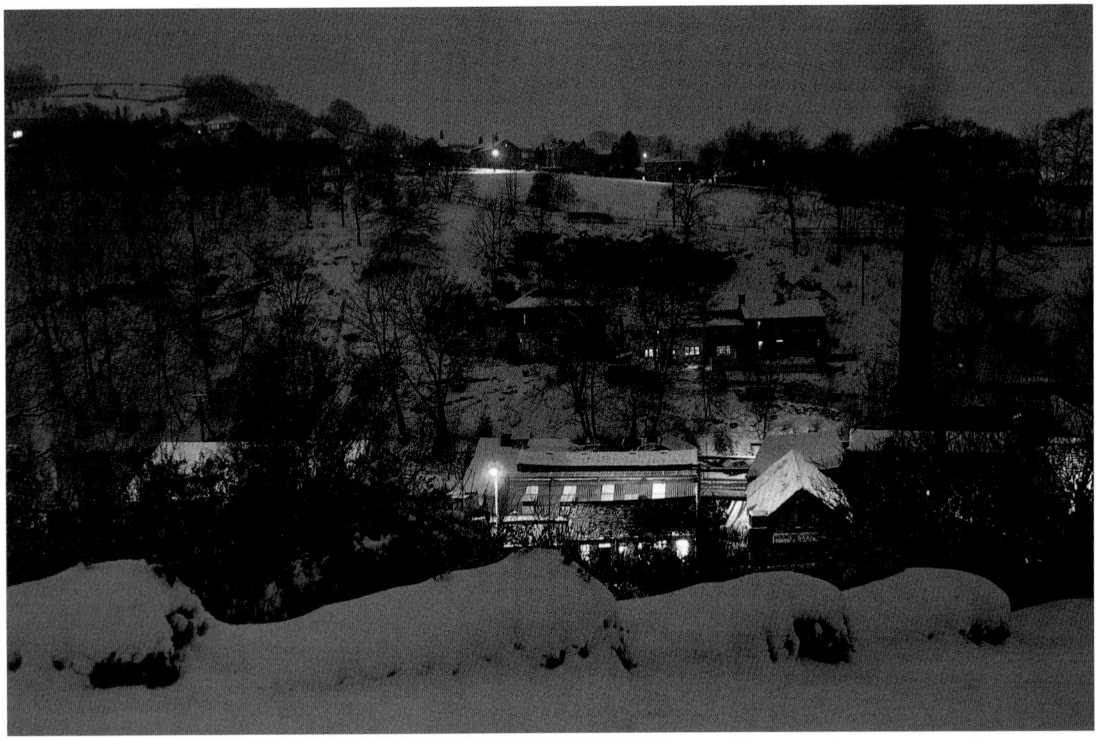

Factory glow

In some situations it is better to represent the white snow as a mid tone to ensure that areas of bright light appear bright.
Ilford HP5 35mm processed in Ilford Microphen.

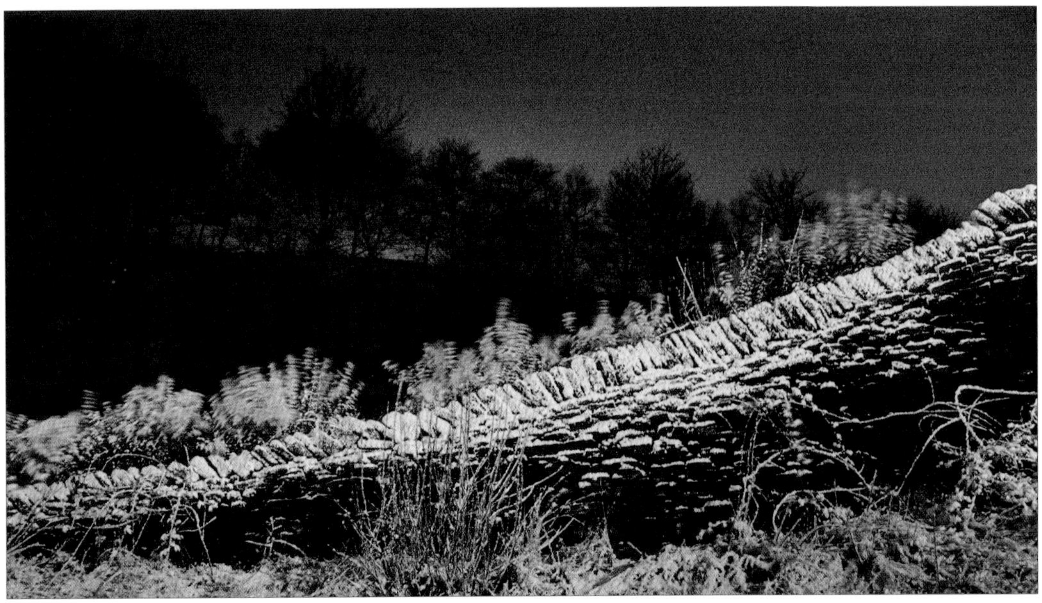

Wall detail

Sometimes a light dusting of snow can highlight detail that would otherwise be lost.
Ilford XP2

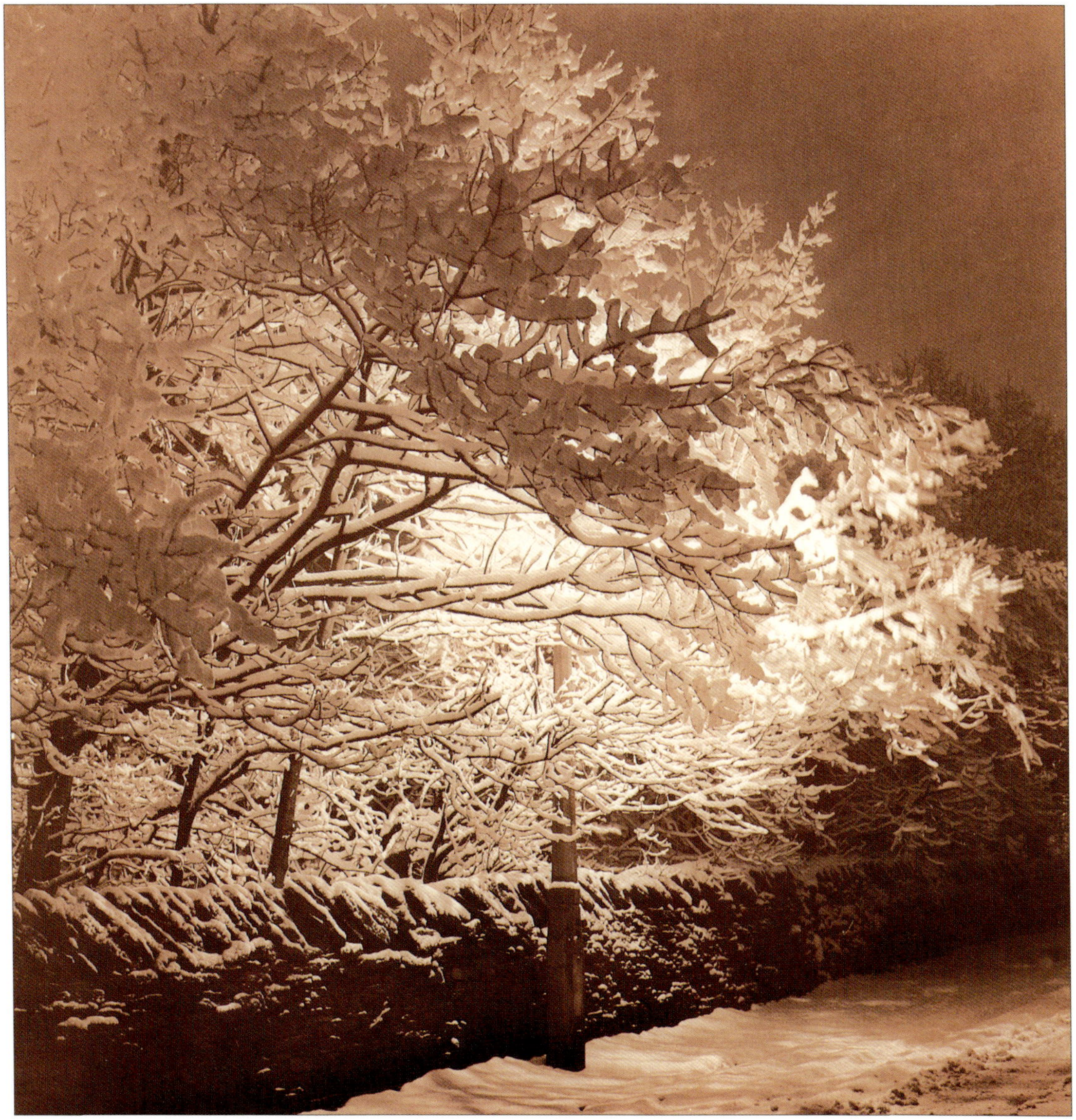

Reducing flare

Snow can cause extreme problems of contrast. To reduce this, obscure the lamp behind a branch or post. Ilford HP5.

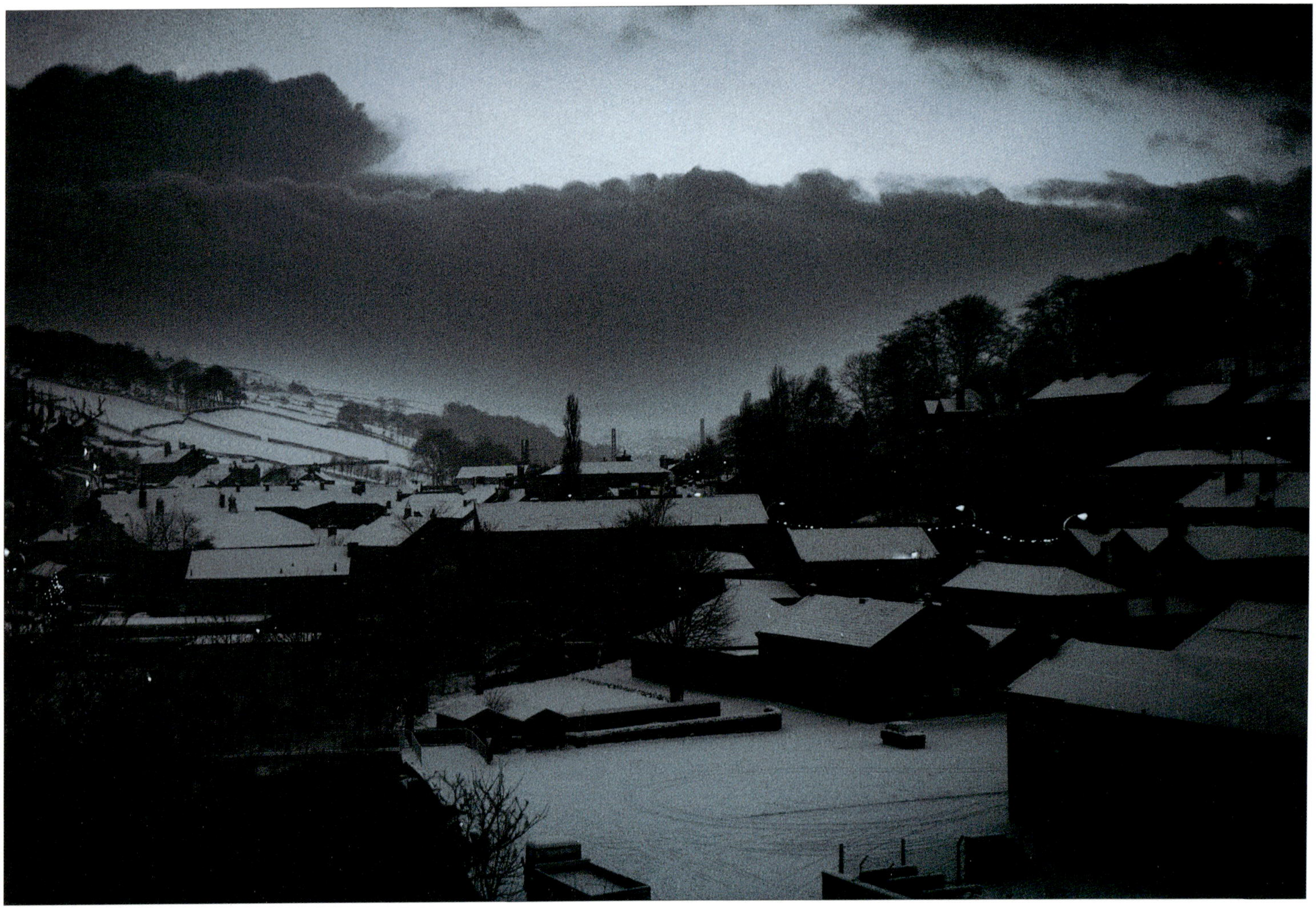

Crown Bottom, Holmfirth

Ilford HP5 35mm processed in Ilford Microphen.

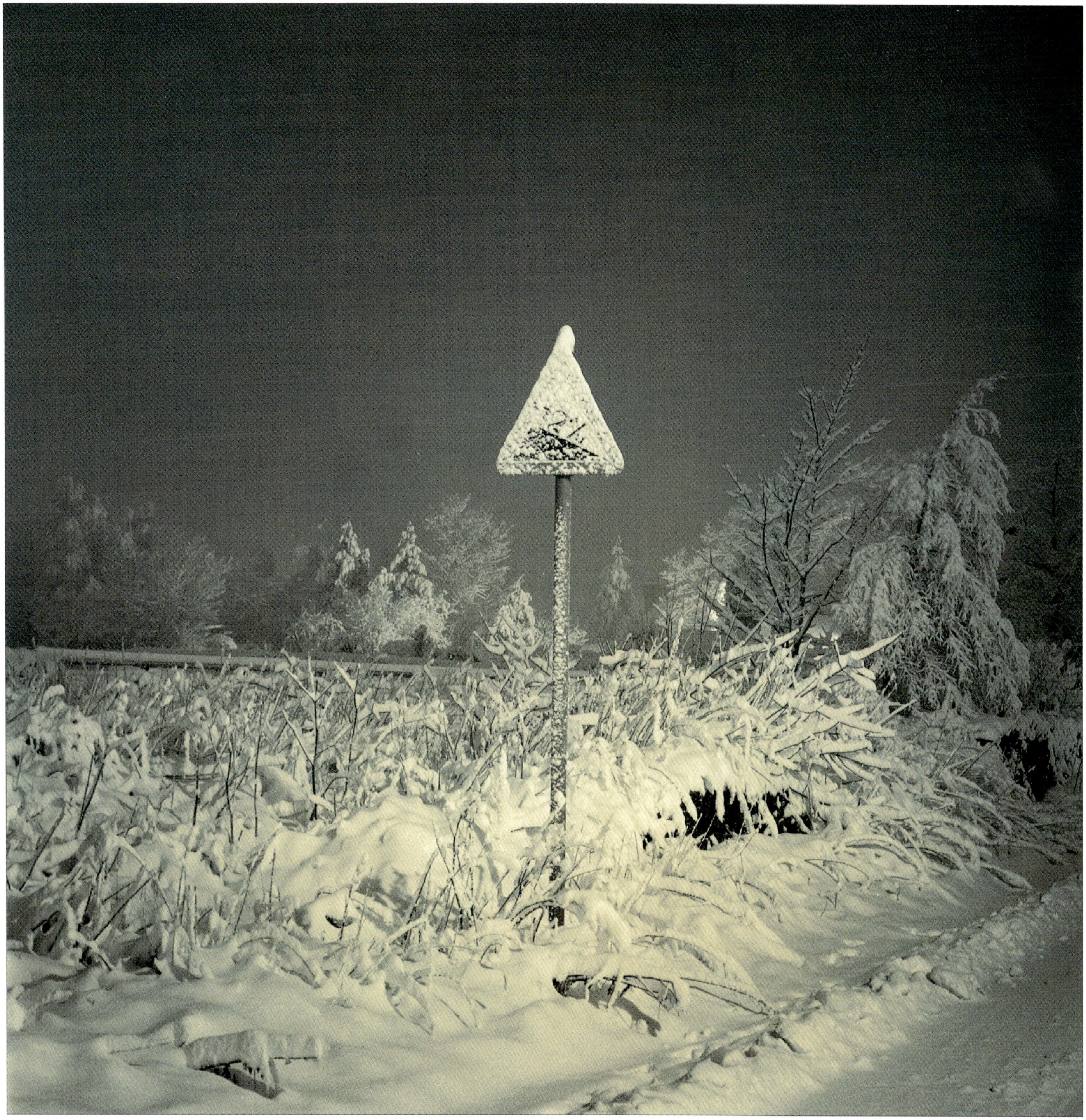

12% incline

Ilford HP5 6x6 negative processed in Ilford ID11.

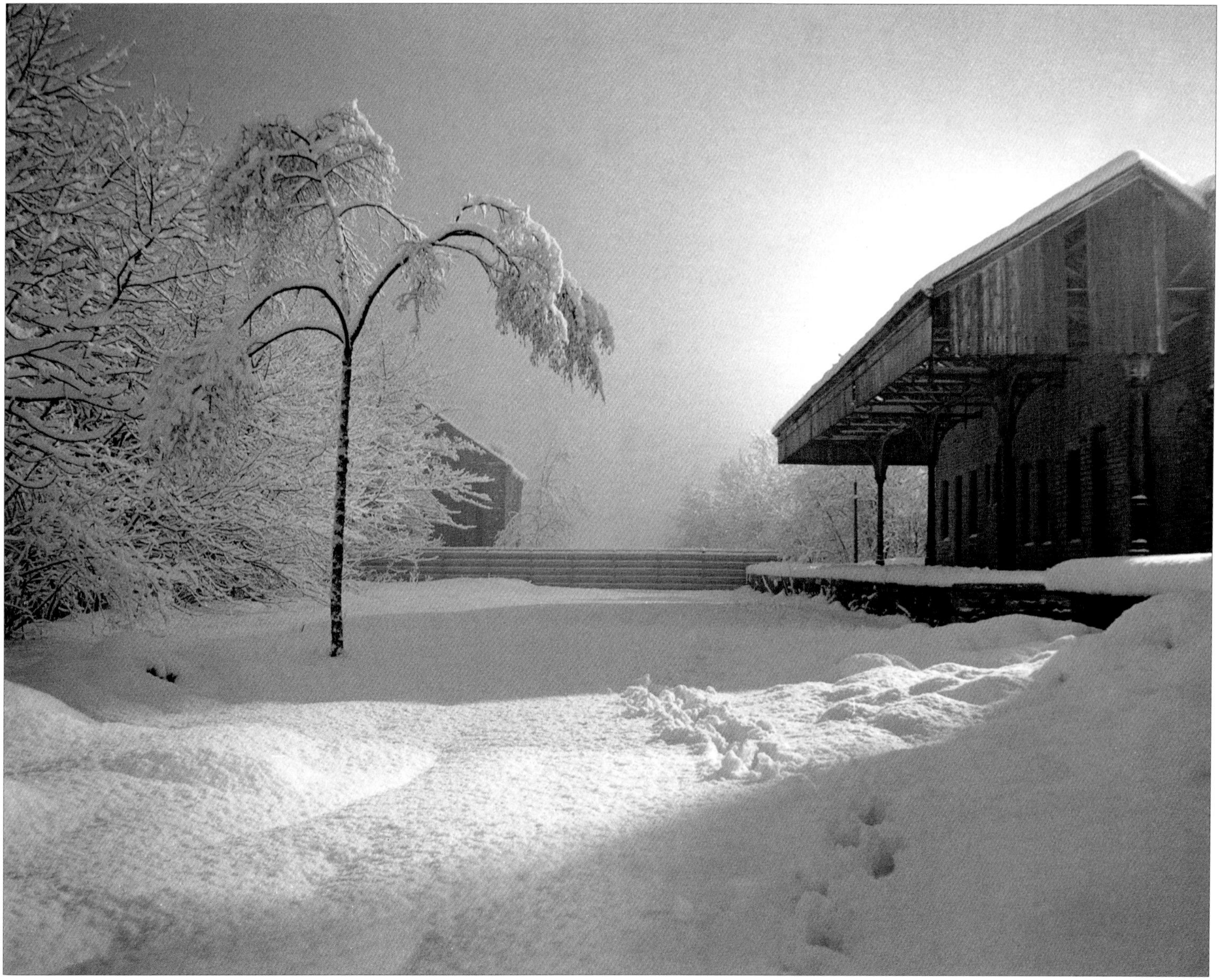

Disused railway

Ilford XP2.

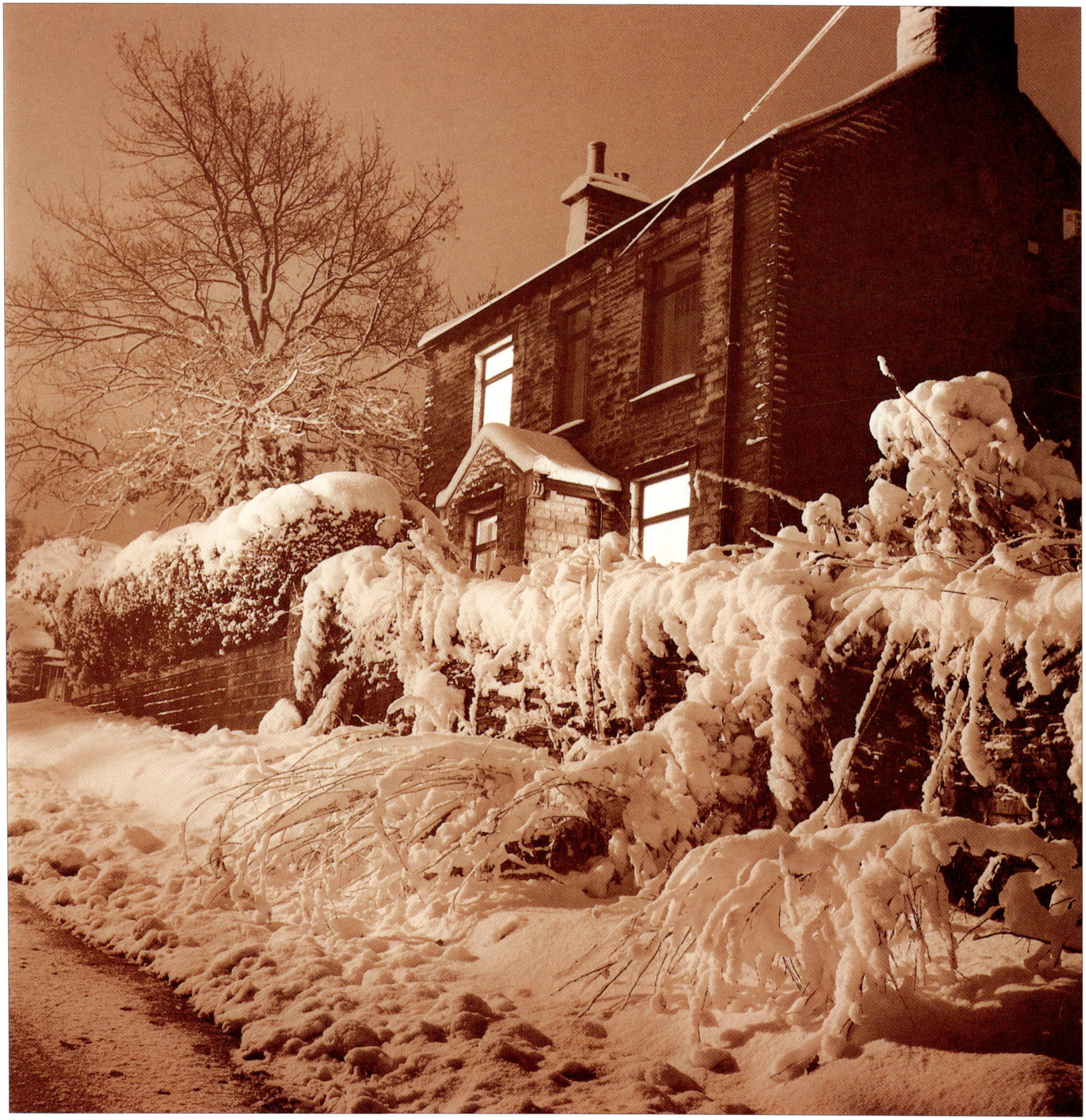

Snowy house

Ilford HP5 6x6cm negative processed in Ilford ID11.

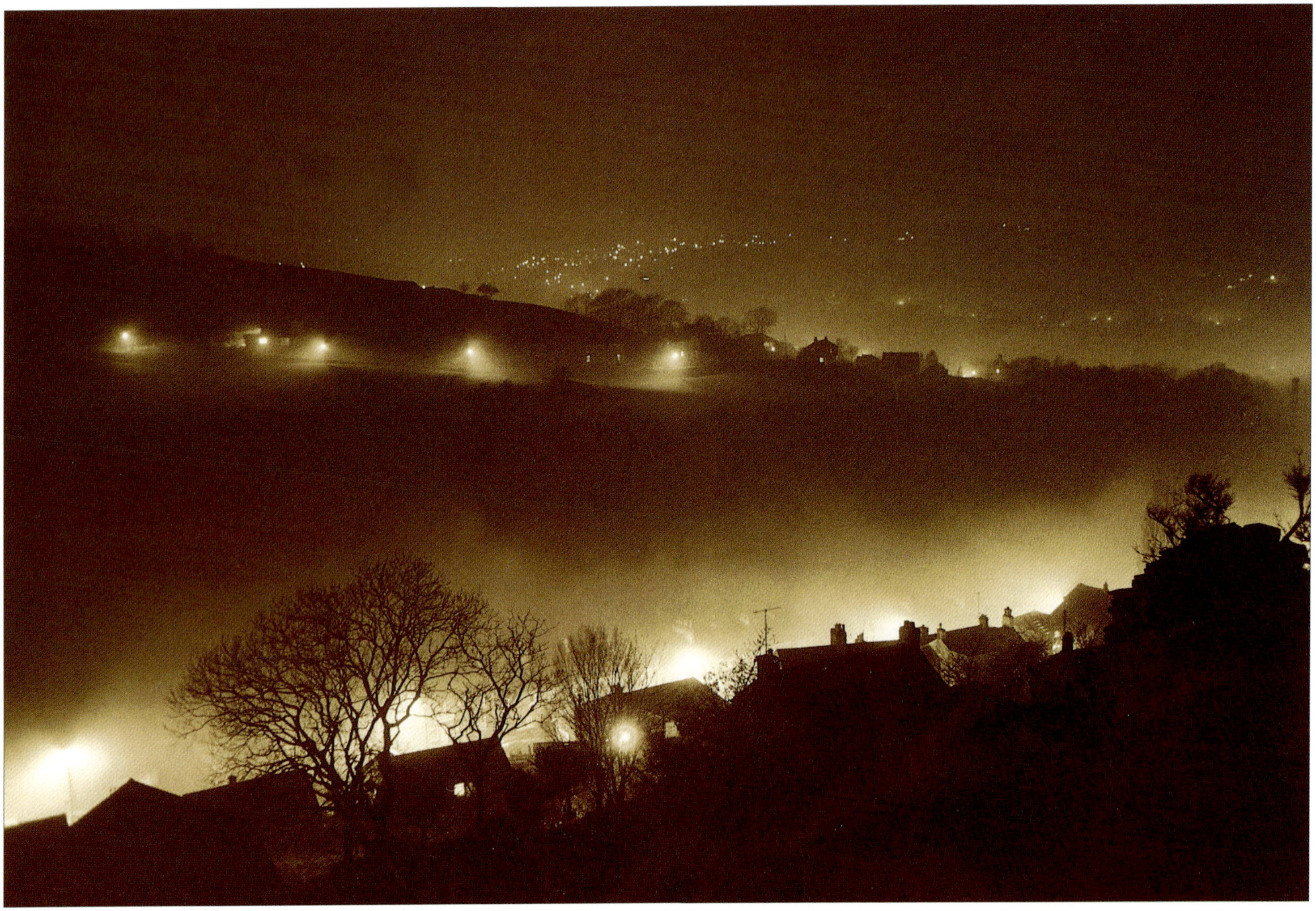

Mist in the valley

Getting a higher viewpoint, if possible, can sometimes reveal a better view of the fog.

Ilford HP5 35mm processed in Ilford Microphen.

Shooting in fog does not require any special technique, and should not, except in very extreme cases, require any extra exposure.

In foggy conditions it is not advisable to use fill in flash or torchlight. The light will illuminate the fog and destroy the strong separation of tones. Sometimes it can be advantageous to make your way to higher ground if this is possible, as the fog may be confined to lower areas.

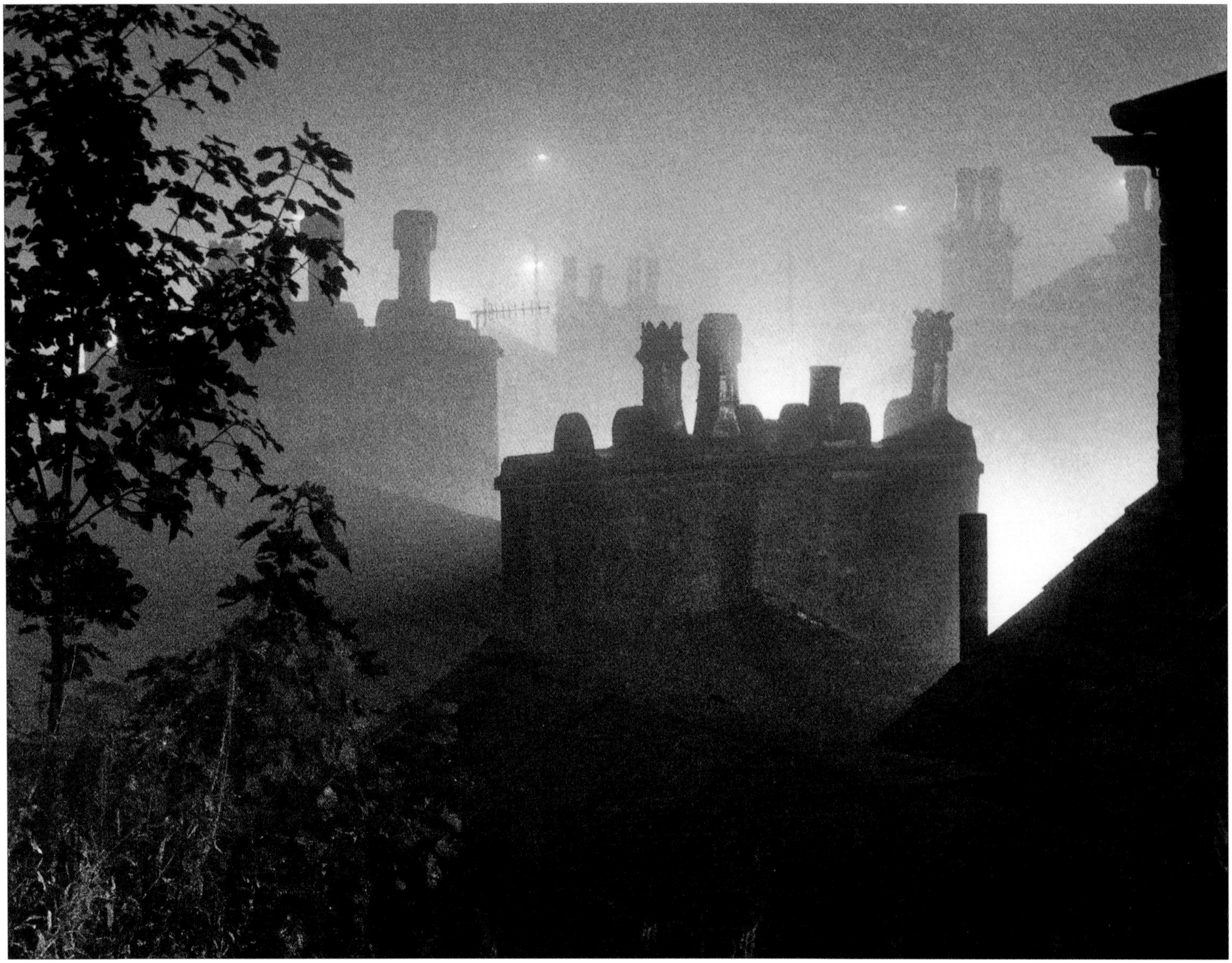

Chimneys in the mist

Fog helps to separate the foreground and background, giving dramatic shapes.

Ilford HP5 6x7cm negative processed in Ilford ID11.

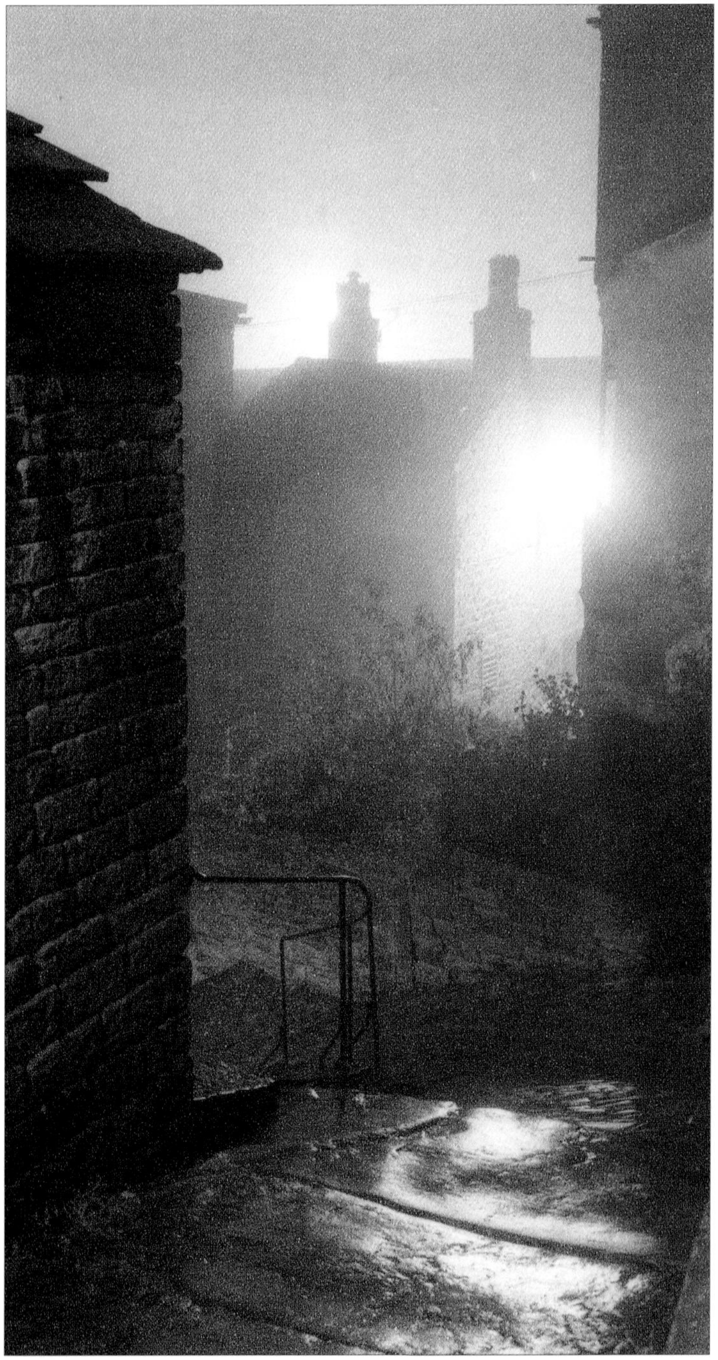

Owd Genn in the mist

A wet mist may not be the best condition for the camera but can give interesting highlight reflections, as well as good separation of tones into the distance. Ilford HP5 6x7cm negative processed in Ilford ID11.

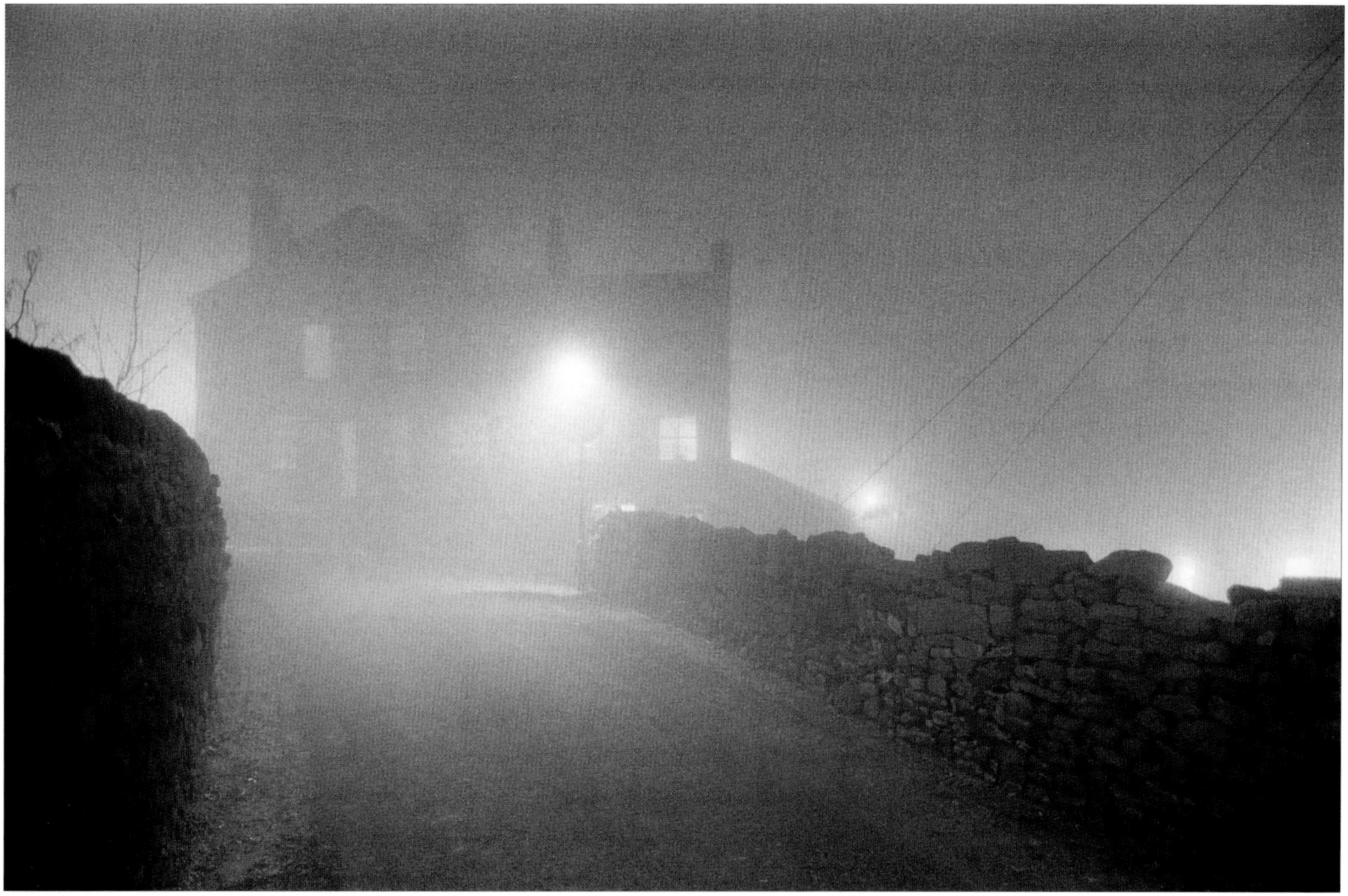

Wooldale fog

Shooting in fog at night makes composition really easy. Here the strong, dark shapes of the walls lead the eye towards the building, eerily emerging from the mist. Ilford HP5 35mm processed in Ilford Microphen.

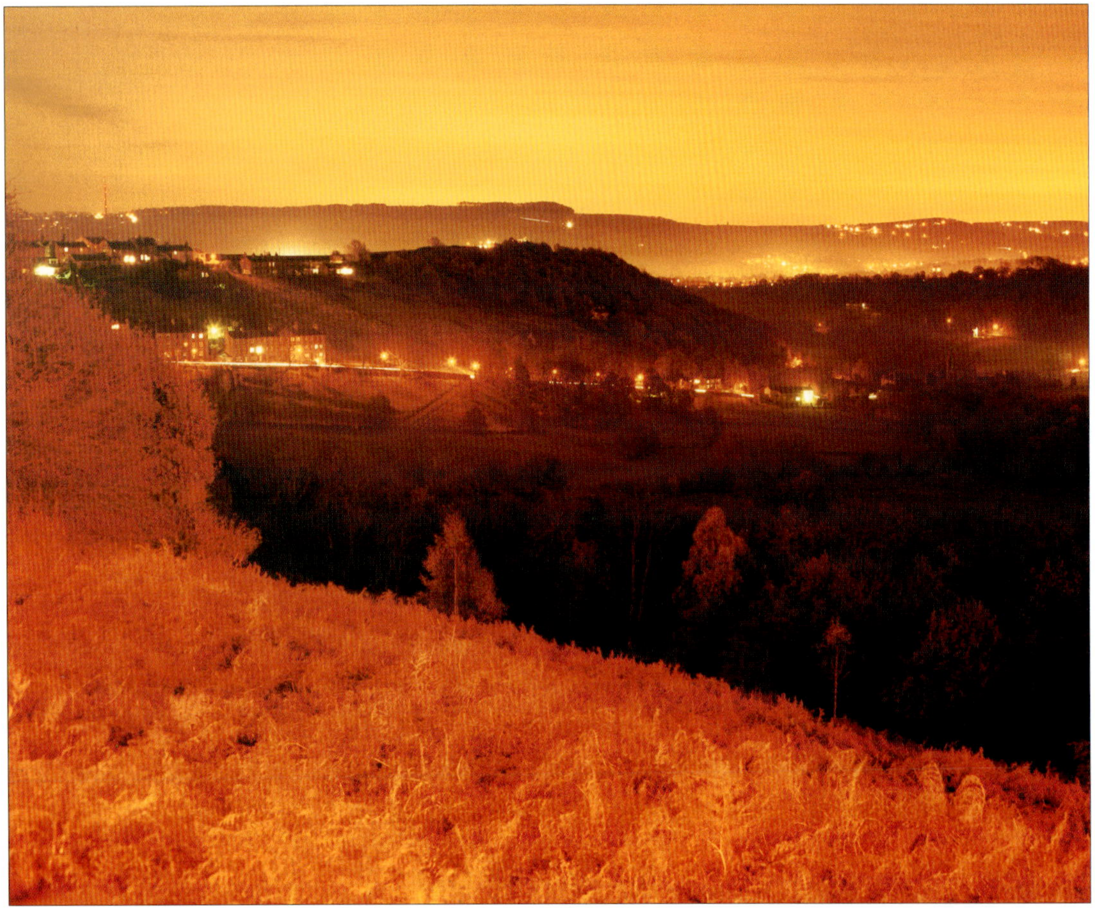

View towards Thurstonland, looking from Netherton
Shooting on colour negative film can give a strong orange/red cast. Fuji NPH 400 6x7cm negative.

Using colour film

The use of colour film for night photography adds another element of pleasure, and of course, extra problems. Be prepared for colours that bear little resemblance to the original scene, especially under orange sodium lighting. I have found that with certain colour negative films, the prints turn out red – not a red cast – just red, which I find overpowering.

The colours can be filtered a little during printing to reduce the excessive orange cast, but too much filtration will cause the shadows and other types of lighting to shift as well, often producing an unpleasant colour. Not all colour negative films display such a deep colour, there is often variation from brand to brand, and also between films from the same manufacturer. Experiment with a few different types to discover the film that creates the effect you prefer.

Colour negative films have the advantage that they can be overexposed by up to three stops and still produce a decent image, in fact, one stop overexposure is usually an improvement.

Transparency films perform better as regards colour balance, but exposure is more critical.

To determine the correct exposure for the shot of the fish and chip shop (opposite), I exposed a few frames for one minute each, and altered the aperture settings as I progressed. I started with the exposure that was indicated by the light meter, and

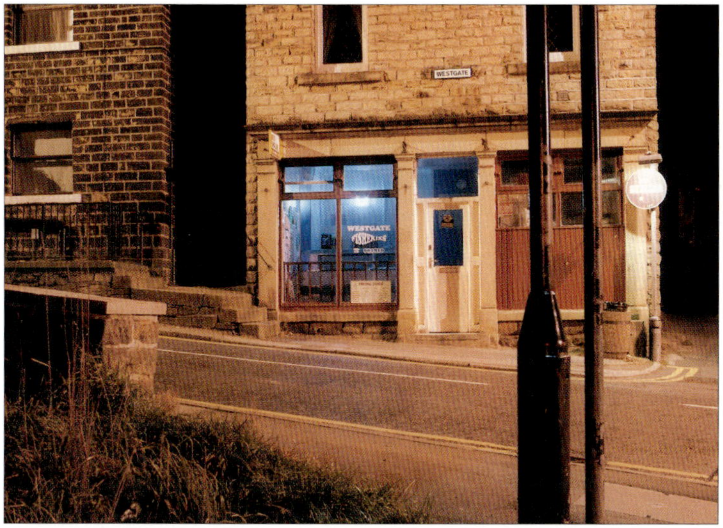

Colour negative

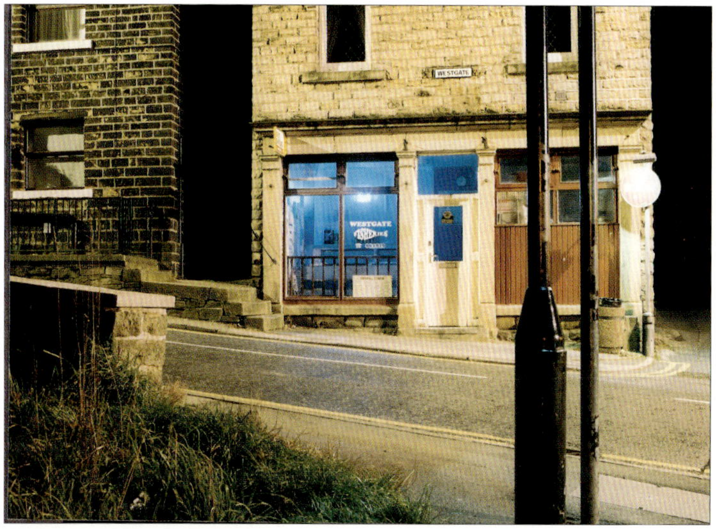

Colour transparency

When the negative and transparency films are compared, it will be noticed that transparency has truer colours and suffer less from the orange cast.

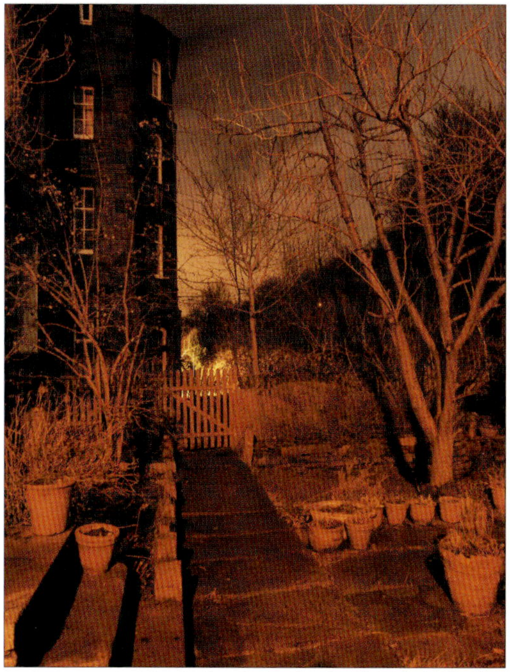

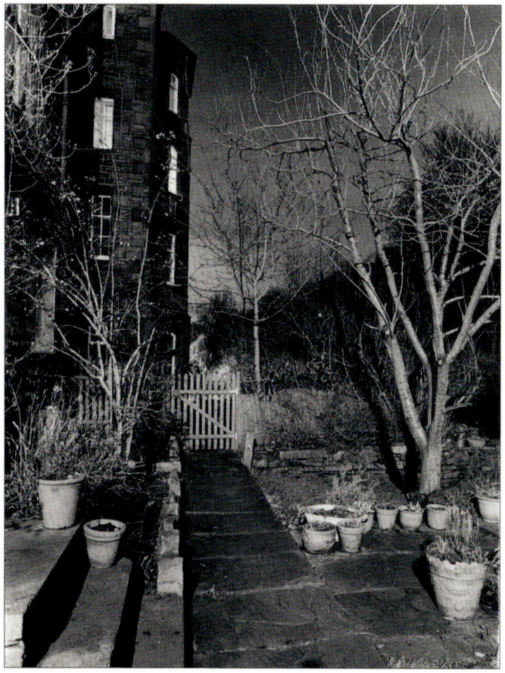

This comparison shows that black and white film reveals much more detail than colour negative. These frames were both exposed at the same settings and both films are 400 ISO.

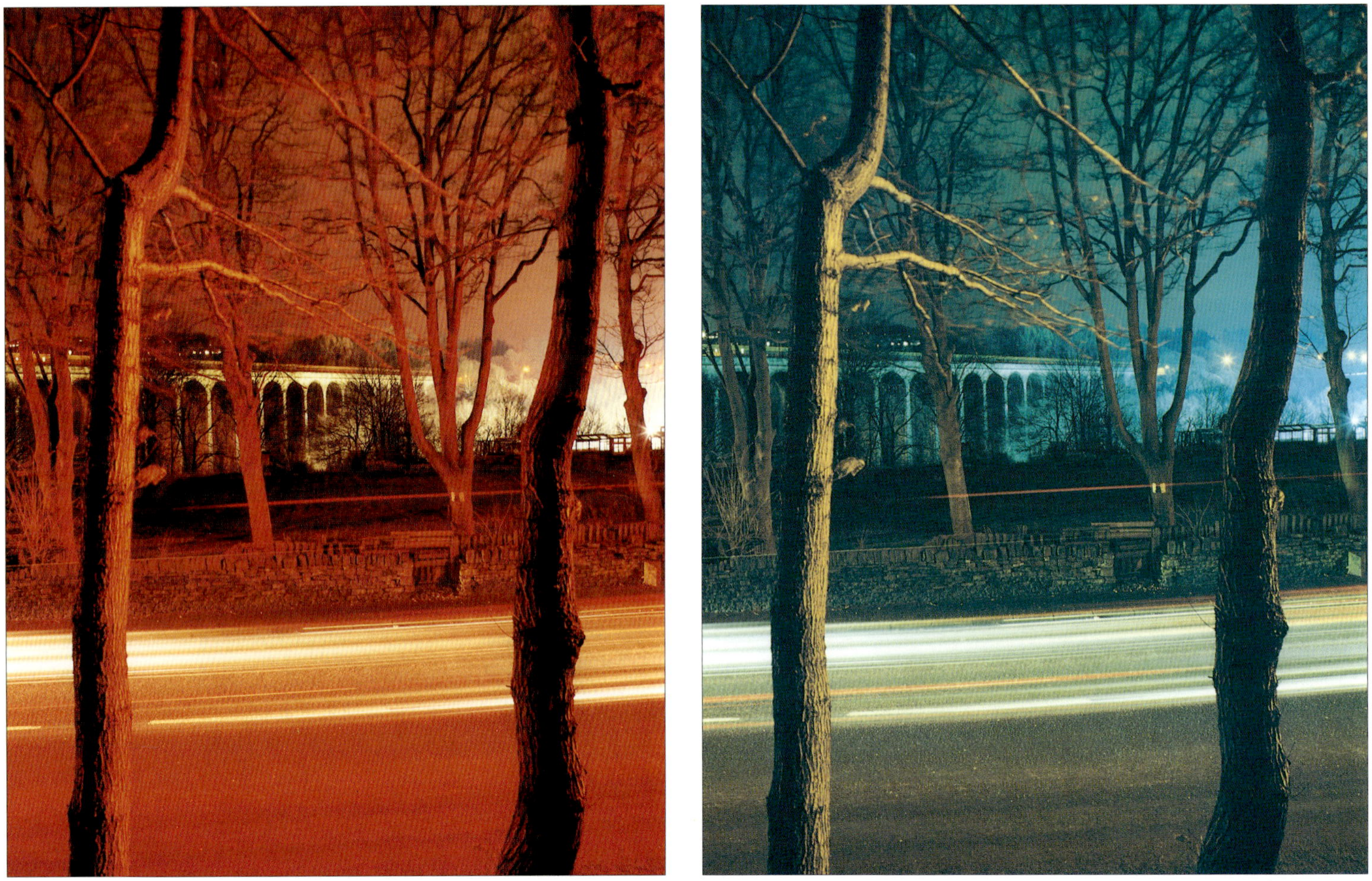

Filtering out the red from a colour negative image can result in the shadows and other light sources taking on another colour.

opened up half a stop with each frame. The frame with the best exposure was one and a half stops brighter than the meter indicated.

When compared with the colour negative of the same scene, it will be noticed that transparency has truer colours, and suffers less from the orange cast.

Colour casts

Some situations offer a mixture of lighting, such as cityscapes, and this can result in various colour changes. Some may surprise you if you have never used colour film for long exposures before, for instance, white streetlights and fluorescent tubes show a heavy green cast, sodium is a strong orange-red, as you would expect, and the evening sky could shift more towards violet.

Other colours will be produced from particular types of lighting, filtered or reflected, and long exposures often exaggerate these.

The film may show colours that hadn't been noticed when taking the picture, where different types of lighting overlap or take on colours from passing vehicles, or window displays and neon signs.

Contrast

Possibilities for contrast control when exposing colour film at night, are not as varied and wide ranging as they are with black and white films. One method of contrast reduction available is fill in lighting, exposing to keep the highlights correct, and using off the camera flash to prevent the shadows from becoming a solid black area.

Remember though, that the scene may be very orange, but the fill in will be white.

It may be necessary to place an orange filter over the lens or the flashgun, though this would obviously reduce the intensity of the light considerably.

Down rating is possible with colour films, but does not have so marked an effect as with monochrome films, and can result in colour changes.

Other possibilities

Cross processing

Colour photography at night certainly opens up a whole new range of possibilities for the creative photographer, and one area that I have just begun to explore is a combination of night photography and cross processing. This seems to produce some very interesting results, but requires that the film be rated four stops below the manufacturers recommended speed, making a 400 ISO colour negative film into a 25 ISO colour transparency film.

This is obviously a bit of a drawback, but worth trying.

Coloured gels

When using colour at night, some photographers use fill in flash with coloured filters or 'gels' over the flash, the scene is given a number of flashes from various positions, and the colour filter is changed with each flashing.

This gives a very different effect, and I include one example here for reference, though this is not the kind of night photography that I would normally undertake.

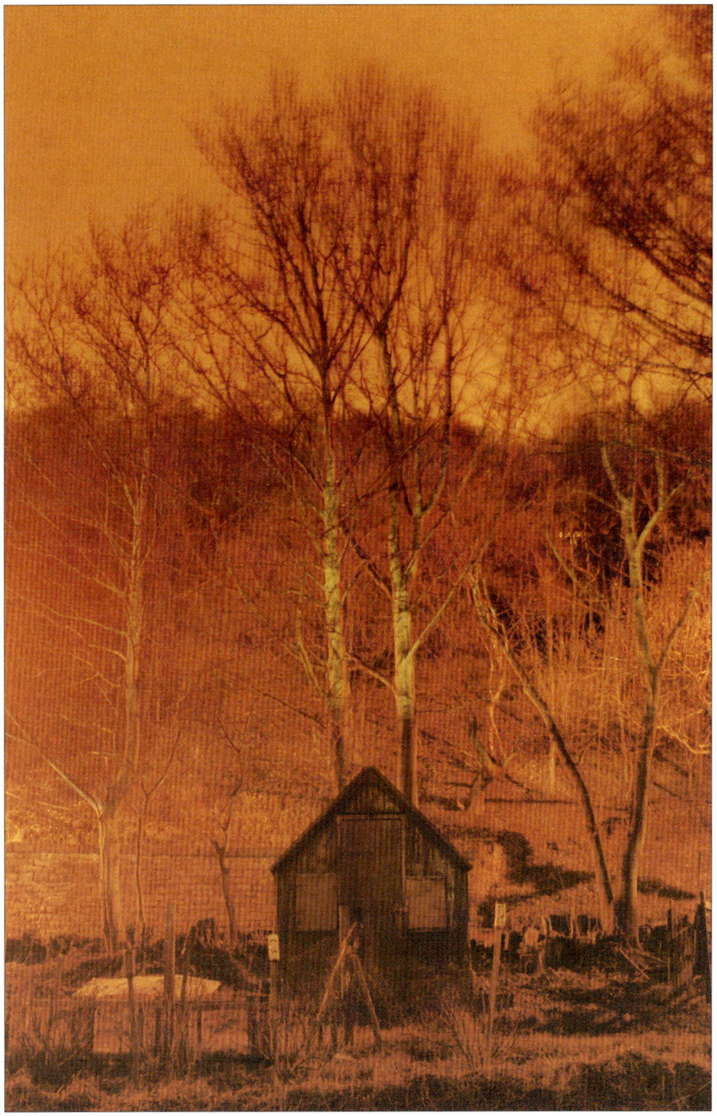

Allotment shed

Fuji colour negative Fuji NPH 400 6x7cm negative.

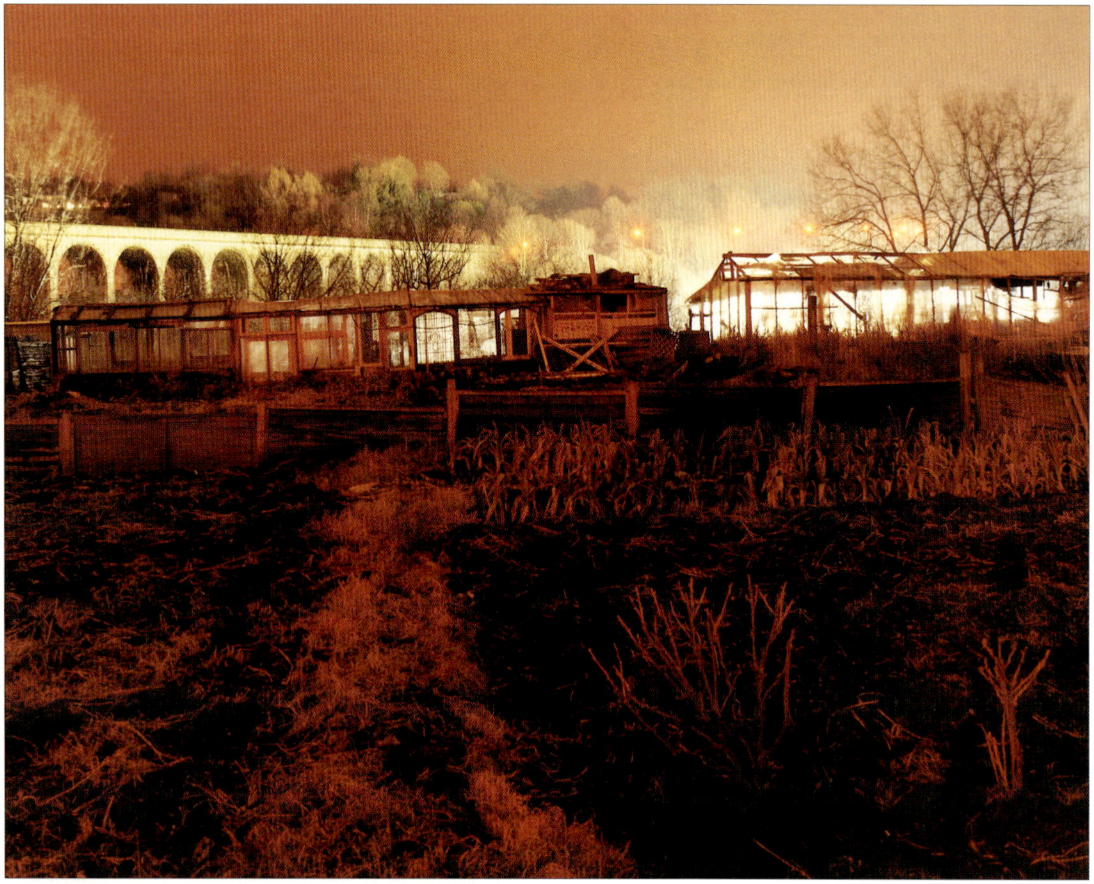

Glow from the floodlights

This picture shows the effect with mixed lighting where long exposures produce strong colour shifts, especially under orange sodium light.

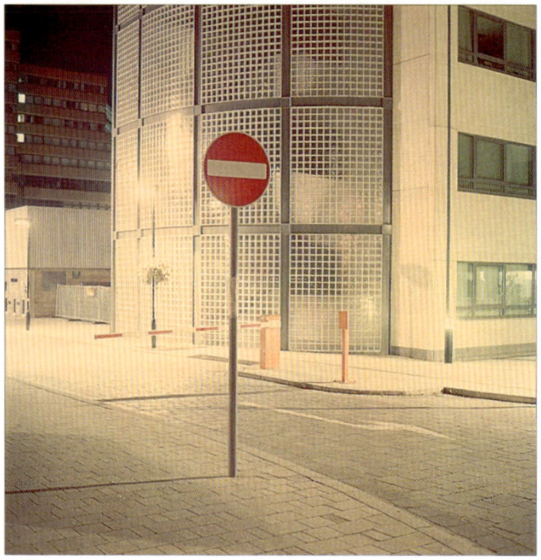

Cross processing

Kodak Gold 200 , down-rated 4 stops and processed in E-6 chemicals.

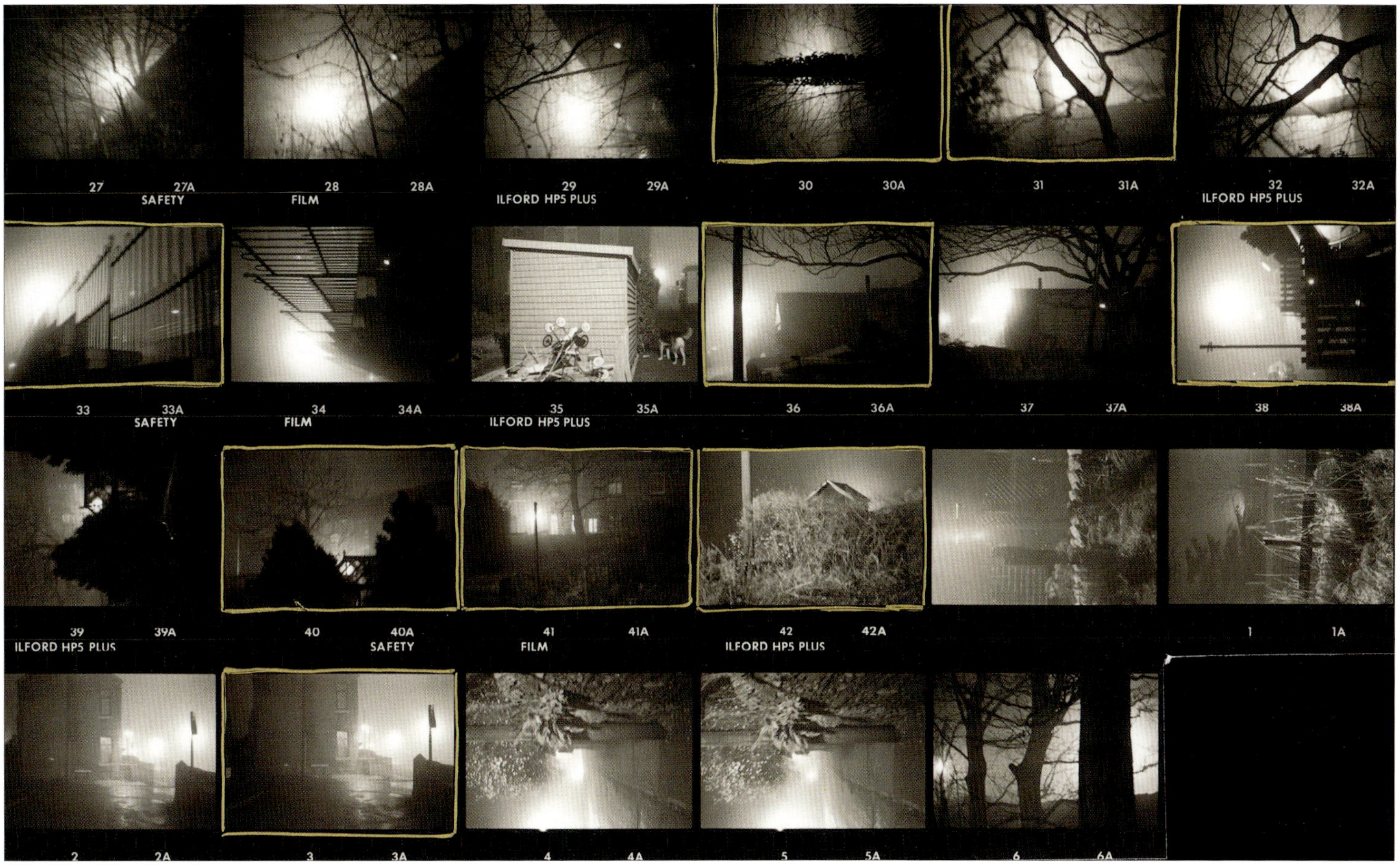

Hand held night photographs

Contact sheet

One foggy night, whilst preparing to walk the dog, I had the idea that I should take a camera out and take a few night shots at the same time. Unfortunately, I had left my tripod back at my studio, some four miles away. The only way I could get any shots would at be to shoot them hand held at 1second @ f2, (400 ISO) this would give me sufficient exposure, but would obviously suffer a fair degree of camera shake, no matter how firmly I held the camera.

I decided to take the camera out anyway and use the pictures as notes, a reminder to go back the next time it was foggy, and re-shoot any that proved interesting. When the film had been processed, I viewed the contact sheet, and there were a few frames that had a certain charm about them, so I did some little prints to get a better idea of the content, and the degree of shake.

These small shaky images looked quite interesting, there was something I liked about them, that I thought would be lost if the image had been sharp and steady. The photographs had the feel of a still from an arty b+w movie; they were more 'urgent', rather than the slow deliberate night work I was used to. They may not appeal to the purist, but I don't think that this method is completely without merit, I include them to offer another possibility for the creative photographer.

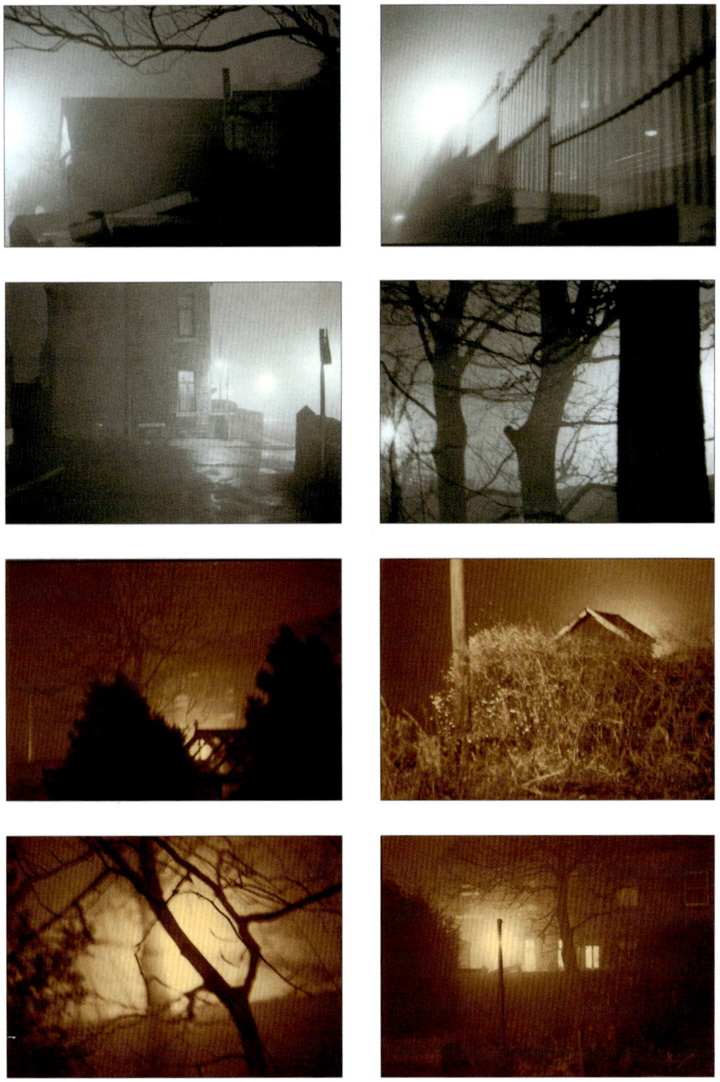

Some of the test prints taken from the first film of hand held night pictures, treated with tea stain and toners.

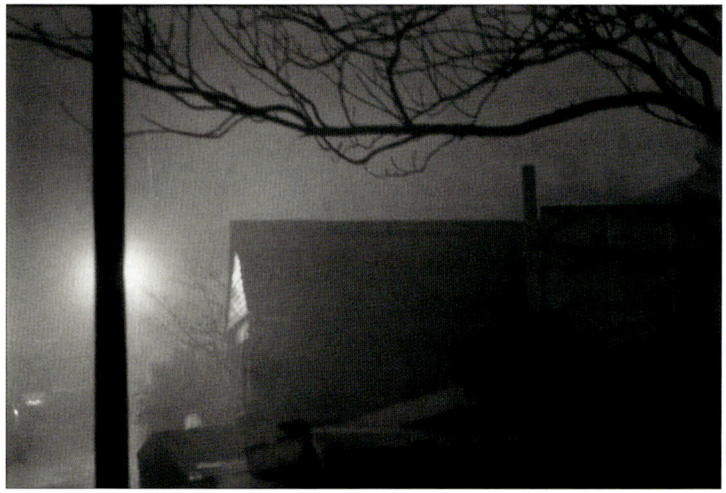

Even when enlarged, this hand held image still works because the picture derives it's strength from shapes and tones, rather than detail.

Exposing by moonlight

A text on night photography would be incomplete without a section on exposing by moonlight,

On nights when there is a full moon in the sky, photography looks like an even more rewarding possibility than usual. In practice, the range of brightness is extreme and causes problems for exposure and development.

To expose for a landscape where it is important to record detail in areas lit solely by the moon, and to keep tone in areas that receive light from a street lamp, is beyond the scope of any film that I know of.

The brightness of the moon is thirteen and a half stops more than areas illuminated by average sodium light and nineteen stops away from the lower tones – way beyond the ability of any conventionally processed film.

The contrast range is just recordable with an extreme compensation process such as pyro, but still leaves a poorly defined landscape in areas where the only illumination is moonlight.

Using pyro as a developer (see processing section), means a reduction in effective film speed, as it requires an exposure to be made for the lower tones, rather than the mid tones. A lower film

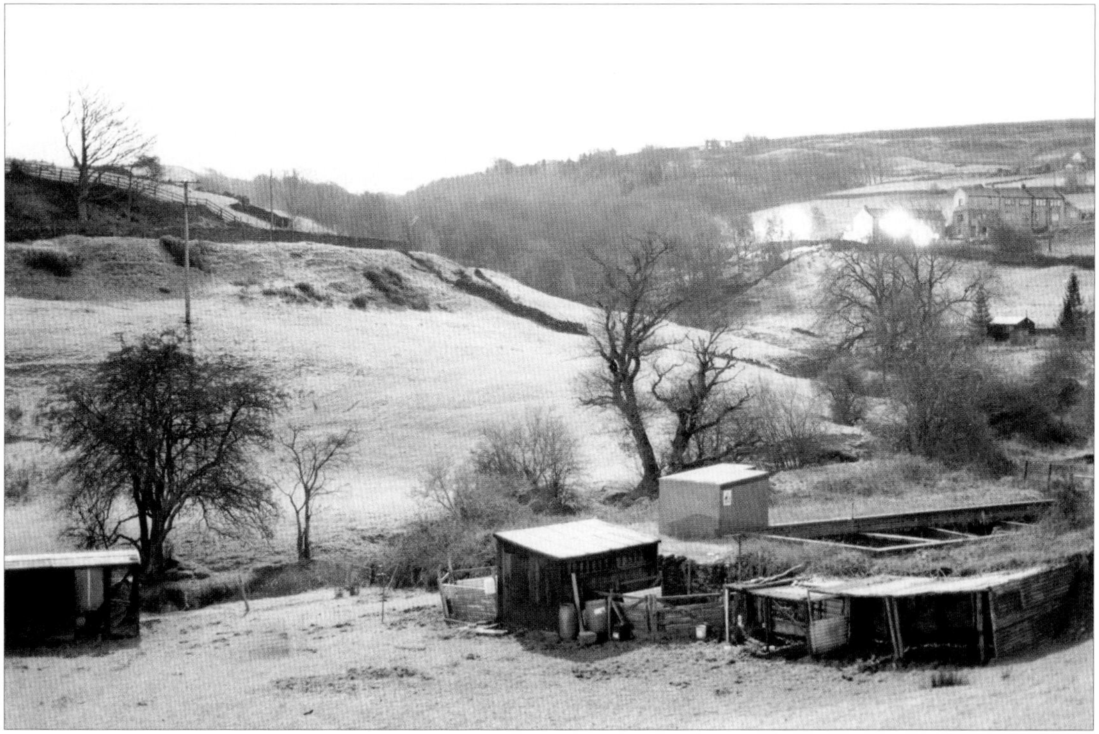

Overexposed moonlit landscape

Pictures taken by moonlight can look like daylight if given enough exposure. This was an experimental shot to see if the automatic setting on the camera could cope with such a dimly lit scene. As this picture shows, it actually overexposed it. Ilford XP2 Super.

speed means longer exposures, and this excludes the possibility of recording a still moon.

A full moon in a totally clear sky can provide enough light to expose by, but exposing for areas illuminated by moonlight will give excessive exposure wherever artificial lighting appears in the scene, to the extent of approximately five stops.

Exposing for moonlight alone in open country where no other lighting appears, can – with a long enough exposure, give a picture that looks very similar to one taken in daylight.

I took this picture of the moonlit field using the automatic setting on my camera, to see if it could cope with such a dimly lit scene, and was surprised to find that it overexposed it!

I deliberately excluded the moon from the frame for this shot, because it would have radically altered the automatic exposure reading, the test was for the dimly lit landscape, so for the purpose I had in mind, I composed the picture to include as much mid grey (grass), as possible.

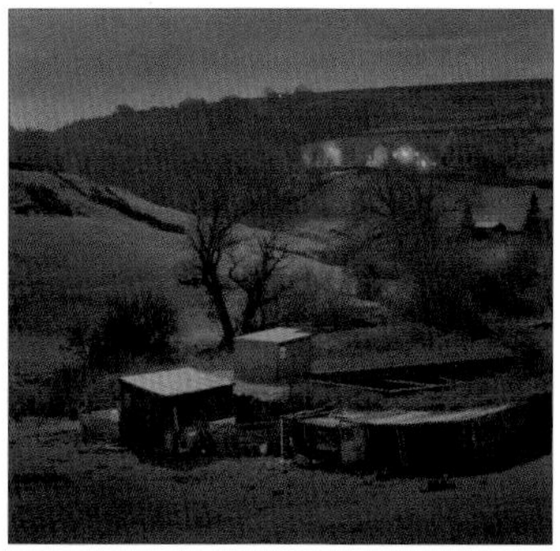

Image title

This is from the overexposed moonlight negative and has been printed down to give a more moonlit impression. I followed this with blue toner and a little tea staining to take the harshness out of the blue. Note how the highlights are unable to gie a clean white. This is the result of the 'flattening off' that happens with overexposed chromogenic films. Ilford XP2 Super.

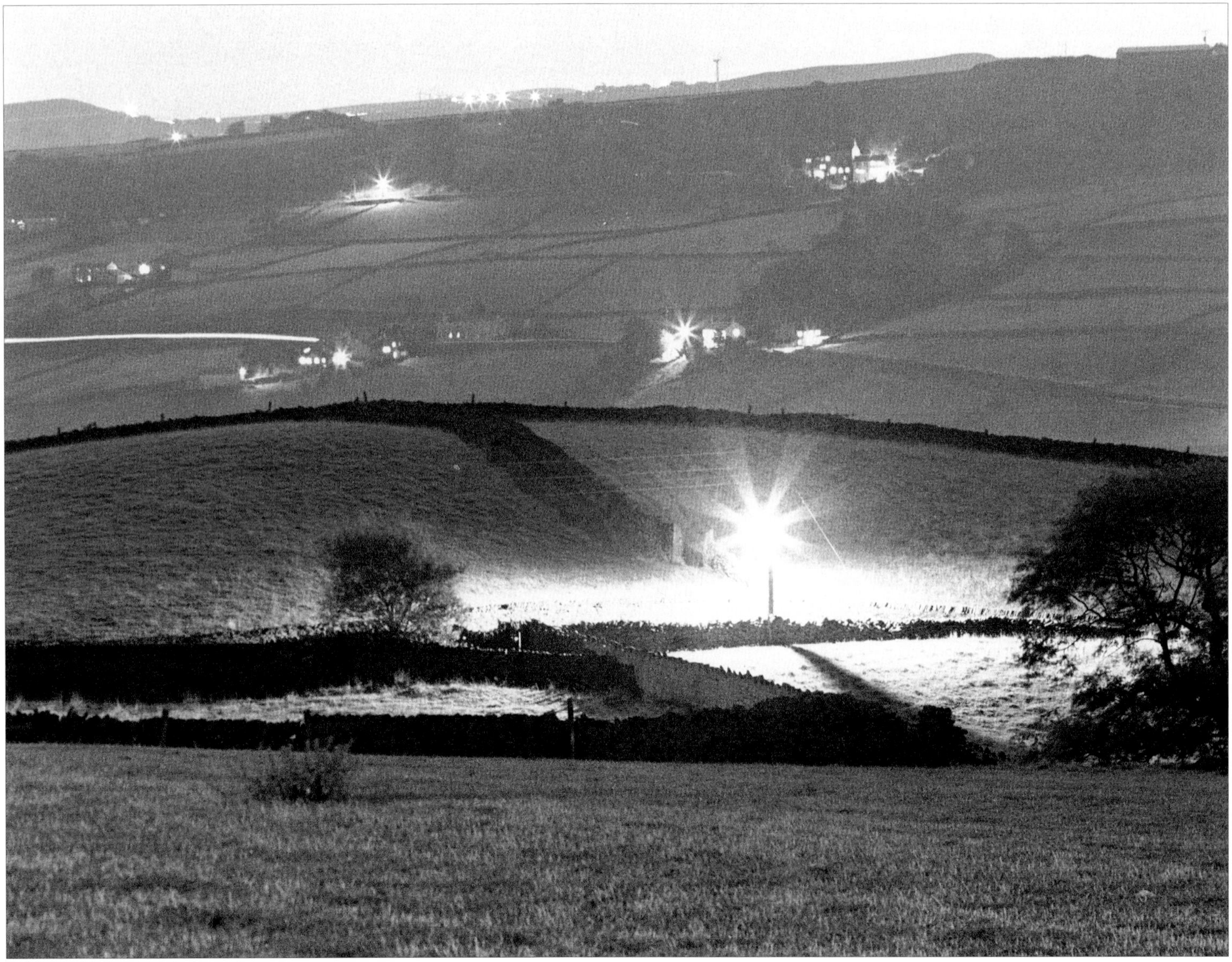

Moonlit landscape

Exposing for the landscape illuminated by the moon will give overexposure wherever artificial lighting appears in the scene.

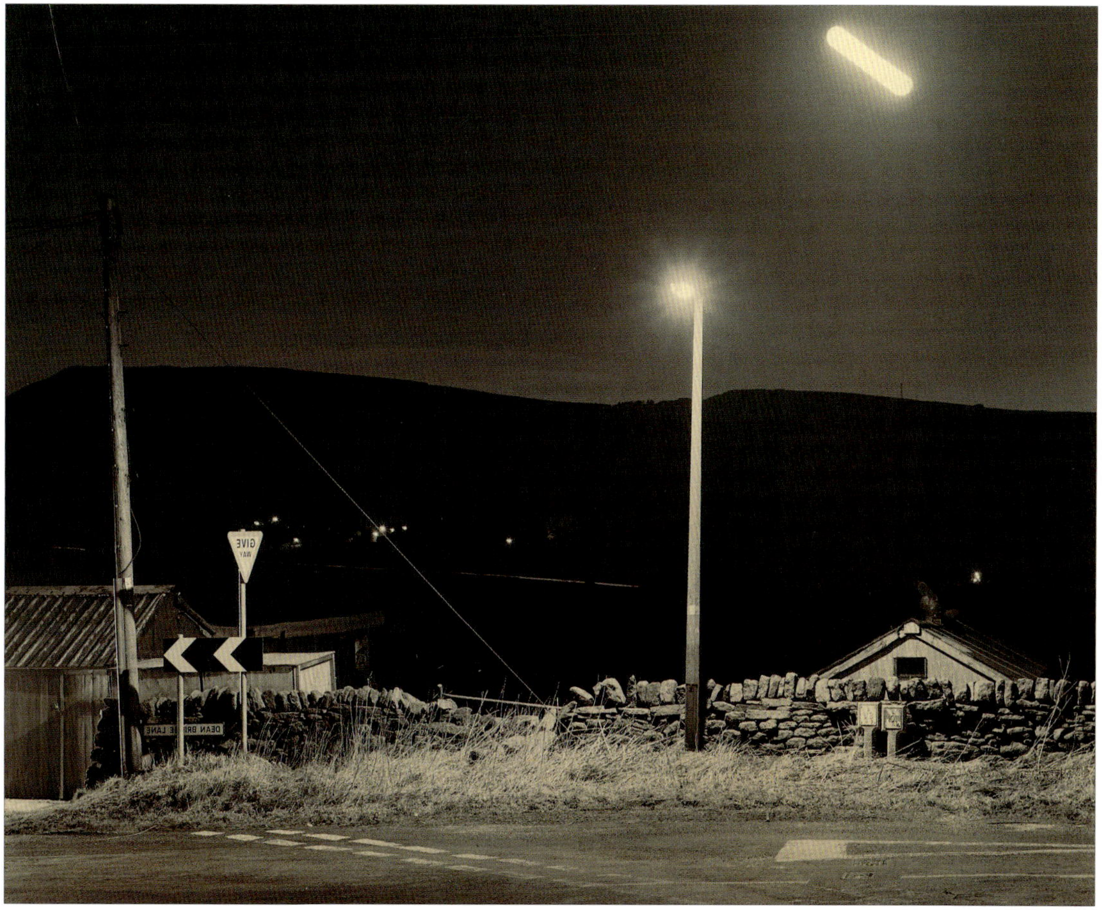

Exposure for moon and streetlighting

This picture shows the difficulty in recording detail in all areas with widely differing brightnesses. The streetlit area was overexposed in an attempt to bring out tone in the moonlit fields behind. Processing in pyro helped to keep detail in the overexposed areas but the fields behind do not have enough density to show separation. Looking at the original print a little detail can be seen but this will be lost in reproduction. Also the moon has moved during the long exposure leaving a streak in the sky.
Ilford HP5 10x8in negative processed in Pyro.

The negative had lots of detail, and after printing the bright landscape here, I tried an overprinted version to give a better impression of moonlight. This was then toned blue to improve the final effect.

As I have indicated, scenes illuminated by streetlights and a full moon, often look more photogenic than ordinary scenes, but they do pose rather a tricky problem for exposure. The moon itself is far brighter than anything you will be exposing for at night, and for those photographers not employing special contrast reducing techniques in processing, it is best excluded from the frame.

Working with moonlight as a supplement to street lighting is the best option, by that I mean shooting street scenes on moonlit nights – this can make for a more interesting shot, the moon giving the scene an extra source of fill in light, although this is a very subtle effect.

GUIDE CHART FOR EXPOSURES BY MOONLIGHT

Film speed	**f8**	**f11**	**f16**	**f22**
100ISO	2h	-	-	-
200ISO	52m	2h	-	-
400ISO	20m	52m	2h	-
800ISO	9m	20m	52m	2h
1600ISO	3m 20s	9m	20m	52m
3200ISO	1m30s	3m20s	9m	20m

The main advantage of a full moon is a brighter sky, and sometimes bright white clouds, which can give better separation for buildings and trees against the sky.

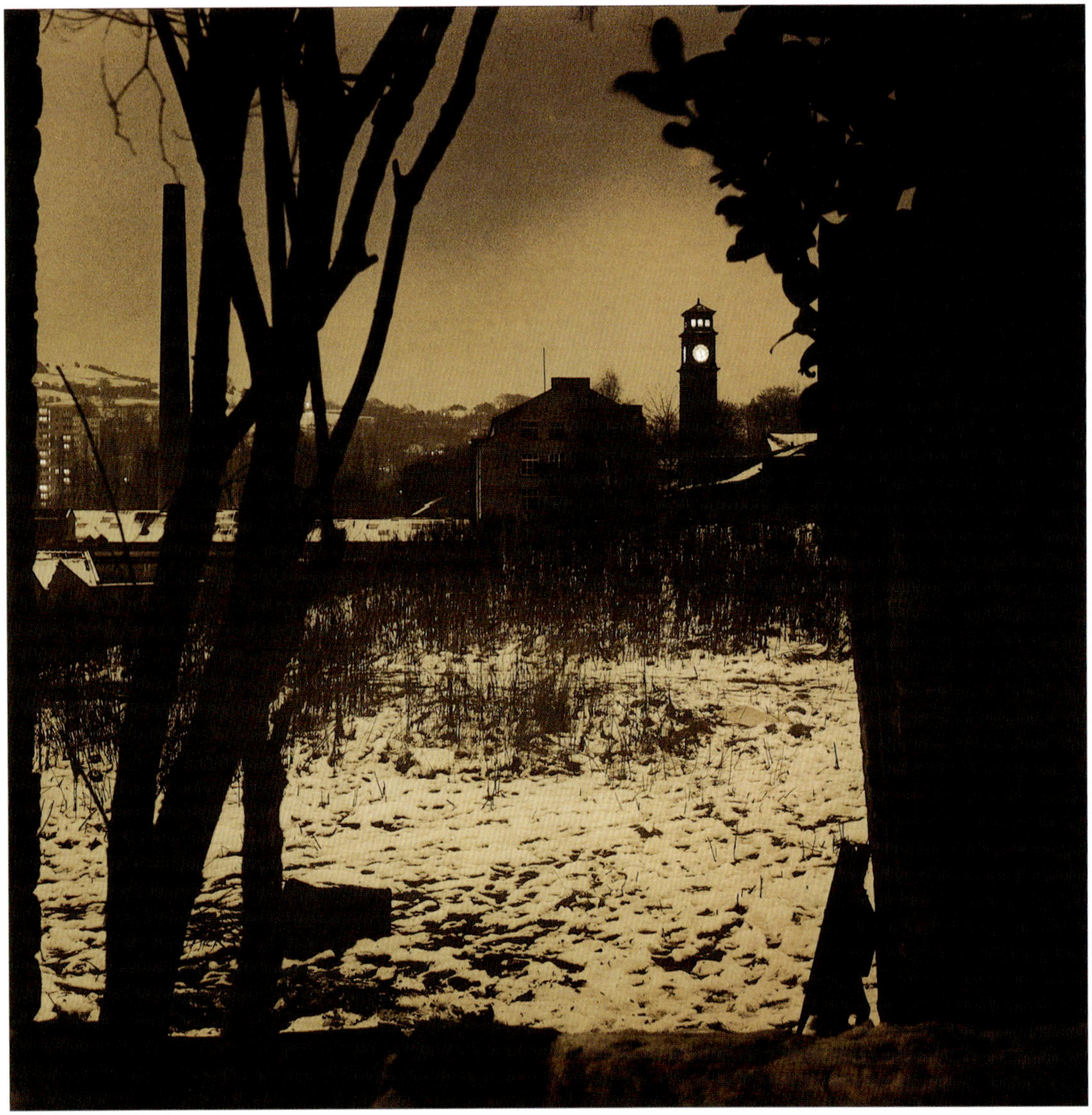

Clock tower

Shooting at dusk can help to bring out detail where there is little or no artificial lighting. Shoot a series of frames as it gets darker and use the one that gives just enough detail. This can look similar to moonlight.

DID YOU KNOW?

Night scenes in movies are shot in sunlight and underexposed to give the impression of moonlight, sometimes with the addition of a blue filter to emphasise the feel of night.

QUICK EXPOSURE GUIDE FOR SHOOTING UNDER MOONLIGHT

(Assuming a film speed of 400 ISO)

The difference between the scene illuminated by streetlights and areas illuminated by the moon alone is five and a half stops,
ie; street lit area = EV 2.5 moonlit area = EV minus3.

Underexpose the moonlit part by two stops, and overexpose the street lit part by three and a half stops. (expose at EV minus1). This should give enough exposure to print both extremes by split grading, or lith printing. (Try an exposure of eight minutes and fifty seconds at f11)

Employ a contrast reducing process such as dilute/static, pyro or two bath if possible.

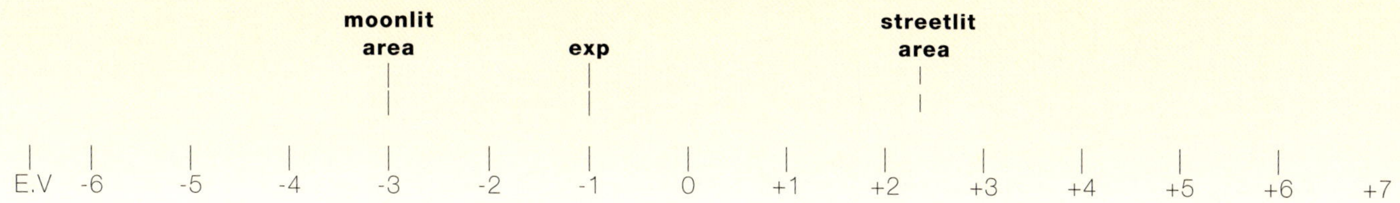

Shooting with the moon out of the frame, or hidden behind a post or tree, will make use of the extra light, whilst avoiding the over bright streak that can result from a moving moon.

Bear in mind that with long exposures, the moon might be hidden behind a post at the beginning of the exposure, but will have moved significantly during it, and by the end, may intrude into a part of the shot where it is not wanted.

Colour film can also be used under moonlight, but don't expect a nice slate-blue moonlight sort of colour. Transparency films will record the colours of the scene as if it were daylight. Some films will veer towards blue (Fuji), and some will give a more red cast (Kodak), but they will record far more colour than you can distinguish with your eyes.

The reason for this is, our ability to see in colour is lessened as light levels drop, and reaches a point when it becomes monochrome.

What is perceived as a dark slate blue, will record as slightly cold sunlight, with grass appearing green, skies blue, flowers (if open) showing their full glory, and all other objects appearing as normal.

Any streetlighting included in the scene will record as orange, as would be expected, but will be grossly overexposed.

Deciding on an exposure

The first step is to decide if the picture is going to be a general street scene with moonlight 'fill in' in which case the exposures are the same as normal, or if the main exposure is a landscape lit entirely by the moon, where streetlights do not feature, or are so distant as to not be a problem. In this case a much longer exposure is necessary. This is only a guide to give you an indication about the length of exposures to expect,

For an important shot I would advise taking three pictures at your chosen exposure, each one with a different aperture (aperture bracketing), even though this may take quite some time.

If you are unsure about how the light is going to balance in a street situation, and whether to expose for the moon or the streetlights, then expose a sequence of frames that span the two exposures.

To lessen the brightness of the moon, give the exposure for moonlight, followed by minus one stop, minus two stops, minus three stops, minus four stops, five stops, six, seven, eight, nine, ten, and eleven stops.

To increase the brightness of moonlight on the landscape, give the exposure for artificial light, followed by plus one stop, + two stops, + three stops, + four, + five, and plus six stops.

With a sequence such as this, a balance can be achieved and a negative or transparency chosen which best suits the effect you wish to create, and your own style of working.

At first glance, this looks well within the range of a normally processed film, but the metered streetlit area is a mid tone, and refers to parts illuminated by the lamps at a normal distance, there are bound to be brighter areas within the frame, which will take the highlights off the scale.

Combining negatives

Trying to show a moonlight scene as you have experienced it, can be frustrating. The contrast, as I mentioned above, is far greater than at first appears, and the moon is not going to keep still, or record with detail. Some other method needs to be employed to recreate what was seen.

The moon and the landscape need to be photographed at different times, and combined to give the impression of one single exposure.

The first method that springs to mind is computer manipulation, but that is a subject outside of the scope of this book. The darkroom technique of combining two negatives, one of the scene, and one consisting of a lone moon in a black sky is simple and effective, and I shall explain a method for achieving good results with this in the technique section below.

One advantage of this method is the facility for ensuring that the landscape and the moon both print to the correct density with one exposure, something that would be impossible if the moon had been within the scene at the moment the picture was taken. Utilising the correct setting for an average street scene would mean an overexposure of the moon by thirteen and a half stops.

Combining two negatives is not a difficult technique, it just requires a little forethought, like, just where you would prefer to put your moon!

Technique

Firstly, shoot the main part of the image, the street scene/ motorway/view/townscape/landscape, or your chosen subject. Perhaps you already have a night negative that is lacking a strategically placed moon.

As you look at your chosen image, decide which part of the sky would be the best position for a moon, then mentally flip that across to the other side, so that if the chosen position is top left, then think about positioning the moon in the top right of the viewfinder (this is because the negatives are to be combined face to face).

The next full moon, go out with your camera and find a location where you can position your moon correctly in the frame, without any other intrusions such as chimneys, lights, wires or telegraph poles etc.

TIP

If this proves impossible, position your moon in the bottom part of the frame, in the opposite corner, pointing your camera higher, and hopefully above the problem intrusions – then turn the negative upside down.

Whichever position the moon finally rests in within the frame, it is probably wise to give yourself a few other moon negatives, with slight variations up/down and left/right to give a few more options when combining the negatives.

To get a usable negative of the moon in a black sky you will need to know how to establish the correct exposure to give a print with density that is realistic and that prints well in combination with the other negative. It is not possible to meter off the moon with anything less than a two degree spotmeter, but for those photographers who do not own a spot meter, a simple rule can be applied;

The exposure for recording detail on the surface of the moon is surprisingly easy to figure out.

The moon is illuminated by the sun, as we are on earth, and is therefore the same exposure as mid day down here – 1/500 at f11 (400 ISO).

When you have the necessary moon negatives, and have chosen the most suitable frames to combine, for best results, place them together emulsion to emulsion. This is to ensure that both negatives will focus on the baseboard at once, but if this places your moon in the wrong part of the sky, then combining negatives with both emulsion sides facing down is acceptable, as long as the enlarging lens is stopped down to about f11, to give a greater depth of focus at the film plane.

Bear in mind that combining two negatives gives twice as much grain to the picture, and the possibility of twice as much dust, be more meticulous than normal about dusting off the negatives before printing.

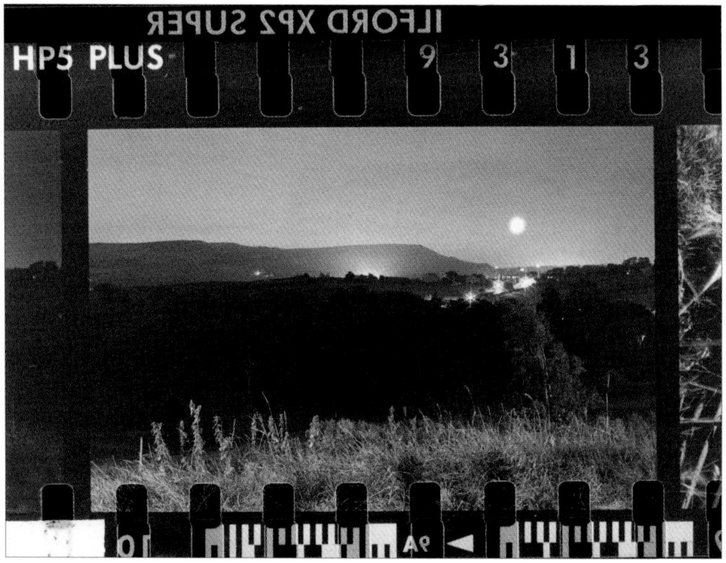

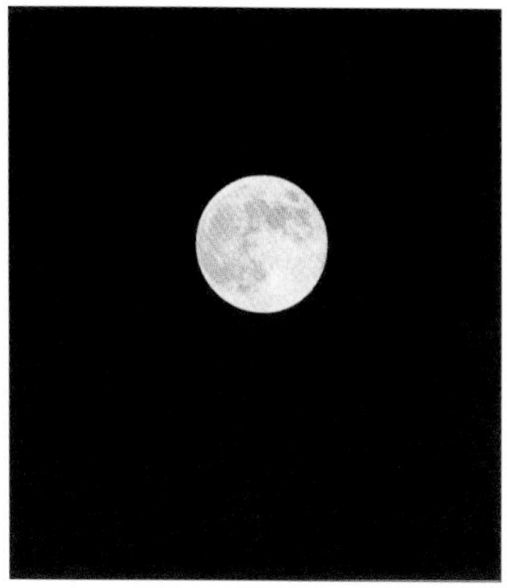

The exposure to record detail on the moon is the same as the exposure to record detail on the earth, they are both illuminated by the same sun.
1/500 f11, 400 ISO

Combination of 2 negatives

This shows the two negatives together. Because the moon film is otherwise completely clear, it can be moved around until the positioning looks correct.

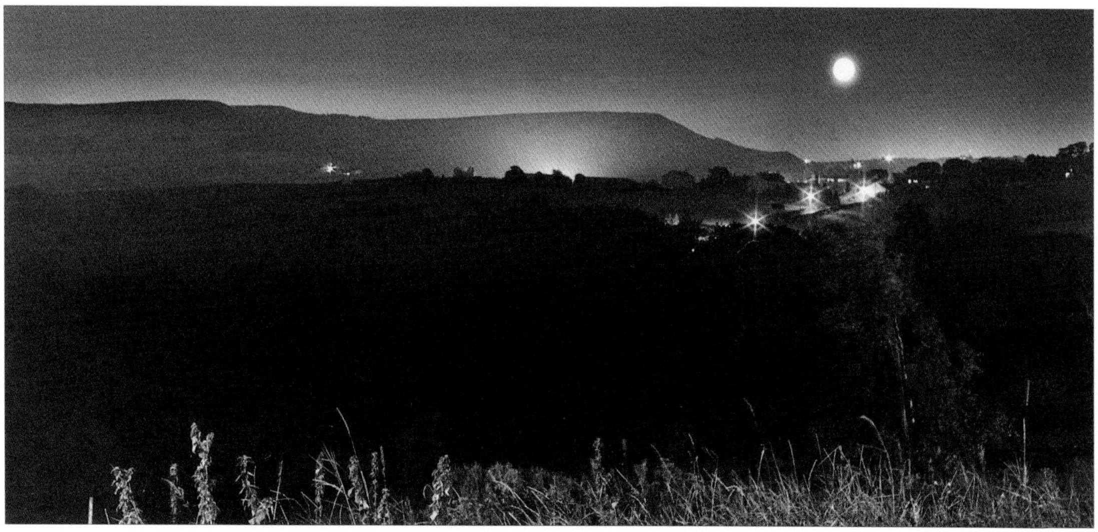

The finished print from the combined negatives.

Grain 'doubling up' is obviously less of a problem when shooting on larger formats, but for those photographers restricted to 35mm, the effect can be lessened by shooting the moon negative with a slow, fine grained film, in which case the exposure will be one of the following;

25 ISO - 1/250 @ f4
50 ISO - 1/250 @ f5.6
100 ISO - 1/250 @ f8
200 ISO - 1/250 @ f11

The image here of the moonlit landscape is completely constructed, using the method I have just described. The moon is from a series of test exposures of it in a black sky, and the landscape was shot in the middle of the day. I combined the two negative strips, and held them together with a small piece of masking tape in the negative carrier.

After testing for the exposure, I decided on an overprinted version that conveyed moonlit clouds, rather than sunshine.

The streetlights that can be seen in the bottom left of the picture were created by adding a few small spots of water soluble black ink to the surface of the print before exposure, these were then rubbed off during development with a bit of tissue, leaving a white spot.

After fixing and washing, the print was then slightly bleached in ferricyanide (sepia bleach), and toned in thiocarbamide, this was to brighten and tone the lighter parts of the clouds to a slight sandy colour.

After washing, the print was placed in a tray of selenium toner and removed when the shadows had changed to a plummy colour. This was followed by a further wash, and then a blue toner was applied to convey the effect of moonlight.

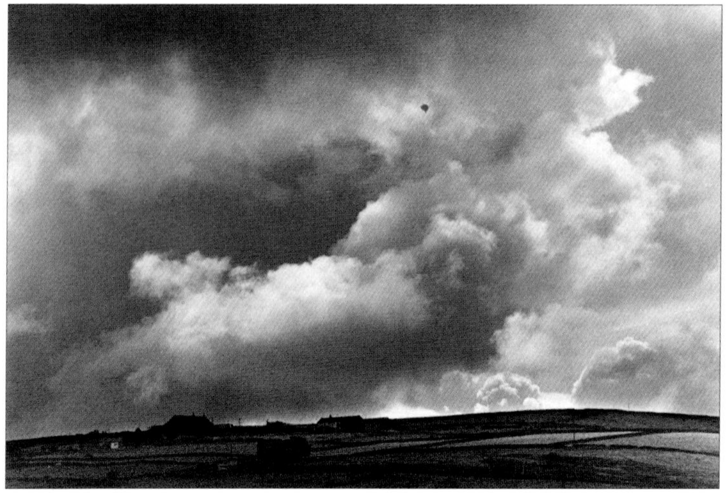

The clouds were photographed in daylight ...

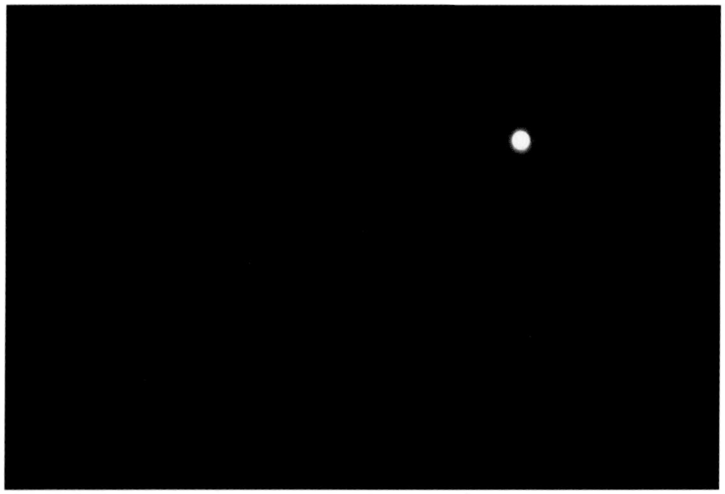

... and combined with a moon negative.

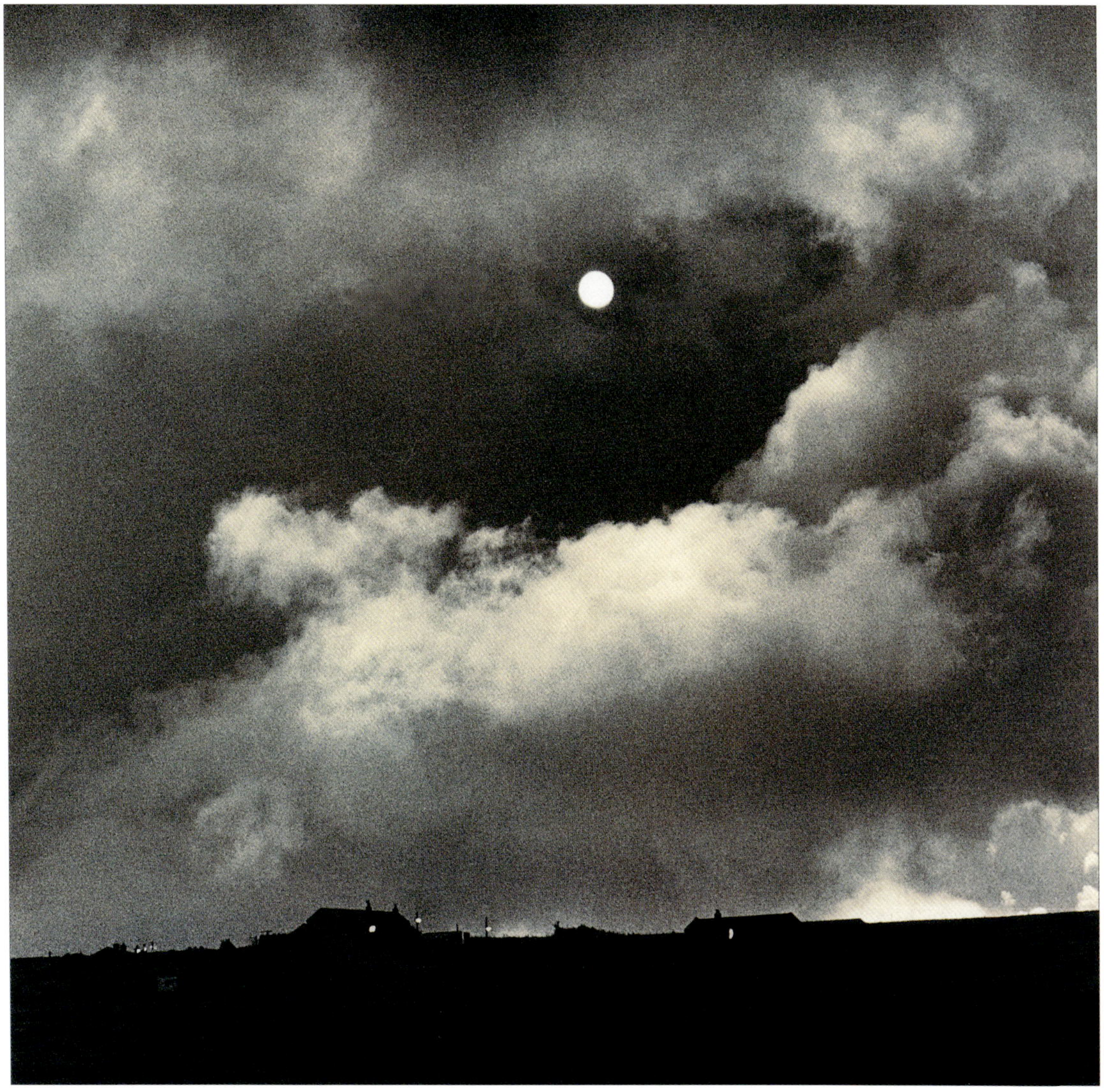

Moon over farms from two negatives combined

This picture was made by combining a moon negative with a landscape and printing down to simulate night. The image was then split toned to emphasise the mood.

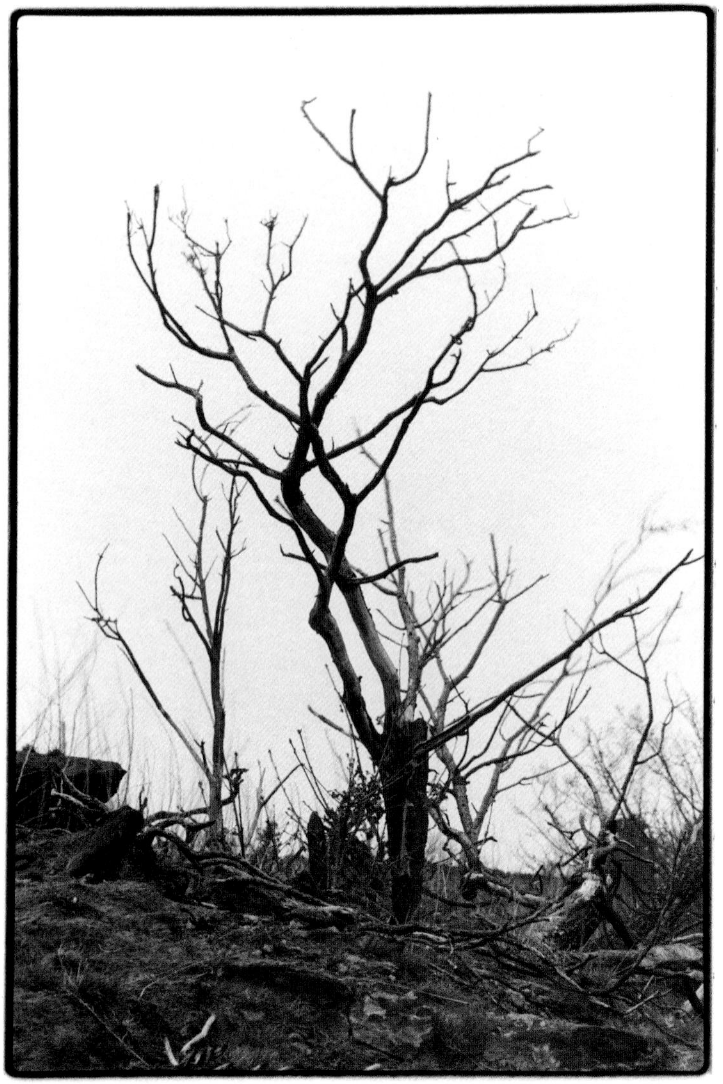

Straight print from a daylight exposure of small trees against a white sky.

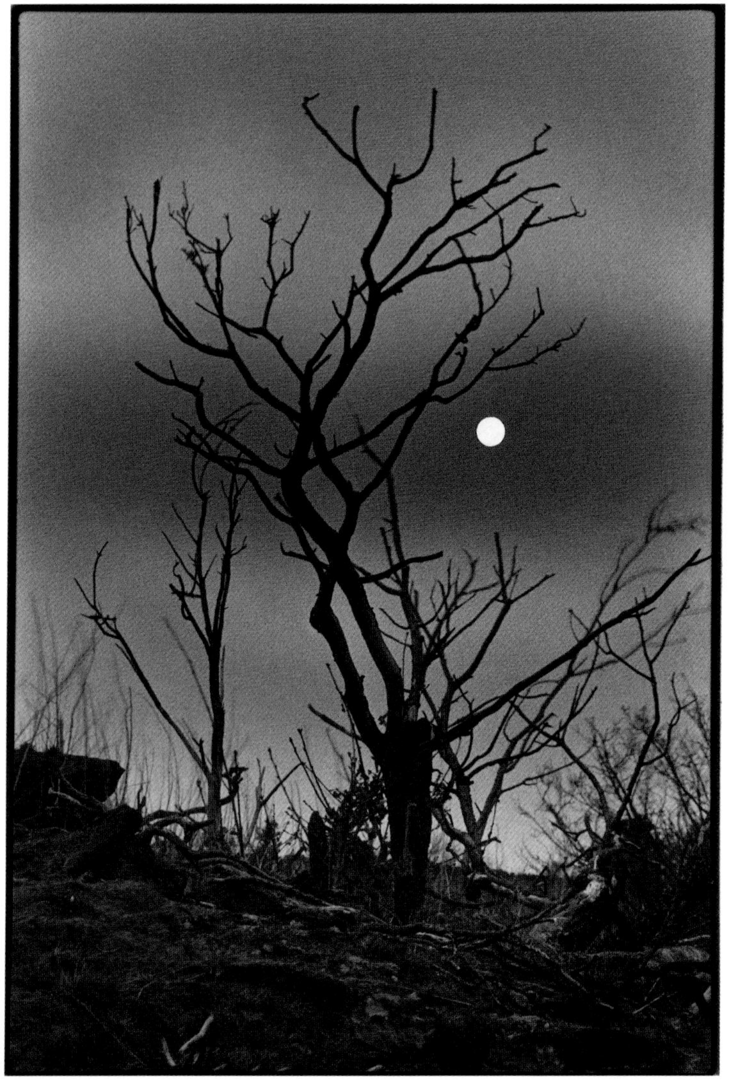

Printed down version with small circular card placed on the paper during the exposure. Clouds simulated by selective burning in.

Another method for creating a moon

A similar effect to the moon negative can be achieved by positioning a small piece of circular black paper (such as a hole punch might provide) on the surface of the paper with the red filter swung under the lens, and leaving it there during exposure, In this way the 'moon' could be sited in the most effective position in the sky.

I find this method is less convincing as a moonlit landscape, because the edges of the moon are too sharp, and there is no impression of flare.

Personally I would never use this technique, I only include it as an example.

Underexposing in sunlight

A simple method for achieving a moonlight effect is to shoot a scene in full sunlight, underexposing by between four and eight stops according to the effect required. The addition of a red filter will help the impression, by simulating the black sky.

This obviously cannot give a very convincing image, due to the absence of street lighting, so is best restricted to unpopulated landscapes.

It would be possible with large format negatives, to apply dots of black dye to the neg to give the effect of distant streetlights. How convincing this would prove, would be down to the skill of the retoucher.

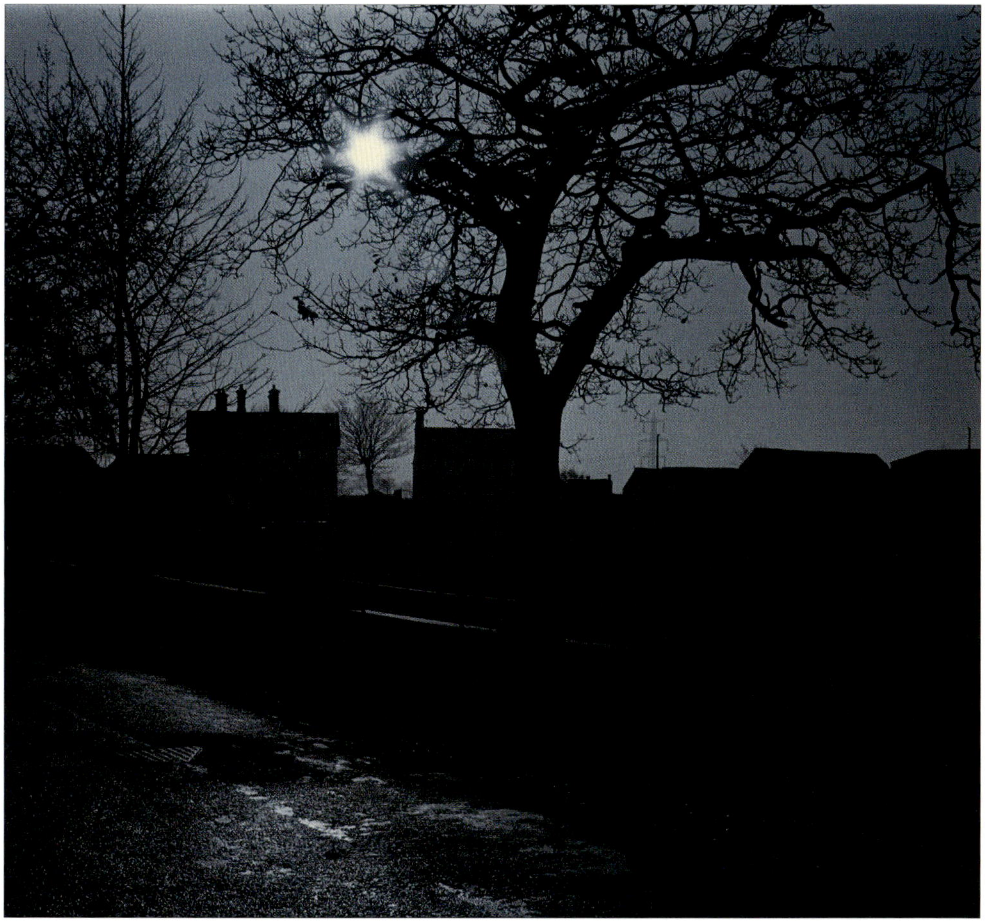

Overprinted daylight picture simulating moonlight. Blue toned and tea stained.

processing and printing

Coping with contrast

Shooting at night produces probably the greatest potential for contrast that you are ever likely to encounter in photography, from raven black shadows, right through to the hot amber brightness of a lamp filament.

Modern films, as good as they are, have great difficulty with these extremes and need a little help to produce a print with detail and tone in all areas.

I actually believe that some areas should be jet black and without detail, as this is precisely what night is all about, and this can be used to dramatic effect. Conversely, the lamps themselves, if included in the frame can be a pure detail-less white – and still look realistic, tonally, provided that all other tones in-between have been represented accurately. However, it is wise to keep contrast to a minimum wherever possible, and to that end I will provide some useful tips and techniques.

Contrast control falls into three categories; control during shooting, control during processing, and control during printing. Utilising just two of these, contrast control during shooting and processing, should greatly reduce the need for contrast control during printing.

The first of these, control during shooting has been covered in the section on supplementary lighting.

The second, control during processing, has several options;- Down rating, Dilute development with static processing, Two bath development, and Pyro development.

Contrast control during processing

An old maxim in photography which still holds true today is, expose for the shadows, develop for the highlights. This philosophy, if carefully applied, will ensure that the contrast of almost any scene is within the range of the film, and give you printable negatives.

Exposure and development are inextricably linked. Exposure determines how much is recorded on the film, development

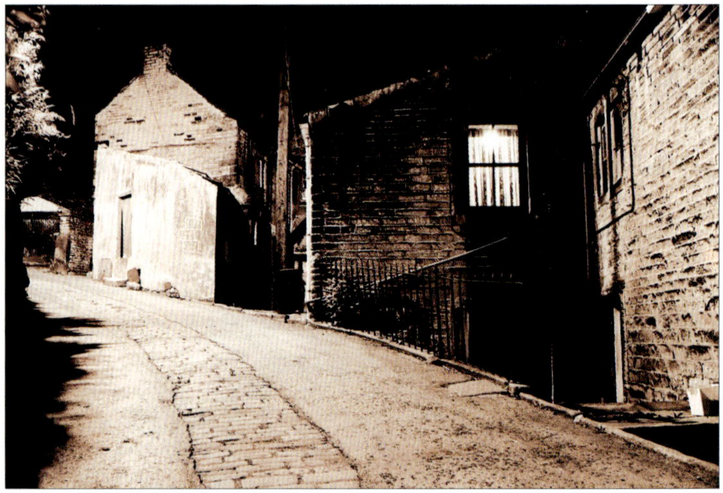

Goose Green, Holmfirth, Yorkshire

Ilford HP5 processed in Ilford Microphen.

determines whether that image is pale grey, grey, dark grey, or black. Stopping the development at the right point prevents the highlights from reaching black, and becoming too dense for light to pass through at the printing stage.

In the early days of photography this was achieved by developing individual glass plates in a tray of developer by inspection. These plates had a low sensitivity and were orthochromatic, they could therefore be developed under red safelight until the correct density had been reached. Judging the amount of development for each image was therefore fairly simple.

These days, development by inspection is out of the question, because of the increased sensitivity of todays emulsions. Also, most people do not shoot individual 'plates' or sheets of film, but use roll or 35mm, in which case, development can only be approximated, and a processing time chosen that will be an average for the whole film, rather than the appropriate one for each individual shot.

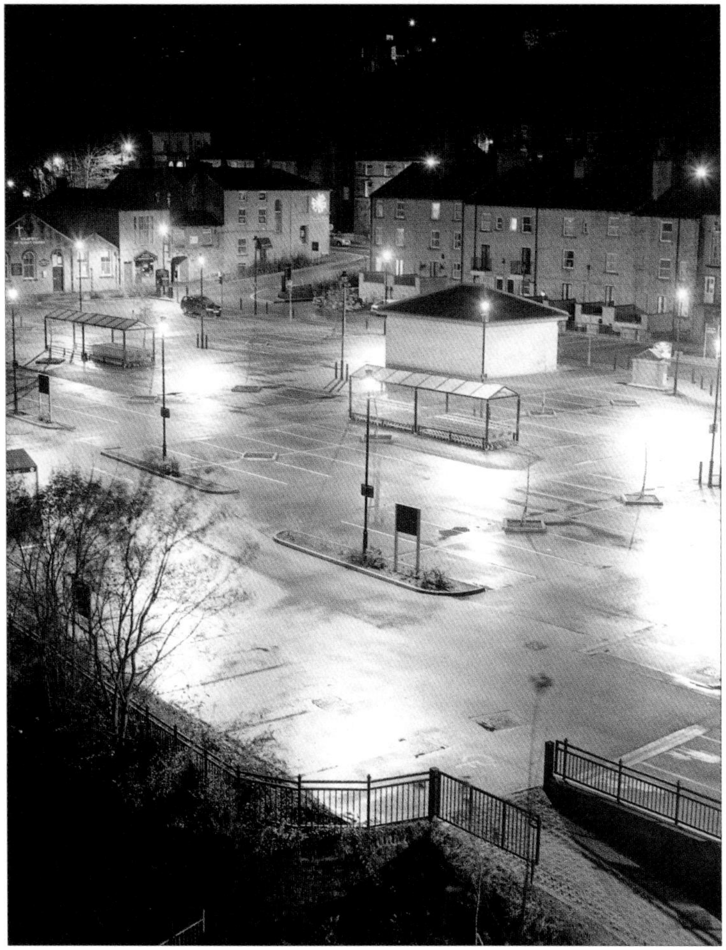

Normally processed

A scene such as this with bright high pressure sodium lamps reflecting off wet tarmac, and very deep shadows, is too extreme for a normally processed negative. HP5 rated 400 processed normally in Ilford ID11.

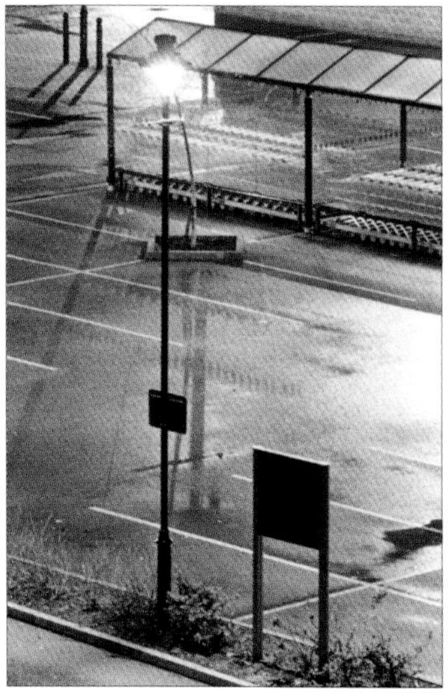

Detail

If you are shooting night photographs, and wish to employ contrast reducing methods in processing, then shoot complete films in particular lighting conditions, and choose a processing option that is appropriate for the whole film.

I know this frightens many photographers, but it will ensure that the process is matched to the exposures. Use shorter lengths of film if this prospect gives you palpitations.

Downrating

The simplest method of contrast control with processing is to over expose the film by one stop (set the ISO to the next lowest number), and reduce the development.

How much to reduce the time in developer is a question that produces different answers from different workers, some recommend as little as a ten percent reduction in processing time, whereas others go as far as thirty percent. My own is twenty percent, but sometimes less, with T. grain films, because these can be more susceptible to changes in development.

At the back of the book will be found a table of development times and percentage reductions, which will assist you in determining a time for your own film and developer. Results from downrating can vary with developer type, and some film/dev combinations are unsuitable for this treatment, so some experimentation and testing may be necessary to establish your own time for the developer you are using.

Two bath development

Two bath development has been around for over sixty years, but the majority of photographers have no experience of it, although this appears to be changing, and it seems to be enjoying a revival. Why it has not been more widely practised is a mystery, in some respects it is easier than ordinary processing.

Two bath development works in a different way from the previous process, but achieves the same results, by preventing the highlights from becoming too dense, and at the same time bringing up the shadows. This is achieved by taking the constituents of a general purpose developer, and separating them into two solutions – hence the name.

The first solution contains the slow working developing agents and the second contains the accelerator.

The film is immersed in the first bath containing the developing agents, which work very slowly without the accelerator, and the film is agitated continuously – though carefully. After a period of time, the developer is absorbed, swelling the film emulsion, but the density does not go very far.

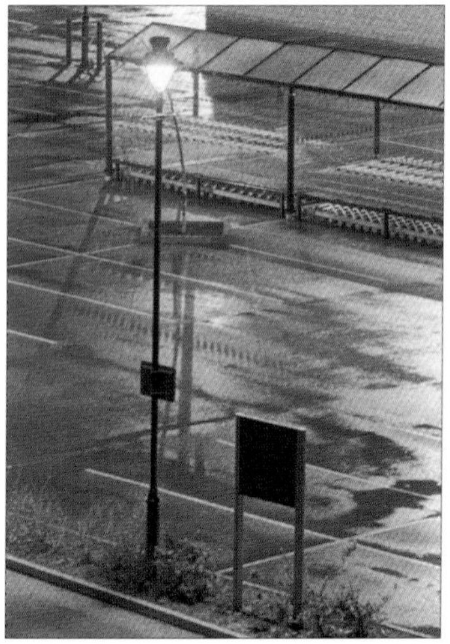

2 bath detail

Notice how much detail is shown in the lamp, and also in the darker tones in the dark sign situated lower centre here.

The first bath is then returned to the storage bottle, and the second bath is poured into the tank (without an intermediate rinse), and is left unagitated for a further 3 mins.

When the second bath, the accelerator, is brought into contact with the surface of the film, development proceeds rapidly, but becomes quickly exhausted in the highlights, where it has had to work hardest. However, the development continues in the shadow areas where action is slower, bringing up the shadow detail.

It is important to make sure that solution B does not contaminate solution A, because this would cause the first bath to work too quickly. Keep bottles (and lids) clearly labled and try not to splash solutions around.

To exercise some control over the degree of contrast, vary the time in the first bath. A shorter time for less contrast, and a longer time for increased contrast. The time in the second bath remains the same.

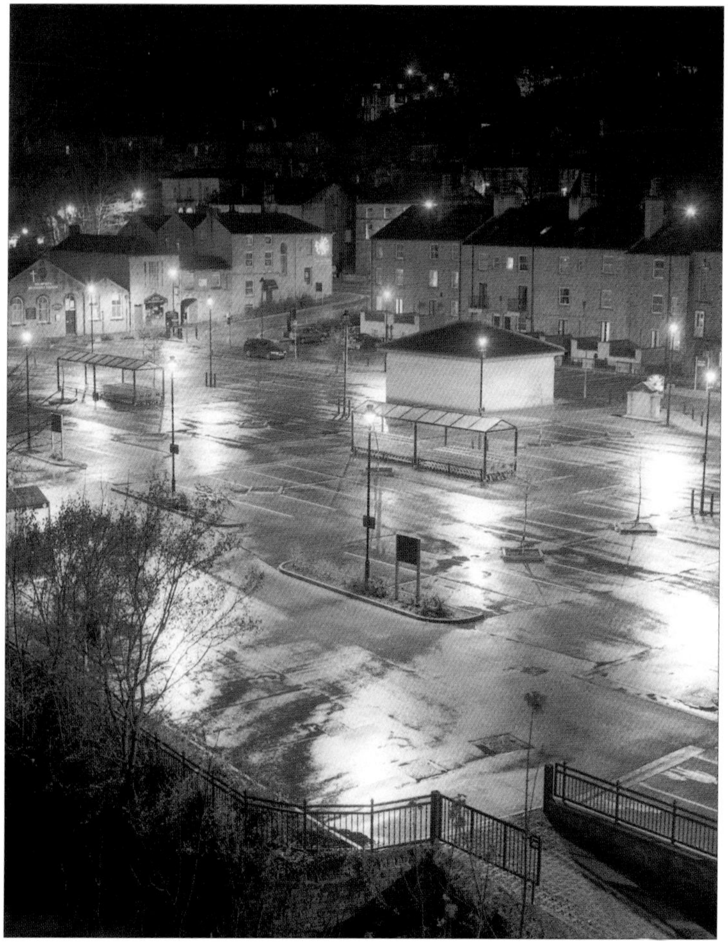

2 bath process

This gives some degree of compression and has rendered the lamps well and kept flare to a minimum. HP5 rated 200.

This is followed by the normal sequence of stop and fix. This method does reduce contrast, but can result in streaky negatives occasionally.

If you find this is happening, I would suggest that when developing films in a spiral, that the spiral is turned slightly as soon as the second solution has been poured in. This can be done with the small plastic twiddler supplied with your developer tank, or if that has been lost, with a wooden, 'dolly' clothes peg.

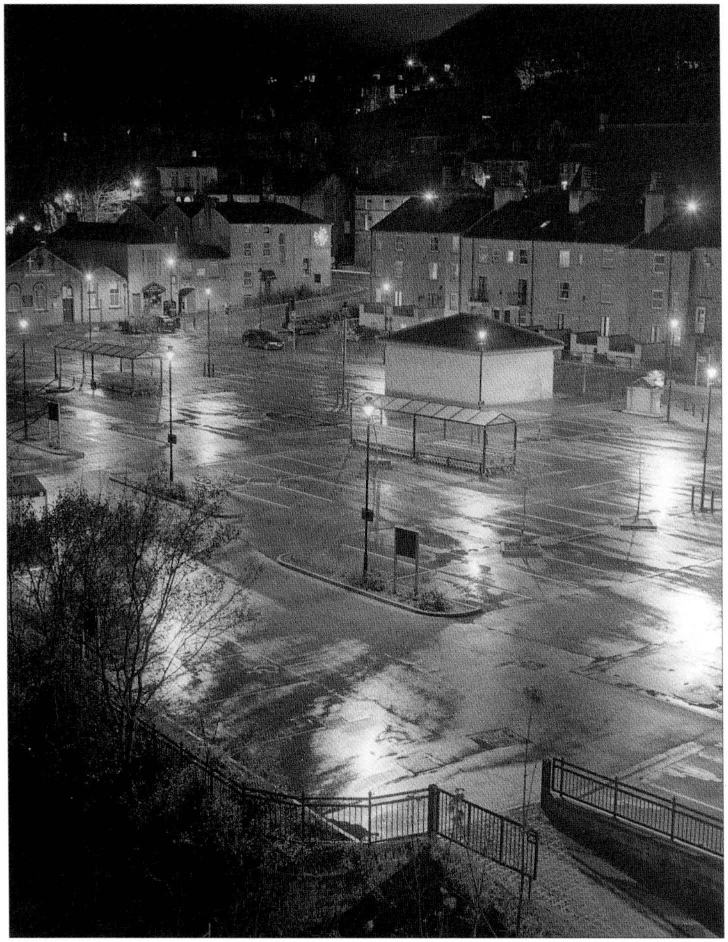

Dilute/static process

The process has compressed the tonal range of the scene, keeping flare under control and revealing shadow detail. HP5 rated at 400 ISO.

However, only turn the spiral a little, otherwise the process will behave more aggressively, and higher contrast will result.

Dilute development/static processing

Dilute development/static processing, is a method that I have adapted from an old process for uprating films which I believe is credited to William Mortensen. It works by preventing the highlights from overdeveloping whilst allowing the shadows to continue to develop. This is achieved by using a solution of developer at a quarter of its working strength and after a period of normal agitation the film is left to sit unagitated for a large proportion of the overall development time.

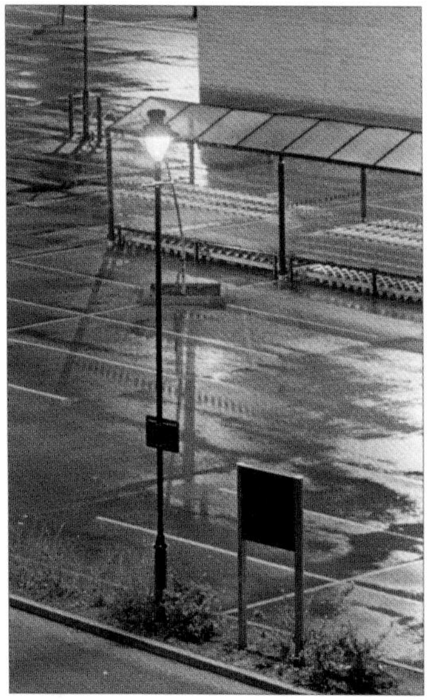

Dilute/static detail

The developer works more vigorously on the denser parts of the image, -the highlights, and becomes exhausted, no fresh developer is brought into contact with these areas whilst the film is static, but the fainter, shadow areas continue to develop and bring up the detail in the less exposed areas.

My formula for working out development times is to find the correct time for a particular film in ID11 diluted 1-3. Divide this time by four to give the time of the first development ie;

HP5 in ID11 diluted 1+3 @ 20 C – time 22 mins.

Divide by 4 – time 5.5 mins.

The second part of the process is to keep the film stationary in the solution for the original time for that particular film/dev/dilution combination.

Static period – time 22 mins.

Keep the temperature constant during this part of the process, and resist the temptation to move the developing tank in any way, as this constitutes agitation.

This is followed by the normal sequence of stop bath and fix.

As can be seen in the test image, the degree of compression is very good, somewhere between results from the two bath process and the pyro process.

There is no speed loss with this particular process.

Pyro development

Pyro development is another very old technique. The film is stained by Pyrogallol during the process, the stain occurring around each developed silver grain, which tends to blend the grains into each other, reducing the granularity of the image.

Modern chromogenic films such as Kodak T400CN and Ilford XP2 Super produce a similar result, but employ a different method to achieve it.

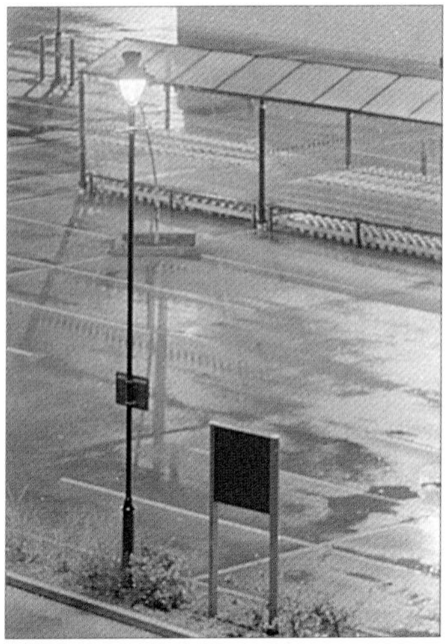

Pyro detail

When processed, the negative appears quite thin, and is actually underdeveloped. The stain brings the density up to a normal level for printing. This prevents the highlights from blocking up, and imparts a delicate tone to the lighter parts of the image, whilst giving good seperation in the shadows.

This processing method is so good at compressing the highlights, that the film can be overexposed by two or three stops and still produce a very nice negative. In fact, for night photography it needs some overexposure to get the best out of it. This can be achieved in two ways; some photographers recommend taking a light reading from the shadows, instead of the mid tones – some recommend taking a reading from the mids with the film speed rated lower.

In night photography, the scene is difficult enough to meter without trying to pick up a reading from the even darker shadows, so apply the lower rating method for this kind of work.

Do some tests of your own to establish the correct amount of speed loss, and only judge the negative by how it prints, NOT by how dense it looks. To get the best from pyro, it is recommended that the negatives are printed on a fixed grade paper, not a variable contrast paper, because the colour of the stain alters the filtration and consequently, the contrast.

Pyro is very well suited to night photography, because of the extreme compression it provides, and its ability to reduce the effect of flare and halation in areas of extreme overexposure, such as when lights are included in the frame during a long exposure.

Halation is a build up of density around a heavily exposed area, which spreads across into adjacent areas. Some of this halation is due to light being scattered, and some is due to what is known as infectious development.

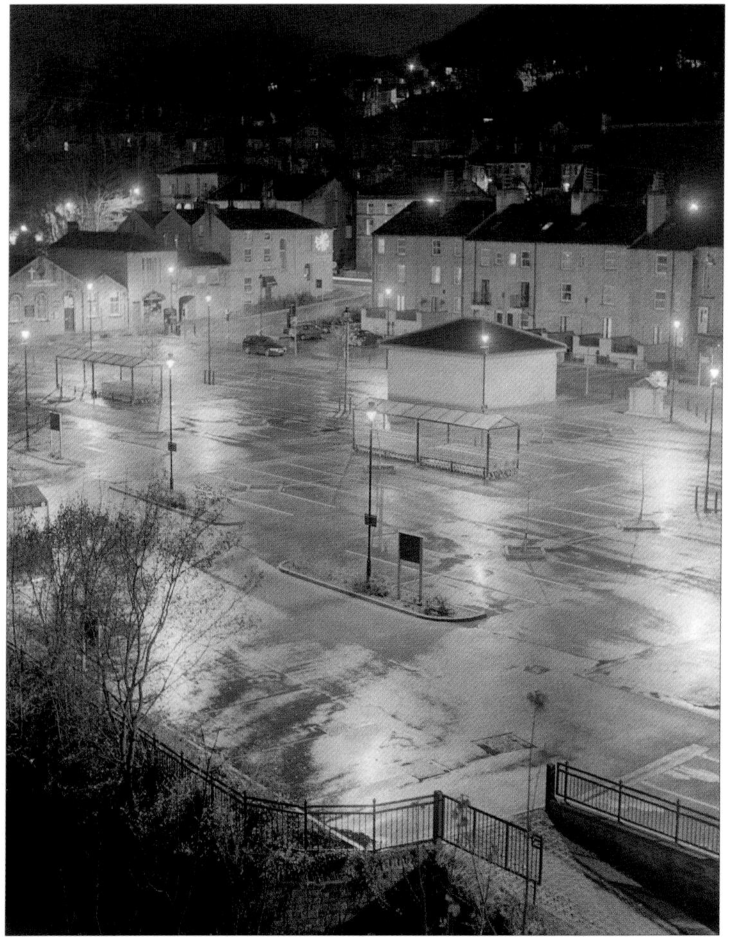

Pyro process

This displays a remarkable degree of compression. The lamps can be seen within the lamp housing and a lot of shadow detail has been revealed.

The main drawback with pyro is the fact that pyrogallol is extremely toxic, and great care must be taken when mixing up from the raw chemicals.

For those who wish to try pyro without mixing the chemicals themselves, there are a few commercially produced pyro developers, and all are good, although it should still be remembered that Pyrogallol is extremely toxic and should not be used in a slap dash way. Purely from a safety point of view, this process should be avoided unless you are willing to work cleanly, and with extreme care.

See formulary section for full processing sequence.

Test exposure

As can be seen in the comparison prints, the view of the car park on a wet night has been represented extremely well. What can't be appreciated is how pyro has the ability to not only keep highlight detail, but also show detail deep into the shadows.

After printing these tests I took the print from the pyro neg to the window from which the test shots had been taken, and was amazed to see detail in the deepest shadow where it isn't even visible to the eye.

I actually walked down into the scene to prove to myself that it wasn't just the bright lights that were preventing me from seeing the dark areas. When I got down there I still could hardly make out the detail.

This process has the greatest compression of any of the contrast control methods I have tried, and I would dearly have liked to have known about it twenty years ago, it would have saved me many, many hours of masking and split grading. It is highly recommended to the serious night worker who is at home with a more careful and time consuming way of working.

A SIMPLE METHOD FOR INCREASING DENSITY IN UNDEREXPOSED OR UNDERDEVELOPED NEGATIVES

If a negative is lacking density, it can be 'boosted' by the simple method of sulphide toning.

The negative must have been fixed properly and well washed.

Place the negative into a tray of ferricyanide bleach, agitate gently and continously, until all that remains is a milky image.

Wash well, then immerse in the sulphide toner.

The image should now be a rich, dark brown. The negative may not look any denser than it did before treatment, but to a blue sensitive paper this behaves like extra density.

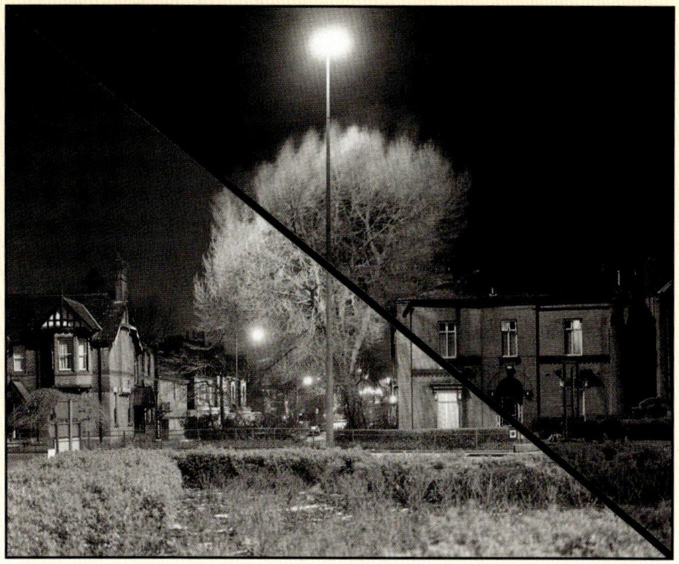

Contrast control during printing

Burning in and dodging

Burning in and dodging are terms used by printers to describe additional local exposure (burning in), or local reduction of exposure (dodging). These are terms that anyone with darkroom experience will be familiar with.

Any photographer wishing to produce good quality prints, is going to have to practice dodging and burning in regularly, especially when printing from night negatives.

It is no exaggeration to say that virtually every picture taken at night is going to have a range of tones which are beyond the range of a single exposure grade 2 print.

Therefore, the night photographer, or to be more accurate, the night printer, needs as many contrast controlling methods as possible to be able to handle a range of negatives.

Dodging and burning in are really the same thing, if you are dodging an area of the image, you are simultaneously burning in the rest. Conversely, if you are burning in an area, you must be dodging all other areas.

They are described as separate techniques to illustrate what is done to the main exposure.

Dodging, (preventing light from reaching an area), is often done with the hands – though this takes a good deal of practice, or, with pieces of card on lengths of stiff wire.

The dodger is held over the print for part of an exposure, to reduce the density in that area, the amount of time that the dodger is used for any part of the image, needs to be established by testing. Too much dodging will leave grey areas, devoid of a proper black.

The skill lies in altering the tones in a way that compresses the information from the negative into the tonal range of the paper, but without this being obvious to the viewer. Taking this technique further produces mood, impact and emotion, if used with understanding.

To establish an exposure for the areas to be dodged is quite simple, place a test piece of photographic paper on the baseboard in the appropriate area, and give it the exposure that has already been determined for the print. During this exposure, move a piece of card over the strip, to gradually cover it up. This is done in stages as with a normal test strip. The individual exposure stages are one fifth (20%) of the original exposure, i.e; if the print exposure is ten seconds, then the card is moved over the paper every two seconds.

The exposure can be divided into anything from quarters (25%) up to tenths (10%), the more divisions you have, the more fine the exposure adjustment will be.

When the test has been developed, it will show the point after which dodging is detrimental.

If more detail is needed in the shadows, I have a particular technique which can 'pull out' far more than ordinary dodging. This is an ideal technique for achieving a split grade effect in a fraction of the time.

This technique is only possible with variable contrast papers, it entails dodging out with a piece of grade 5 filter on a length of stiff wire.

Technique

Repeat the test described above, only this time cover the test strip using a grade 5 filter instead of the card. See on the processed strip how much more is revealed.

Now you will need to cut up the grade 5 multigrade filter to make a high contrast dodger, I usually try to get a few different sized dodgers out of one filter. Try drawing out the possible shapes on a similar sized piece of paper first before you commit yourself.

This technique works best when the main print exposure is done without any filtration at all, this is equivalent to a grade2 contrast.

Once the amount of dodging has been established, apply that to the use of the cut up grade 5 dodger.

Split grade printing

If you have admired the work of other photographers and printers during the last ten to fifteen years, and wondered at the luminescence of good quality work, and how it was achieved, then wonder no more, this is the tecnique.

Split grading gives the printer an amazing range of possibilities in the darkroom, in the hands of a modern printer it is able to give results that were impossible only a couple of decades ago.

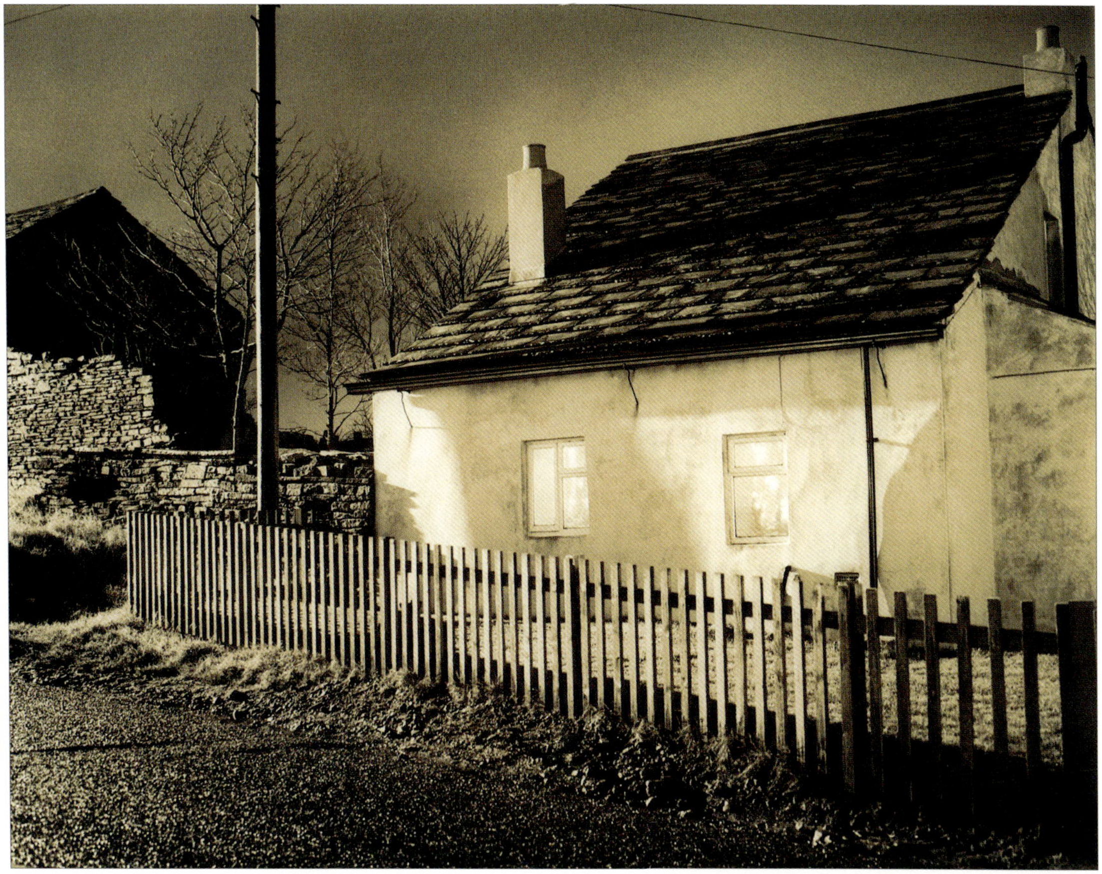

Farm house near Castle Hill, West Yorkshire

The combined effect of both filters with a little extra burning in on the wall to the left, the sky, and the tarmac in the foreground. Ilford HP5 6x7cm negative processed in Ilford ID11.

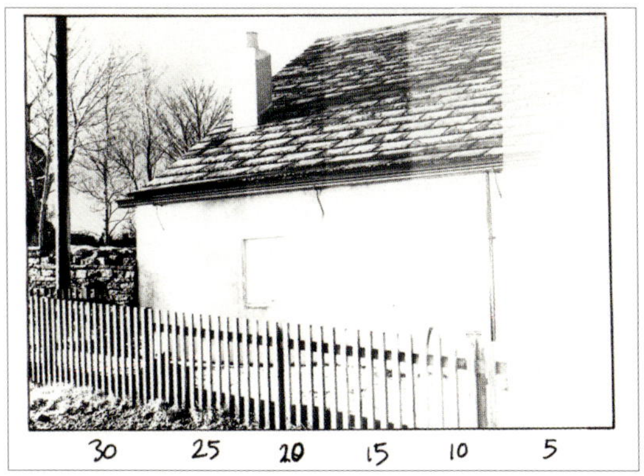

Test strip through a grade 5 filter in 5 second increments.

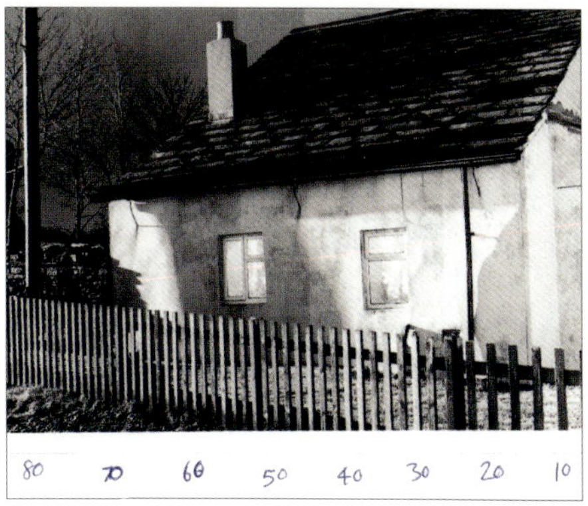

Test strip for grade 00 filter in 10 second increments, plus 15 seconds at grade 5.

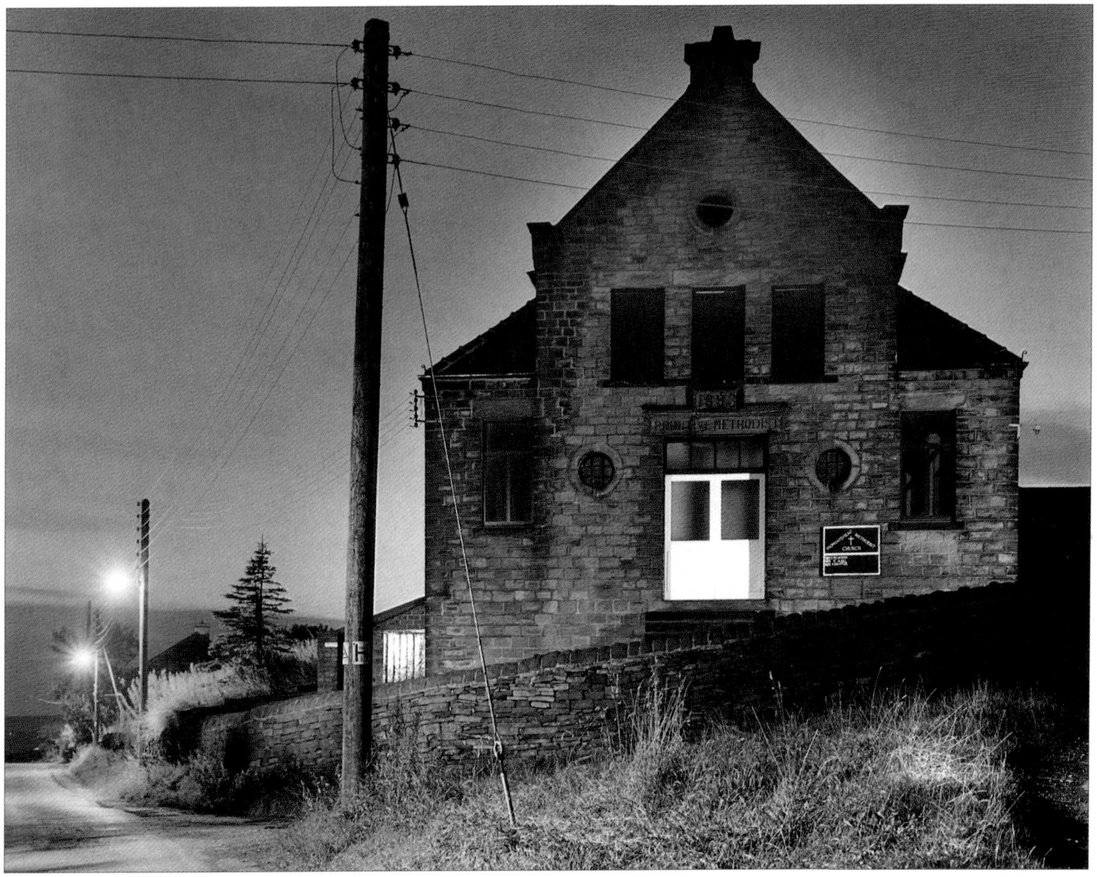

Snowgatehead Primitive Methodist church

Ths print involved a fair degree of manipulation. The six separate operations are described below. Compare this with the same image in the section on Lith Printing. Ilford HP5 5x4in negative processed in Ilford ID11.

This method has radically changed the way photographers print, and is well worth practicing, even if it seems a little complicated at first.

Split grading is a method by which the paper is exposed through two or more contrast filters to show detail and tonal separation throughout the image.

I have read at least three variations in the method for employing separate filters during printing, and I won't confuse you by explaining them all. My own method consists of one exposure through a high contrast or 'hard' filter (Grade 5), to print in the shadow detail, and another exposure through a low contrast, or 'soft' filter (Grade 00), to print in the mid and highlight detail. The proportions of each are arrived at by testing, and differ according to the effect required. The contrast is raised or lowered by varying the amount of exposure through each. The larger the proportion of exposure through a particular filter, the more dominant that contrast (or lack of it) will become. Equal exposures through each filter will give a mid range contrast (Grade 2).

Sometimes, the two exposures cover the full image area for both, and sometimes, the 'soft' exposure is done selectively to certain areas, so as to prevent a degradation of the contrast in subtle darker tones – the shadows.

Contrast can also be added or reduced locally, by burning in through the individual filters, and this is the real beauty of variable contrast papers. Their flexibility can give a more varied result and, in the hands of a master, a print that can take your breath away.

Printing maps

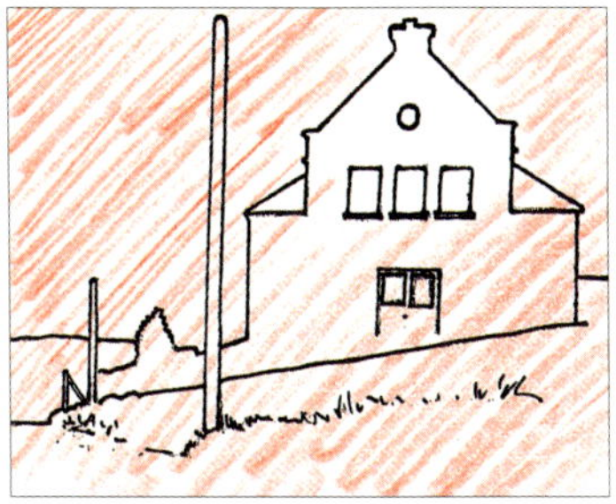

20s G5. Using shaped card on wire.

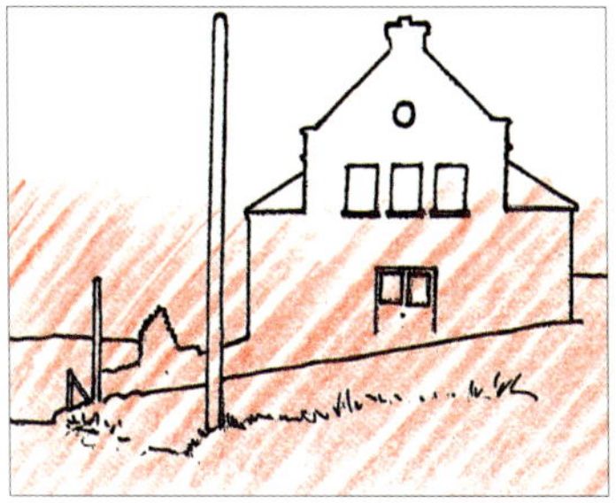

20s G5. Using moving card.

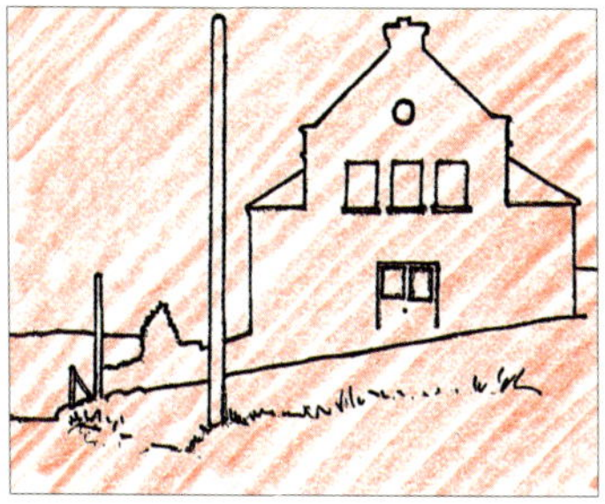

25s G5.

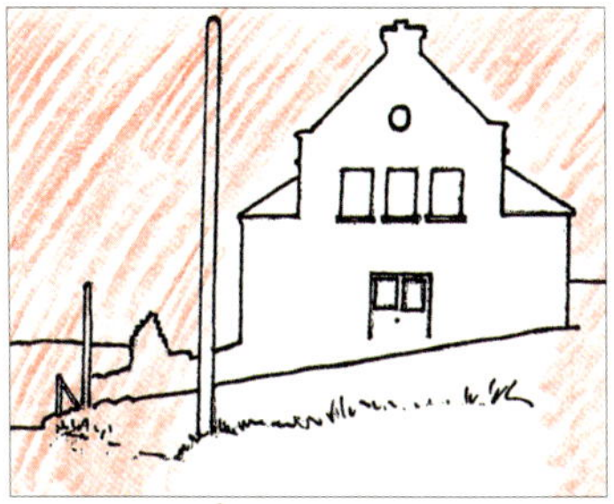

20s G00. Dodged by hand.

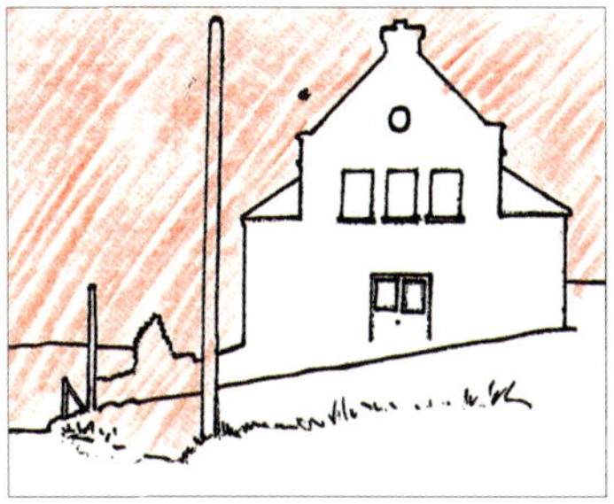

20s G00.Card mask.

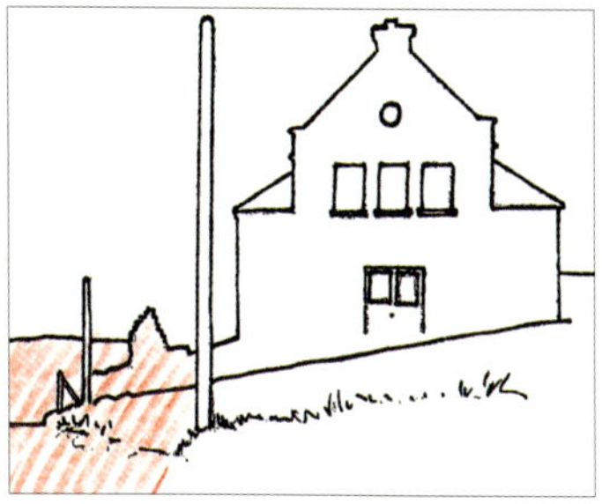

30s G00.

The fine control with this method comes when areas are dodged during one of the filtered exposures.

Consider a basic situation where equal exposures are given through each filter, resulting in a grade 2 all over. If a dodger is held over part of the image during the low contrast exposure, that area stands out as having a high contrast within a predominantly medium contrast scene, because it has only received light from the other filter. Conversely, if a dodger is held over part of the image during the high contrast exposure, the area stands out as having low contrast, within a predominantly medium contrast scene.

The dodger in this basic example is held over the paper for the duration of one exposure to simplify the explanation, though in practice this may produce too extreme an effect, and may only need to be used for part of the exposure, resulting in a lessening of the effect and a finer control.

Obviously, this has unlimited possibilities and could become very complex, but it is an extremely exciting way to print because of the control and variation that it gives.

When using more of one filter than another, it is not necessary to know which grade of paper is being approximated, only that the contrast is correct for that print or part of a print.

If the negative needs to be printed again, and the contrast recreated, then the exposure times through each filter are repeated, giving the same effect.

When establishing the printing exposure, the first test is done through a grade 5 filter, and the shortest exposure chosen that will produce a black from the thinnest parts of the negative. In the example on the previous page, this time is fifteen seconds.

The second test is done through a grade 00 filter, but must have the chosen exposure from the previous test given first.

The second test therefore, is given fifteen seconds through a grade 5 filter, followed by a series of exposures through a grade 00 filter to establish the point at which the lighter tones look correct. In the example here, the grade 00 test indicated an exposure of 45 seconds.

The final print is then given fifteen seconds through a grade 5 filter, followed by forty five seconds through a grade 00 filter. This was followed by a little burning in for the sky, and some extra exposure through the grade 00 filter for the wall at the left of the picture. The tarmac road which occupies the lower left corner was

Test strips to determine correct exposure for pre-flash

Correct test.

Too little exposure.

Too much exposure.

given extra exposure through both filters to darken it, and to subdue the highlights where the light was being reflected off the wet surface.

The example I have given here is not too involved or complicated, the image could be printed to reveal more in the darker tones, such as the roof, by preventing some of the grade 00 exposure in that area. This would have increased the contrast and shown the tiles much better. It could also have been given extra exposure through the grade 5 filter in the light parts of the wall of the house to bring out the mottled tone of the old cement rendering, the possibilities are many, and each printer tackles a negative differently.

For sequences of printing that involve a number of different operations, it is important to keep notes to refer back to. It is very easy to omit one part of the sequence, ruining the print completely.

A lot of photographers, myself included, draw little boxes and indicate with shading, the areas to be flashed, burned in, dodged, filtered, or whatever else is necessary for the final print. These are drawn out as the various tests are done, to ensure that no part of the sequence is forgotten. These are known as print maps

Pre-flashing

Pre-flashing is a technique for giving extra detail in the highlights of a print. It is sometimes described as a technique for lowering contrast, this is true, as it gives the impression of lowering contrast by bringing the lighter tones out, but this is quite a different effect from using a lower grade of paper.

Exposure inertia

An unexposed sheet of paper needs a certain amount of exposure before it will 'get going' and produce tone. This is referred to as exposure inertia. If the paper is given a very short exposure all over to a diffused white light, this inertia is overcome – the exposure is on its way, this means that areas of the negative that pass little light have more of an influence on the print tone.

It is obvious though, that this carries the risk of fogging the paper, so the pre-flash (not really a flash, just a brief exposure) must be controlled.

The light used to create the pre-flash needs to be of a low intensity, to allow controllable exposure times, so switching the

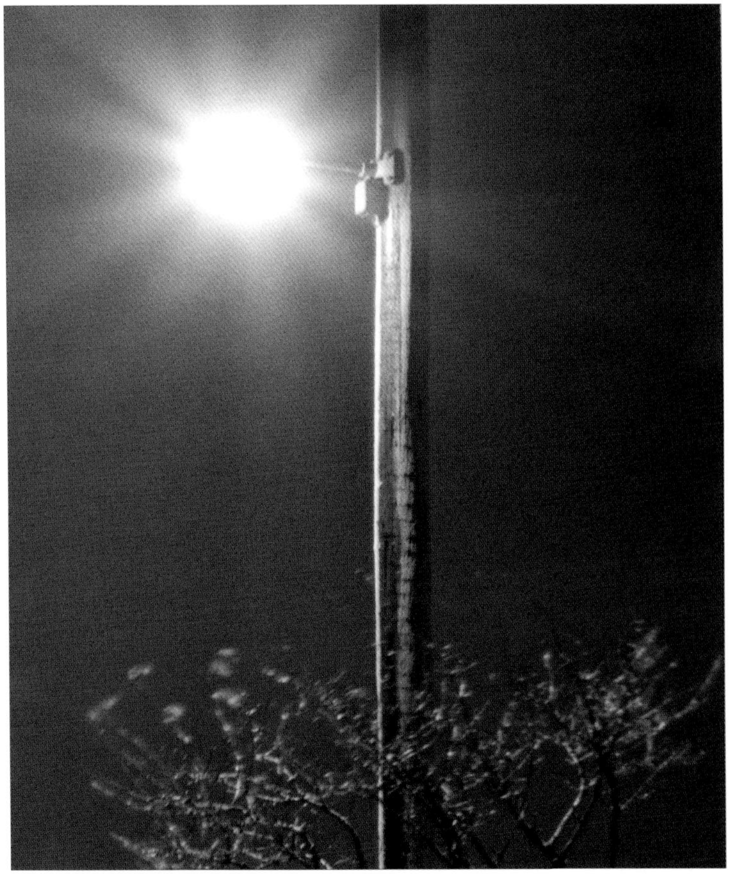

Enlarged section from snowy field showing amount of flare before the flashing

Printed normally the lamp appears burnt out with no detail.

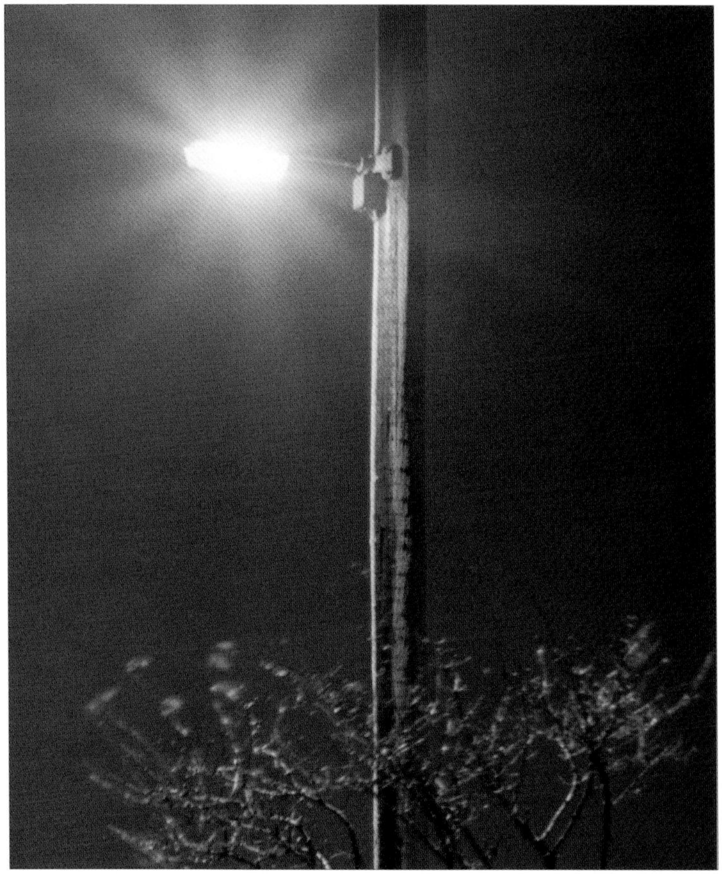

Enlarged section from snowy field showing effect of pre flashing

After a pre flash this print was exposed exactly as the previous example. The flare has been reduced considerably.

light on and off in your darkroom is likely to give too much exposure to be of any use, even with a low wattage bulb.

One method is to raise the enlarger to its full height and close the lens aperture down to its smallest position, to reduce the light output.

The negative needs to be taken out before the flashing exposure is given, and this may be done by simply taking the film strip out of the carrier, or by removing the carrier completely if it is important to ensure that the image is projected in the same position when the carrier is returned to the enlarger.

If the carrier is to be completely removed, then the gap left by the carrier needs to be covered up with electricians tape or black paper and affixed with sticky tape – this is to control stray light pouring out of the opening. Also, a little tape on the neg carrier itself could prevent the negative from moving when these manoeuvres are taking place.

The paper is then tested to discover its threshold exposure. This is the point at which pre-flash becomes real fogging.

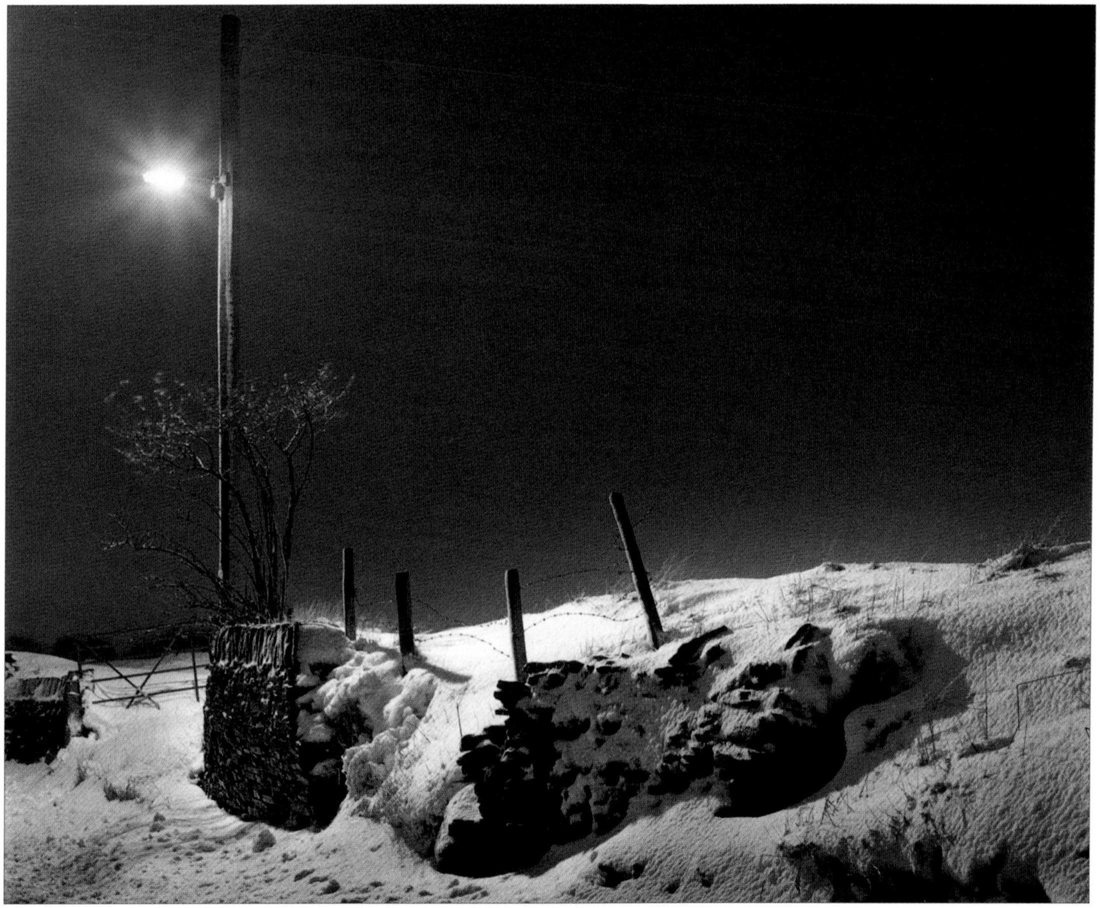

Snowy field and broken wall

When printing this image I restricted the flashing to the upper half of the paper to preserve as much detail in the wall as possible. Ilford HP5 6x6 negative processed in Ilford ID11.

Technique

The enlarger is prepared as described in the last paragraph, and a piece of photographic paper is placed on the baseboard. The paper is then exposed to a series of small exposures, as would be done when making a test strip, but of a much lower intensity. These individual exposures will be quite difficult to see when the test is developed, so keep the distance between them the same – a finger width is ideal.

After development, the strip should range from white to light grey, if the paper is all white, repeat the test with exposures doubled, if the paper is displaying very dark tones, and has no white strip at all, then the individual exposures need to be much shorter.

You may find that your timer is overexposing the test on its shortest setting, this is because with some timers it is not possible to give very short exposures accurately, so the light output of the enlarger needs to be reduced by other means. This can be done by placing one or more pieces of tracing paper over the lens, or resting on the swing filter holder (red filter removed) below the lens. The test is then resumed until a white to light grey strip is produced.

Several layers of trace can be used to give a pre-flash exposure with the negative still in the enlarger, in situations where removing it would cause registration problems.

This is my preferred method. With only two layers of tracing

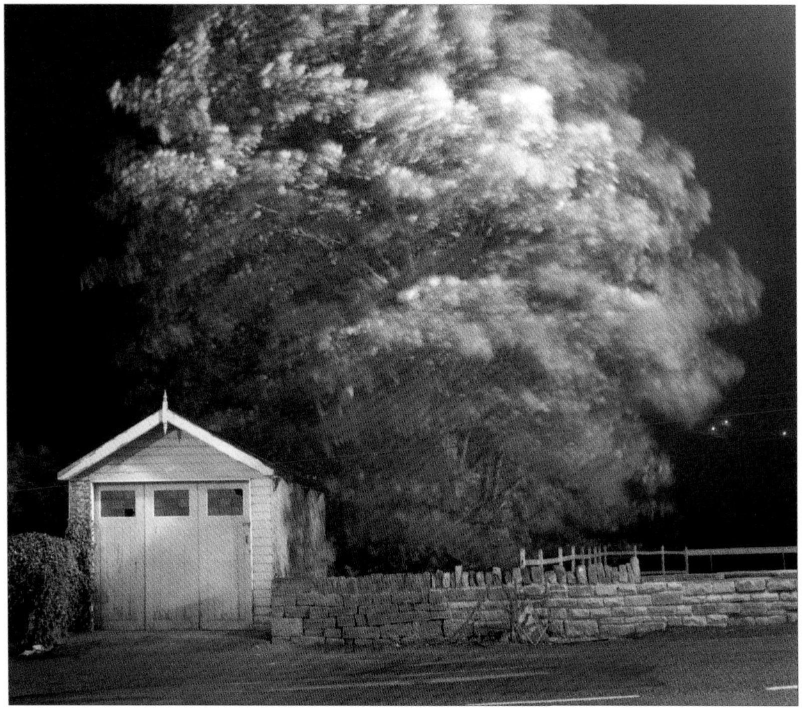

Flashing was used here to control the lighter tones in the foliage towards the top of the print. Ilford HP5 processed in Acutol. Untoned print.

paper, the light is reduced to a manageable level, and the image is totally diffused, giving an even light. The only thing to remember is that the amount of exposure needed to give a pre-flash, varies with the density of the negative in the carrier.

When the test has been developed, look to see where the first signs of tone appear.

To assess this test properly, it should be given a short wash and dried, this is because all papers darken slightly when dry. This density change is known as 'dry-down', and when judging the threshold of a paper it can make quite a difference.

As you view the test strip, count the exposure increments (finger widths) up to, but not including, the first show of tone. The reason for this is that the slightest exposure from a negative is going to provide that little extra which will take the paper into tone. If you choose the first exposure on the test that shows tone, your final print will have no clean whites.

One point I should mention is, don't pre-flash a lot of paper in advance, the effect of the flashing will wear off fairly quickly (days), only flash what you can use in one session of printing.

Having arrived at a pre-flash exposure, flash some paper to put aside for test strips for the image. The pre-flash is going to affect the whole image exposure, so it must be added to the test strips for an accurate assessment.

If you are printing on variable contrast paper, and you wish to use pre-flashing to bring out subtle highlight detail in night shots, for best results, do the pre-flash with grade 00 filtration.

In situations where very faint detail in the shadow areas of the negative is important, extra exposure could be detrimental. For this kind of print, pre flashing should be confined to the appropriate area, either by using the hands, card masks, or Lith masks.

The card or Lith mask can be placed over the paper, a flashing exposure given through tracing paper, the mask and tracing paper removed, the main exposure given, and the Lith mask replaced for the burning in. In actual fact, the burning in can be done before the main exposure, so that the mask needn't be removed and replaced. It makes no difference.

No matter how many separate exposures or flashings are needed to produce your print, they can be given in any sequence, as long as the exposures add up to the same amount, exposure is cumulative.

Selective flashing can also be used to remove distracting parts of the image, by giving far more exposure, and fully fogging the area before (or after) the main exposure is given.

If a print requires flashing and split filtration, and perhaps burning in too, then the seperate tests in the sequence would go like this;

1. Test for pre flash exposure.
2. Give pre flash exposure, and test for grade 5 filtration
3. Give pre flash and grade 5 exposure, and test for grade 00
4. Give pre flash and grade 5 exposure, and grade 00 exposure, and test for burning in

Because each exposure affects the whole, and affects every other exposure, they must be added to each test as you go along.

Burning in can be done in several ways. The extra exposure can be applied by using the hands or specifically cut pieces of card to cover the shadow areas.

Using card masks is more accurate than using the hands, and might be a good idea for some images, but hardly a possibility here.

Cutting card masks needs a fair amount of skill in most situations, though I think that anyone can see that for this negative, this would be impossible.

Using the hands is an even more unlikely scenario, there are so many small highlights to burn in, that many of the subtle darker tones could easily be lost when playing shadow puppets under the lens.

What is needed is some method of burning in many areas, large or small, hard edged or graduated, preferably with one exposure. Step forward Lith masking.

Making and using lith masks

To explain the use of Lith film for improved burning in or dodging, I have chosen an image (opposite) that would be very difficult to alter by conventional means.

This picture displays a range of tones that it would not be possible to print on one grade of paper with one print exposure, and many small areas which would be impossible to burn in by hand, without losing adjacent shadow detail.

Printing with an extremely soft low grade filter such as a grade 00 might produce a print that showed nearly everything on the negative, but not in a way that would accurately represent the scene, with its deep blacks and strong lighting. Printing on the lowest grade filter alone tends to produce prints that look flat, with muddy shades of grey – not very exciting.

What is needed, is a way of keeping each area tonally 'alive' by respecting its local contrast, whilst keeping its relation to other areas of the print compressed, but still appearing realistic. This is where an appreciation of the prints tonal values is invaluable.

The photographer Ansel Adams referred to tonal values as being separate from the actual recorded tone, and this is what must be kept in mind if a print is to look real and alive. An understanding of print values is as important as the ability to operate a light meter.

When a print is judged to have the correct tonal values, (and this might not be a conscious opinion), then the photograph is believed to represent what the eye saw.

When viewing a scene, our eyes adjust to the brightness of each area that we look at and see a normal contrast in each. We might look into the brightest areas of the scene and see everything clearly and then look into the shadowed area, and see plenty there too.

Unless we understand that our eyes are seeing things inaccurately, and that film can not respond the same, we will be constantly disappointed.

Our brain and eye work together to compress the tones without us being consciously aware of it. Film can compress the tones, but not selectively, like the eye.

A night photographer needs to be able to assess a scene, and decide (before the shutter is fired) how to meter it, what particular process is to be employed, and what the individual areas of brightness are going to look like on the final print. This may, in turn, cause a reassessment of the meter reading or the process to be employed, to give a print with all the information and the correct tonal values.

The one piece of advice that I was given as a novice photographer, that has affected virtually every frame of film I have

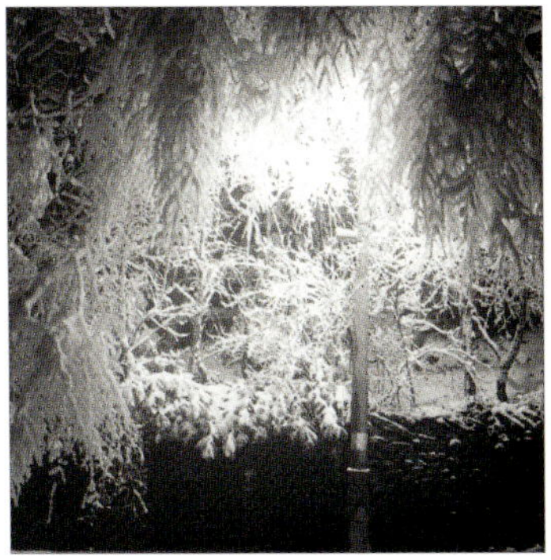

Grade 2 print for the shadows

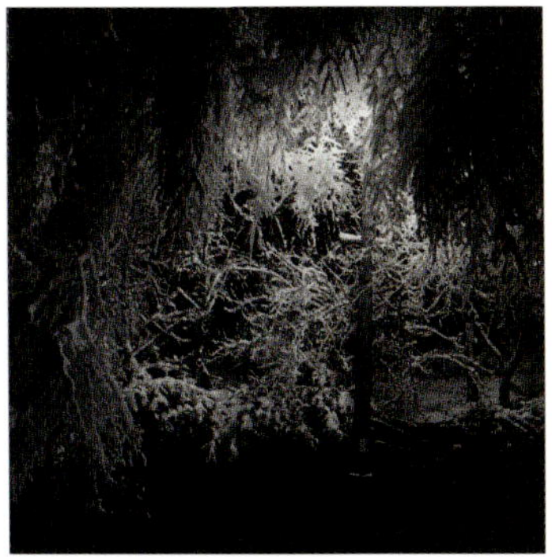

Grade 2 print for the highlights

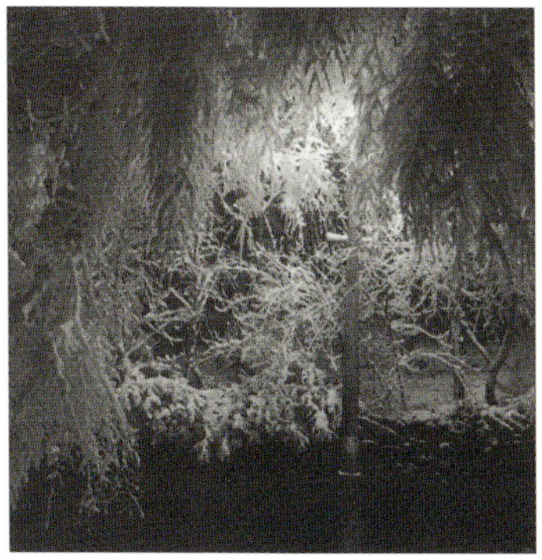

Grade 00 print

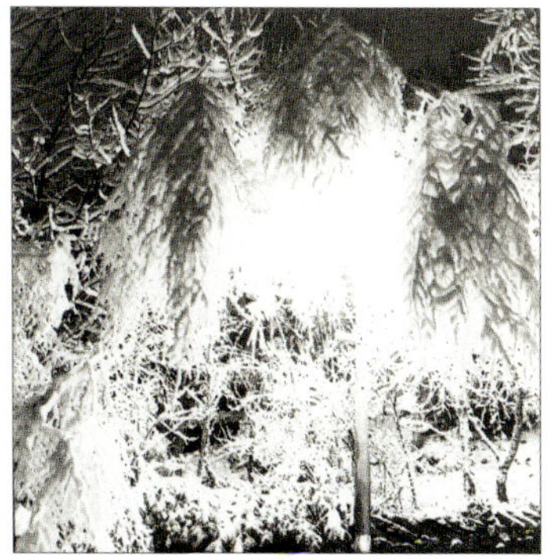

Grade 5 exposure

The print was given the shortest exposure that would print black to reveal the subtle shadow detail.

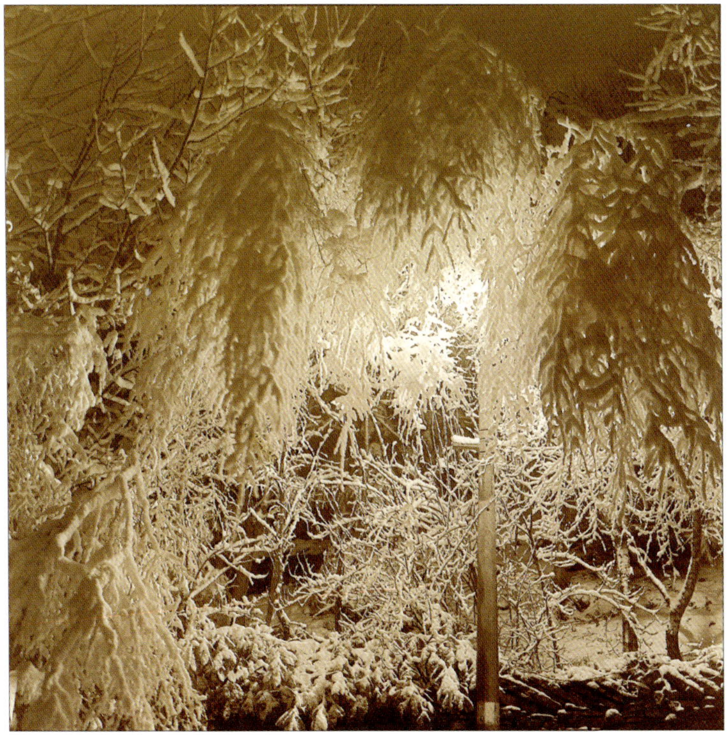

Heavy, snowy branches

The final print combining the grade 5 exposure for the shadows and the grade 00 exposure selectively applied to the highlights.

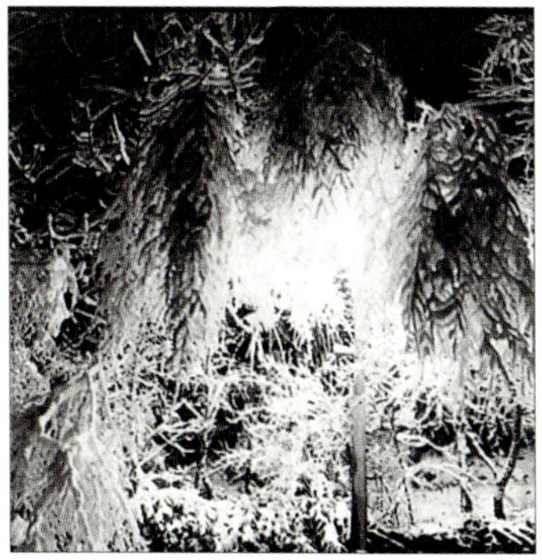

Lith mask exposure

Exposure through the lith mask with a grade 00 filter. When this is added to the grade 5 exposure the print displays a full range of tones.

See page 92 for more information.

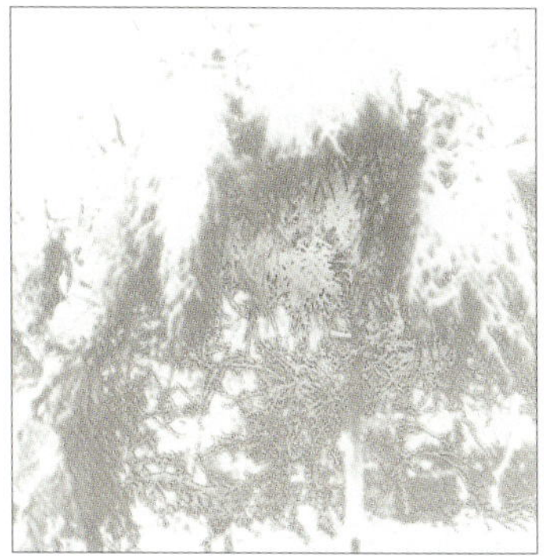

Lith mask

ever exposed, and has been invaluable, is; Always have the finished print in mind before firing the shutter.

If you can develop an ability to 'see' your picture – cropped, printed, burned in, toned, or whatever, whilst looking through the viewfinder, you will reduce the amount of failures per film dramatically, and of course, simultaneously have a higher proportion of successes. With this visualisation technique and an understanding of metering, one exposure is usually all that is necessary for any situation.

I can honestly say, that all of my favourite pictures come from this visualisation method, and none of them have spare negatives. All are from one exposed frame, with no spares and no variations. This is a discipline as well as an aid, and discipline creates repeatability and quality.

This is a very important skill to develop, whatever photographic genre is practised.

The pictures on page 91 show the principle of lith masking a difficult negative.

The first print, exposed at 15 seconds on grade 2, shows the detail that is in the shadows. Notice how the paper is unable to hold the lighter tones.

The second print, exposed at 35 seconds on grade 2, gives the information in the highlights, but at the expense of the shadow and mid tones, which are overprinted.

The third print is on grade 00, which has a long enough tonal scale to encompass the full negative, but lacks sparkle, and tends to make the lower shades blend together.

These prints would indicate that the shadow exposure on grade 2 be given, followed by some method of burning in the highlights, to encompass the complete range on the negative.

The fourth print and fifth prints: for maximum effect I did tests to establish the exposures for the most contrast (image 4 – grade 5), and for the lowest contrast (image 5 – grade 00). Combining these two extremes pulls virtually everything out of the negative

Lith masking

Lith masking involves exposing a negative onto a graphic arts film known as Lith film. Lith film is a high contrast emulsion on a clear base, which gives a positive image, and can be developed under red safelight.

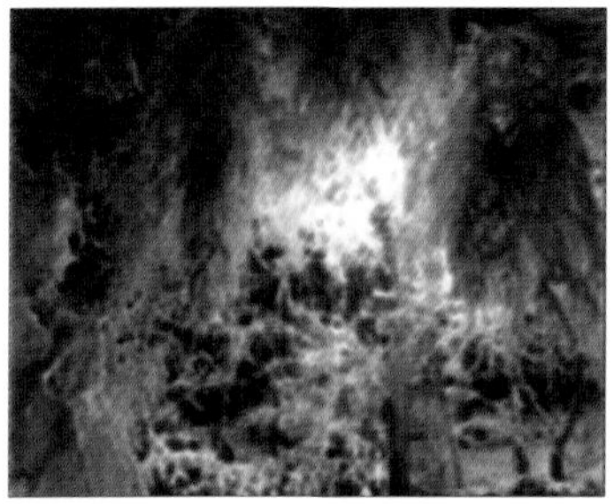

1s 5.6

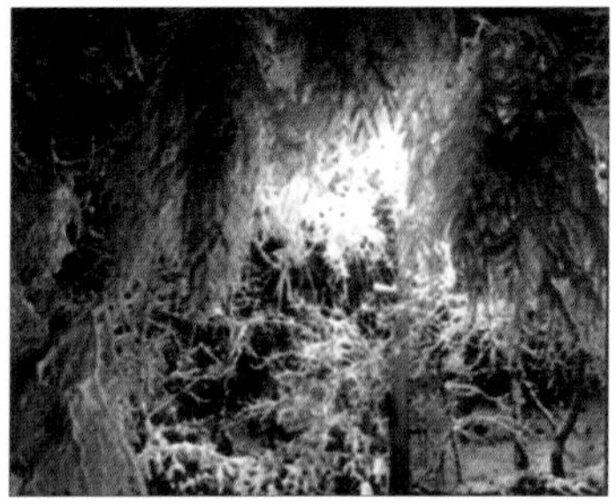

4s f11

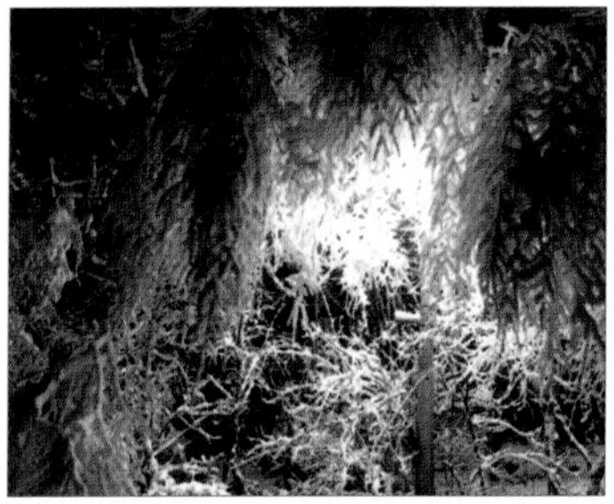

16s f22

Three lith masks made at different aperture settings, with the film placed about 5cm above the baseboard. Stopping the lens down will give a sharper image on the lith mask.

Once processed and dried, it is positioned above the photographic paper during part of the exposure. The image is projected through it, and the print is affected by the tones on the Lith film. Areas of deep black prevent light from reaching the shadow parts of the print, whilst the clear parts of the film allow light through to burn-in the highlights.

The Lith mask must be positioned in register for the effect to be utilised properly, otherwise the burned in areas will not fit the spaces where they are needed.

The image on page 93 shows the bas relief effect that can result from a mis aligned Lith mask – xaggerated here for effect.

Aligning the mask can be done in several ways, the mask can be laid on top of the paper, or positioned a little way above, (but only if this was the original position it was exposed).

A Lith mask exposed 3 - 5cm above the base board will have an out of focus image, this is not detrimental, it will do the job just as well, though any higher than this will cause light to spill across into other areas. If it is neccesary to position the Lith higher up

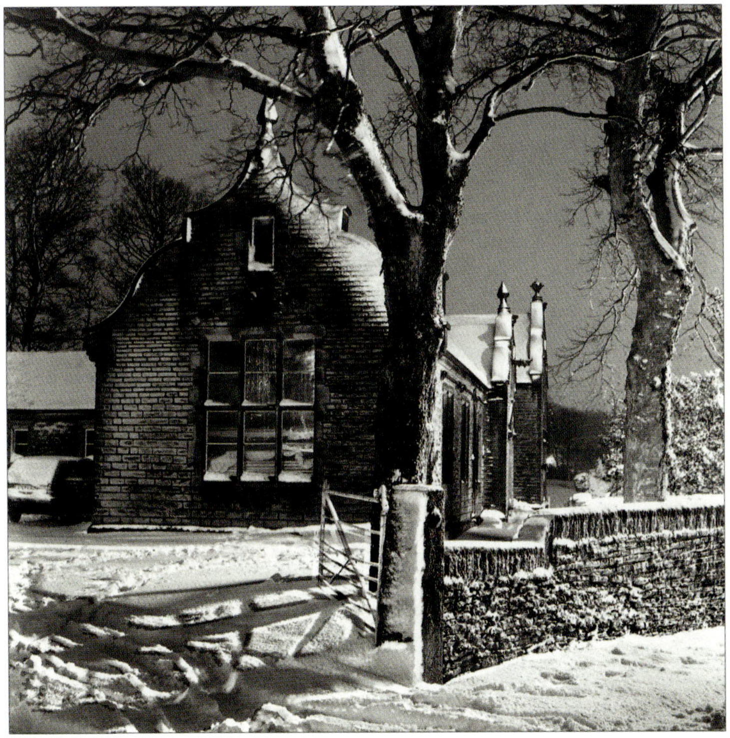

Misaligned lith

When a lith mask is mis-aligned, or the registration system is knocked out of position, a bas-relief effect is the result as can e seen here in the lower left corner.

for any reason (eg to allow access to the easel), then the image can be sharpened by stopping down the lens.

When using an out of focus mask, it must be positioned accurately with register pins or card buffers, because it cannot be aligned by eye.

A Lith mask made on the surface of the paper will have a much sharper image, this can be aligned by eye in many cases, with the red filter swung across under the enlarger lens.

To ensure that the image on the Lith is an exact fit with the printed image, it must, as I said before, be used in the exact position that it was exposed. When using a pin register system this is not a problem, but it is worth bearing in mind that if you are considering using the mask directly on the paper, then the Lith mask will need to be exposed whilst resting on a spare piece of photographic paper to ensure the exact height when in use.

If a masking frame is not used, then the paper will need to be taped to the baseboard, to prevent any movement during the two or more exposures.

There are a couple of other techniques that can be employed, that need very little in the way of pre constructed equipment. The first of these is quick and easy, but a bit hit and miss, the second is fairly quick and is probably easier, so I would suggest that this should be the method to try before attempting to construct a pin register system. In both cases, place a clean sheet of black card/paper under the film, to prevent halation.

First method

Stand two boxes of paper, one on top of another on the baseboard, directly under the lens, lay the Lith film on top and expose (after testing of course).

When processed, washed and dried, clip the Lith to a piece of card such as a window mount, using pegs or bulldog clips.

For burning in, just hold under the lens, and move up, down and around, until the projected image matches that from the enlarger, -have a few tries before exposing the paper, it takes a little practice.

Second method

Support a sheet of 2mm picture glass on four childrens' building blocks, lay the Lith film on the glass and expose (after testing).

The film, when dry can be rested on the glass again and aligned using the red swing filter. (Marks made on the glass from sticky labels or masking tape can help here.)

IMPORTANT

Glass is hard enough to see in daylight and it is all too easy to catch yourself on a raised sheet of it in the dark. Stick masking tape around the outside to cover the sharp edges and draw zig-zags or stripes on the tape with a black marker, so it can be seen easily in low light.

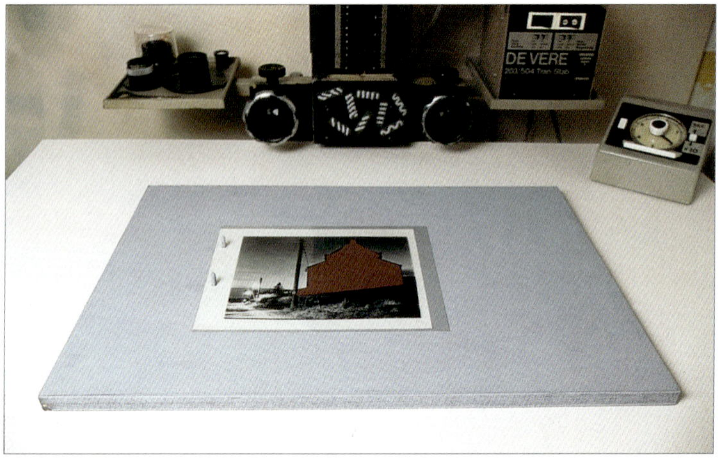

Register pin system for aligning lith mask

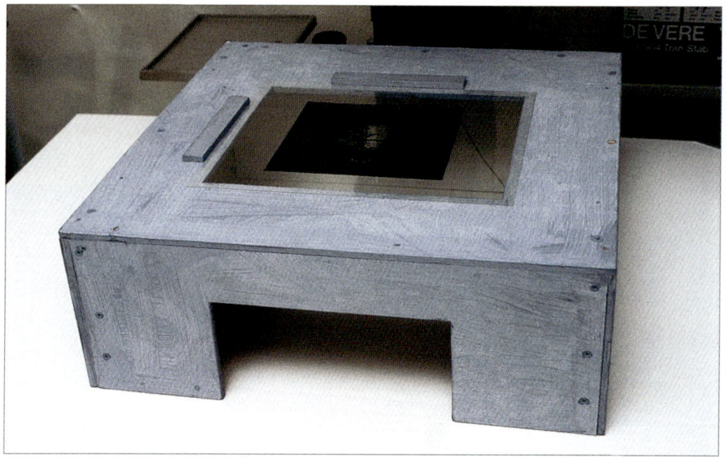

Buffer system for aligning lith mask

With lith masking, whichever method you eventually become familiar with, it will provide a great degree of control that is very difficult, if not impossible, to detect afterwards.

TIP: Use film which is at least 2cm larger all round than the paper you are printing onto. Similarly, using the glass method, requires a much larger sheet of glass.

Buy only the Lith film on the thicker base .0007in. Some Lith film is produced on a much thinner base and tends to sag, which will ruin any registration you may have prepared for, excepting the glass support method.

When producing a lith mask it is not necessary to employ a dedicated lith developer, as this produces an extremely high contrast image. A better method is to use your usual paper developer, but this can also produce excessive contrast if the film is left in the solution for too long.

I use paper developer at its normal strength, and process for one minute if I need a contrasty mask. When I need a more graduated tone, I dilute the working developer with an equal amount of water. The development time is the same.

Using a developer which is too strong, and trying to pull the lith film out early, will only produce streaky results.

Stop and fix as usual, (fix for twice the time it takes to clear the milkiness from the film), wash, and dry with a hair dryer or fan heater.

In some situations it may be necessary to make two or more liths, each one successively darker than its predecessor, or in some cases, the second lith with areas painted out to customise the burning in. This can be done with opaque masking paint, or a black marker pen applied to both sides.

Positioning the lith mask

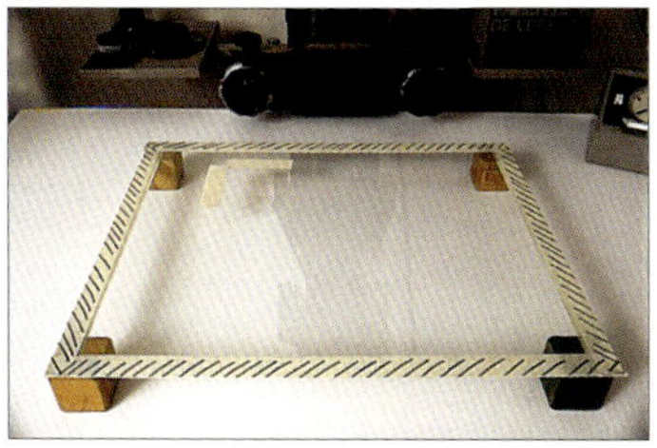

Glass resting on wooden blocks. Note masking tape around the edges clearly marked to avoid accidents in the dark.

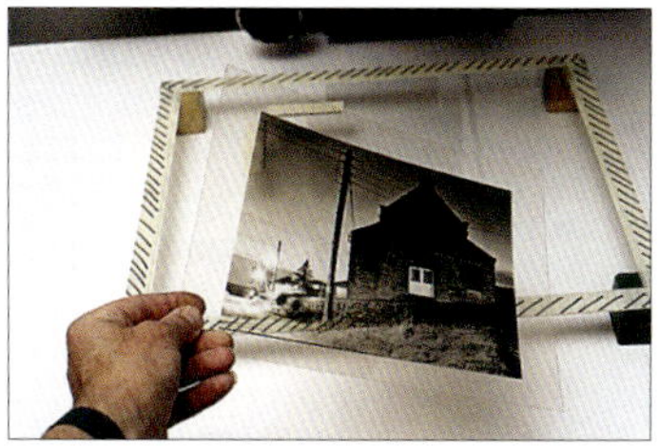

Lith mask being located.

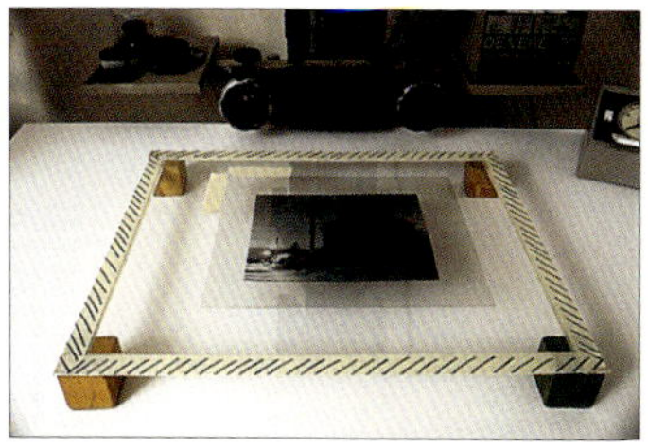

Lith mask positioned up to locating marks at top left.

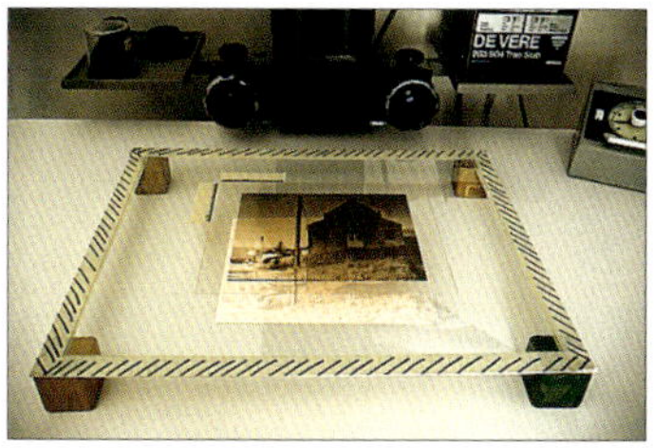

Exposure made through lith mask to burn in highlights.

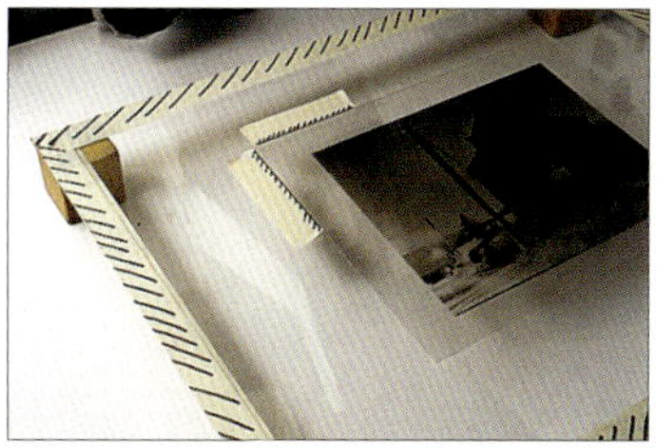

Clearer view of locating tape markers.

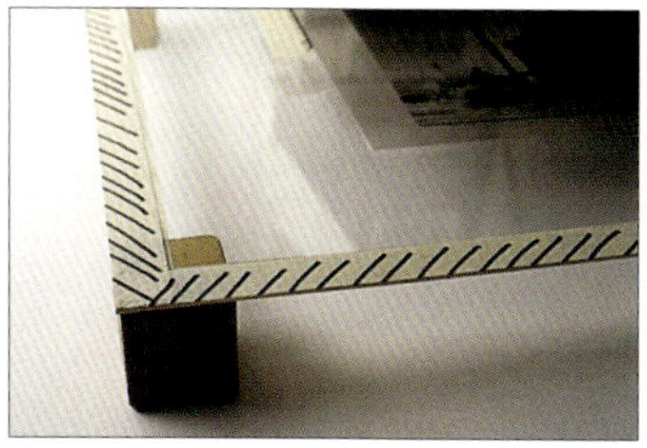

Detail of marked edge of glass.

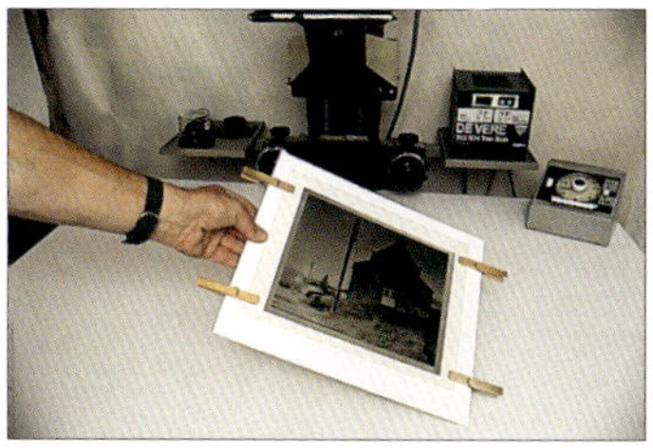

Lith mask secured on card window with pegs.

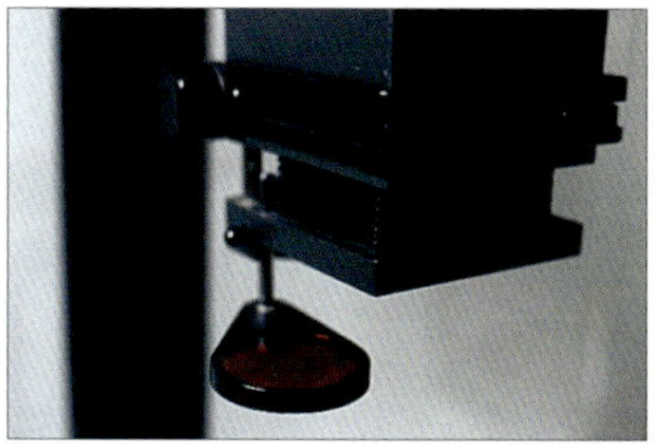

Red swing filter.

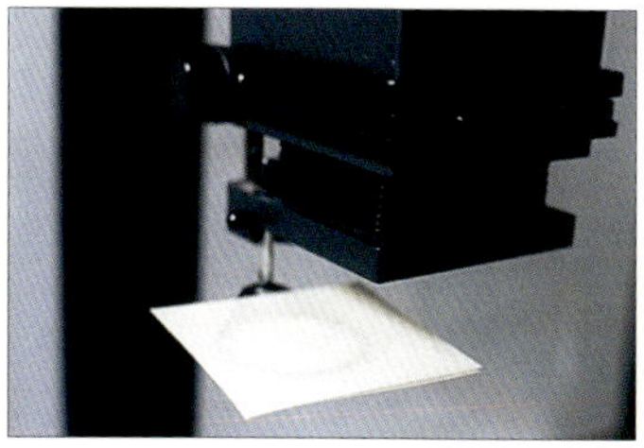

Red filter removed, tracing paper in position for flashing.

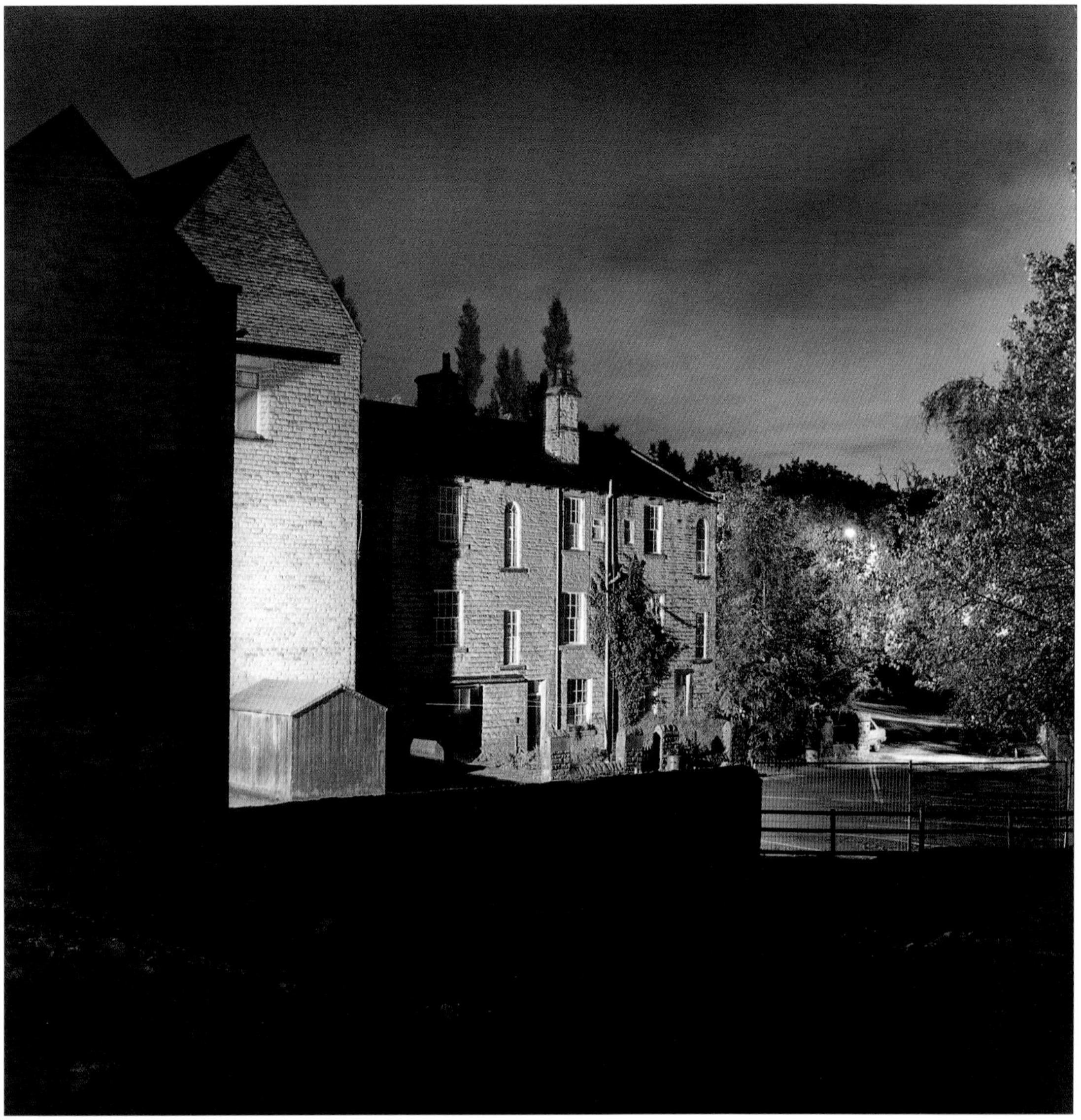

Behind the terrace

Using a lith mask has allowed the print to show all the detail that was on the negative and at the same time keep the local contrast specific to each area.

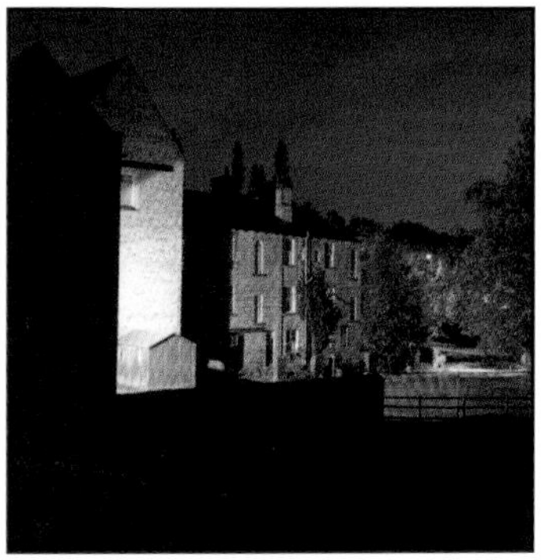

Straight print

This shows how contrasty the image was when printed normally.

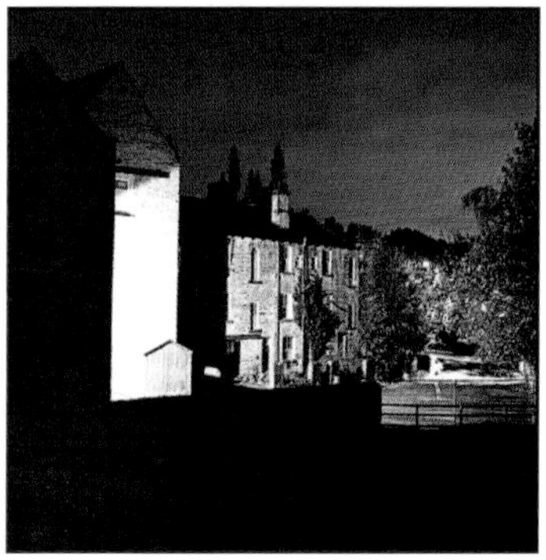

The lith mask

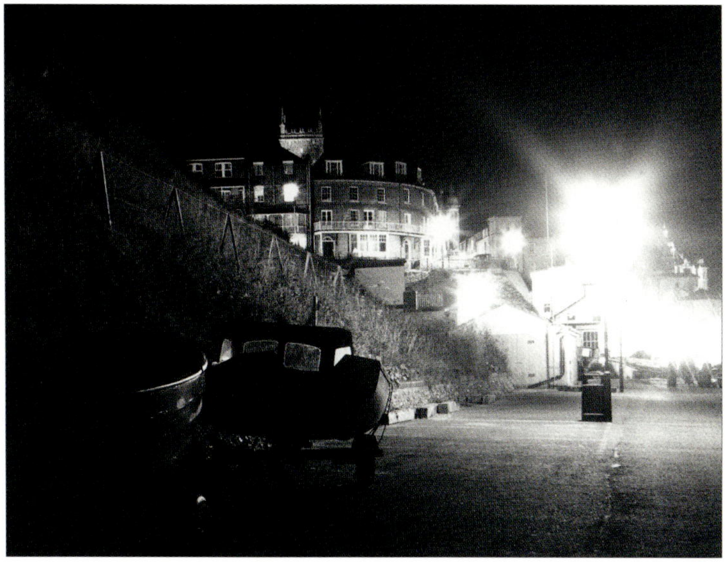

Cromer seafront without lith masking

This was the maximum amount of detail that I could squeeze out of the shadows by giving a short exposure on grade 5. All the highlights have been lost due to the high contrast.

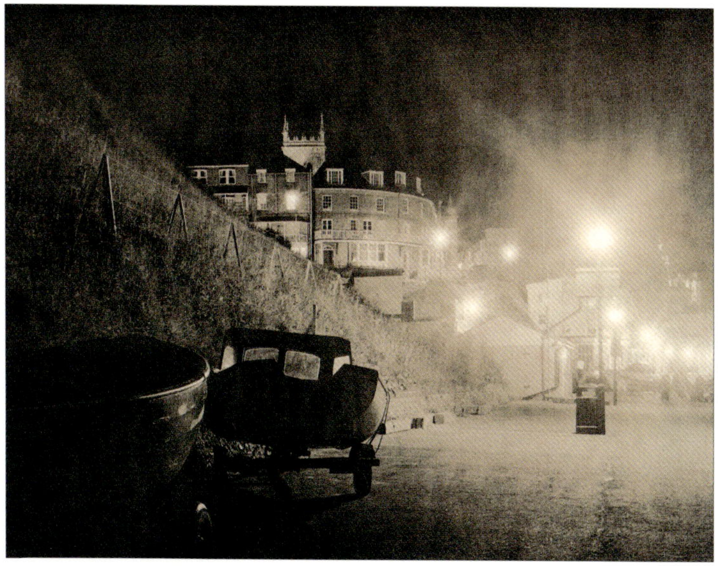

Cromer seafront

Using the lith printing technique I managed to show more detail in the shadows and, at the same time, keep detail in the highlights with the added bonus of a nice colour as well.

Lith printing

Lith printing is currently enjoying an increase in popularity, and for a full explanation of this method of printing the reader is recommended to investigate Tim Rudman's excellent book, 'The Master Photographers Lith Printing Course'.

Lith printing should not be confused with Lith masking, which is a technique that utilises materials from a common origin, but has no similarity in operation. This process has the ability to give a contrasty image in the shadows and simultaneously, a full range of tones in the highlights. The prints are characterised by a colour which can vary from brown, though a mushroomy shade, to pink according to paper type, developer dilution and a host of other influences. Another excellent property of lith prints is that they also respond very well to toners, the most marked improvement is with gold, and to a lesser degree, selenium.

Technique

A specifically made Lith paper, or a warmtone chloro bromide paper, is over exposed to a negative to the order of about four stops, and processed in a very vigorous lith developer which has been highly diluted.

The weakened developer takes much longer to produce a black, but shows a fainter image earlier in the process, representing the full range of the negative.

When development has reached a point for black to be produced, it does so in areas corresponding to the faintest parts of the negative first, ie those that passed the most light.

Pretty soon after the first appearance of black, the process accelerates, and the print is removed swiftly from the developer before the deep blacks have crept too far up the tonal scale. If the print is not 'snatched' in time, the acceleration of blacks takes over the print completely. This reaction is known as infectious development.

If the print is removed at the correct point, the photograph displays a full range of tones in a browny pink shade, with the shadow detail revealed by areas of strong black. (These colours

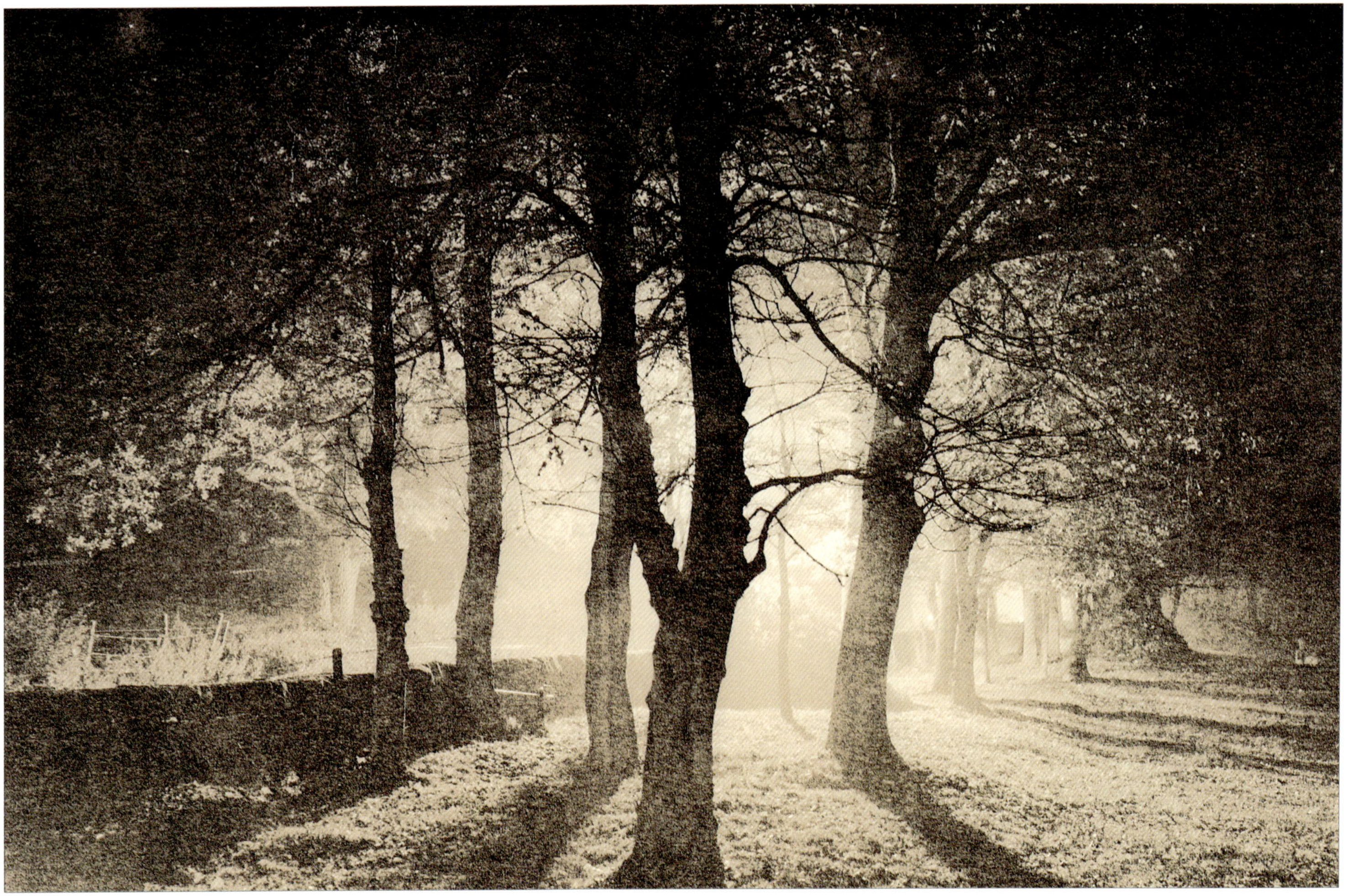

Street light behind trees

Lith printing and night photography were meant for one another. It can show delicate highlight detail in warm tones and simultaneously reveal faint details in the shadows. Ilford HP5

vary with paper type, developer type and dilution, length of exposure, etc.)

As a printing method, this is heaven sent for night photography: to have faint shadow detail brought up with good blacks, whilst showing everything in the brighter tones, with one exposure – no burning in.

Lith printing is not a technique that demands years of printing experience, it can produce very good results from the beginning, The difficulty lies in being able to repeat results, control it, to understand why it goes wrong – and how to remedy it.

Snowgate Head Primitive Methodist church

Lith printing comes in extremely handy for difficult night negatives. Compare this single exposure lith print with the other version in the section on split grade printing. Print from 5 x 4 negative.

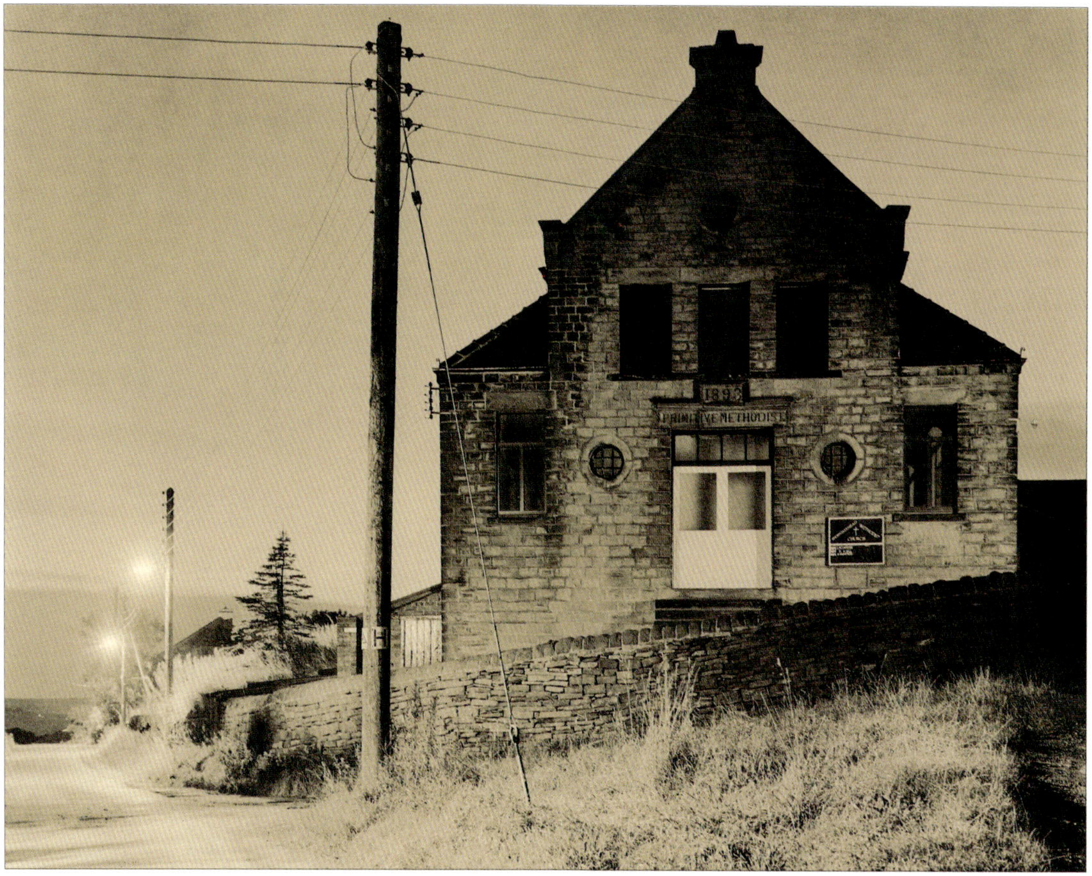

It may seem like a long process to go through to achieve a print, but compared to making masks or split printing with its many tests it is relatively quick.

When printing the negative of Cromer seafront, it was important to me that the faintest detail in the shadows was revealed.

The film used was Ilford Delta 3200 rated at 3200 ISO, and this was the first time I had used it for night photography, so I was unsure about how well it would cope with the contrast of the scene. The lamps are quite dense on the negative, and I tried split-grade printing first, to keep the two extremes of negative detail on the print, but this was proving difficult. The grade 5 wasn't pulling enough out of the shadows and the highlights were tricky to burn in, even with a lith mask.

I decided to switch horses in mid race, and give lith printing a go – the print shown here is the result and was the first print. The lith print has kept the detail in the lamps and brought out more in the shadows than I could get with the grade 5 using the previous method. After spending hours, testing, developing, making lith masks for the split grade method, this had worked perfectly first time.

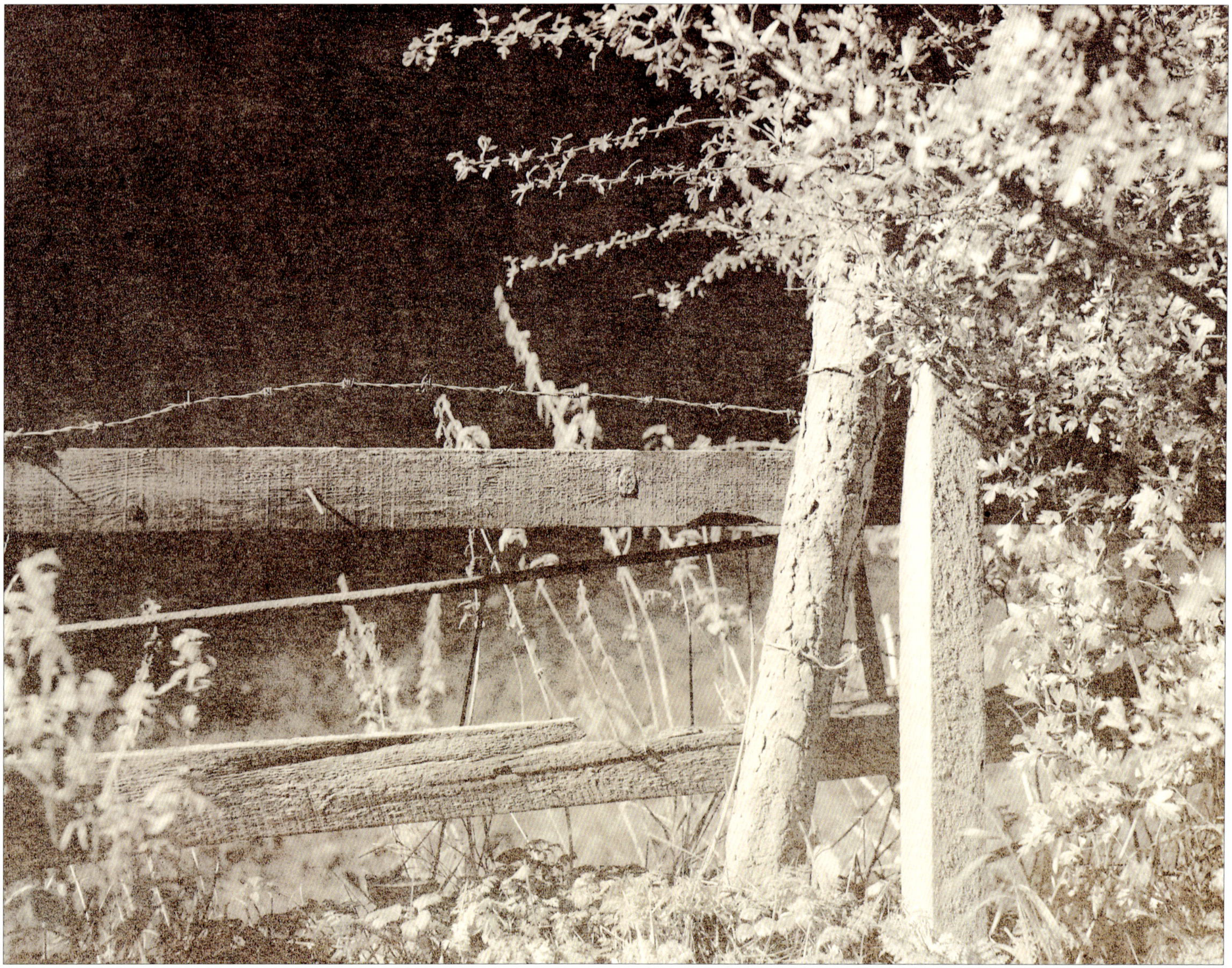

Fenceposts and hawthorne

Lith printing is capable of beautiful delicate tones. Here it has been partially selenium toned. Ilford HP5.

Improving the print

Toning

Toning is used for two reasons in black and white photography;

1. For changing the colour of a print.

2. To increase the permanency of a print. This second purpose is known as archivalling.

Toning for colour change

Changing the colour of a monochrome image can be a way of elevating a good print to that of a fine print, using a subtle colour or colours to convey mood and add drama. Unfortunately it is more often used as a way to 'rescue' a duff shot, making it into a brown duff shot or a blue duff shot and so on.

Monochrome is a wonderful medium and a high quality black and white print can be breathtaking, so don't assume that every shot is going to be improved by changing its overall colour. Toning needs to be applied with care, restraint, subtlety and respect if it is to work to your advantage,

Toning for permanency

Photographs are constantly under attack from chemicals in packaging and storage, as well as pollutants in the air. If an image is to be processed archivally, that is, treated in such a way as to maximise its 'life', and prevent attack as much as possible, then toners are often used as part of the processing sequence, though they are used in a much more diluted form. This provides protection, with little, or no colour change.

Sepia is the only one that must be used at its normal dilution, giving the corresponding brown tone.

Toners protect the vulnerable silver in the print by replacing it, or coating it with a protective layer, such as gold.

The toners, sepia, gold and selenium can be used either separately, or in combination to increase the prints resistance to image attacking pollutants.

Regarding archival processing, I must say that the current fashion to treat everything as worthy of archivality is unnecessary, time consuming, wasteful (water), and lastly, vain.

Photography is an extremely fascinating and inspiring practice which should be enjoyed as much as possible, and this enjoyment can easily wane if the process becomes a rigid scientific exercise bordering on drudgery.

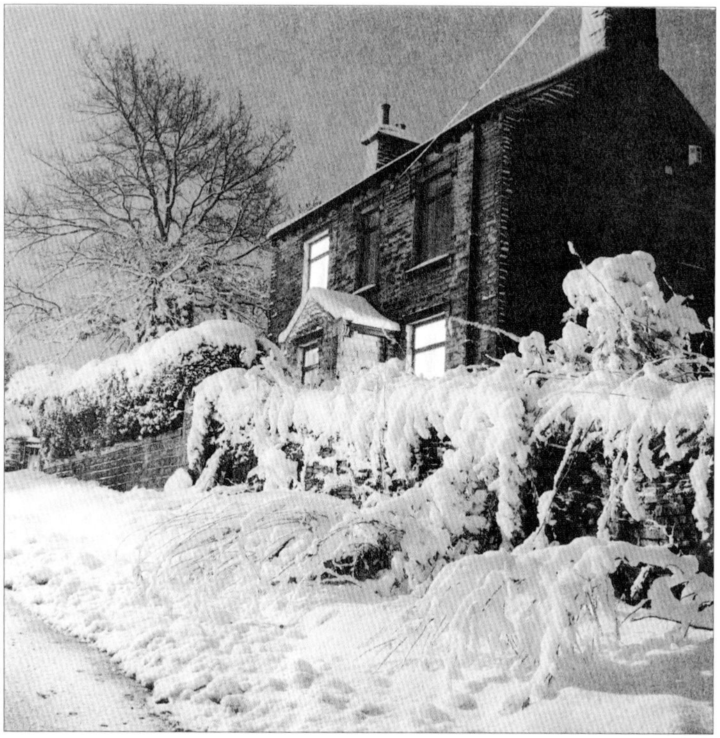

Snowy house

A lith print toned in gold tower produces a very nice, delicate shade of blue which can suit a night snow scene very well.
Ilford HP5.

I don't want to give the impression that I am against archival processing – far from it. I archivally process everything that I produce for sale, but for all the many working prints that are produced, I do not.

I recently had a clear out of photographs that I had lost interest in, either because my style had changed and I was no longer interested in a particular way of working, or because my printing had improved so much that I couldn't bear to look at my old prints any more.

Altogether, I threw out over 300 ten by eight prints – how much time and water could I have wasted archivally processing that lot?

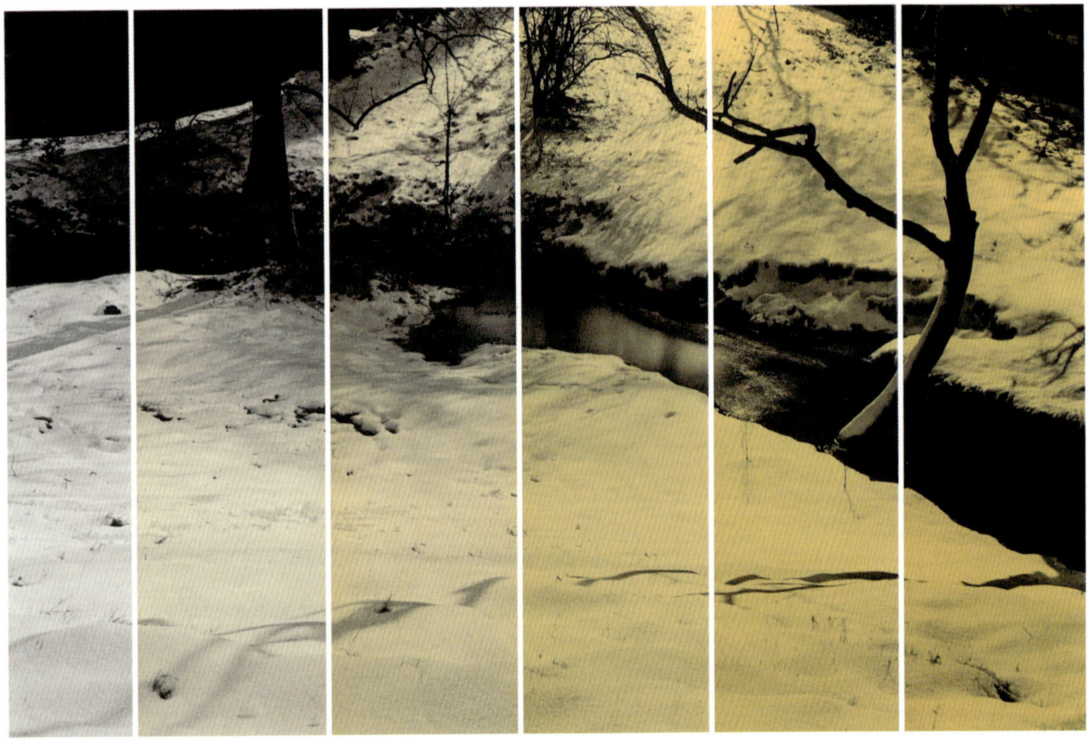

0 seconds *30 seconds* *1 minute* *2 minutes* *4 minutes* *8 minutes*

Tea staining test

A print was cut into six sections and given differing degrees of stain apart from the first section which was left untouched for comparison.

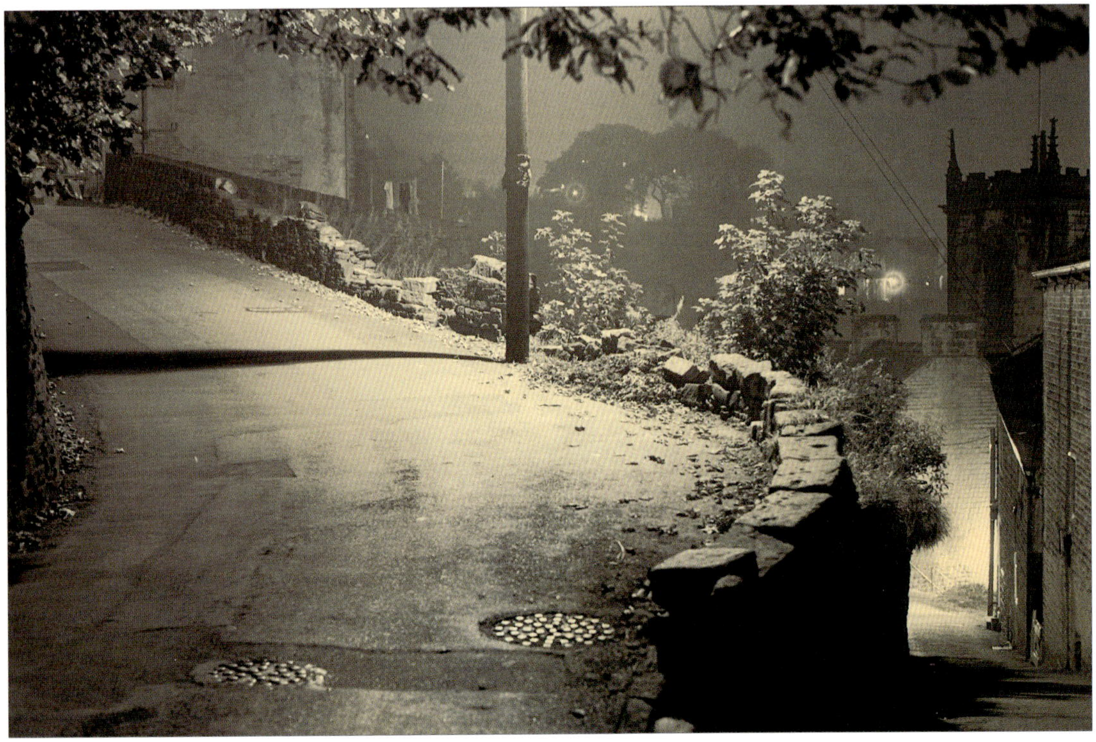

Back lane and church

Tea stain, because it affects the paper and not the image, can be used to colour the highlights, in this case simulating the colour of the streetlights. Ilford FP4 dilute/static process in ID11.

Staining with tea

Not all of the colour changing techniques described here are what is termed 'archival'. The following method of changing the colour of a print is not a toning process because it does not affect the silver salts that make up the image, it merely stains the paper base. But it can produce results which vary from an antique paper look when used faintly, through to a deep amber which can mimic the colour of common orange streetlighting. Used in combination with one or more toners it can produce very nice results.

Even though the permanence of tea staining is unknown, I still use it for images intended for publication or personal work that I display at home. Because I have no idea of how it will behave long into the future, I am reluctant to sell work treated this way.

Technique

This has got to be the easiest technique in this book.

A solution of tea is made up with two tea bags in a litre of hot water, and the solution is stirred occasionally to get the maximum from the tea. The solution is then allowed to cool to about 40 or 50 degrees Celsius, the bags are removed, and the tea poured into a tray.

The print is immersed in the tea and gently agitated until the correct tone has been reached, then washed thoroughly.

If the tea stain is to be used in conjunction with blue toning then the print will need to have a longer wash time than normal. In fact, I usually leave my tea stained prints to soak in a large volume of water overnight, after giving them a long wash. If the tea stained print is not washed well enough, the tannin reacts with the toner and leaves a kind of blue/grey stain in the whites of the print.

Sepia toner

Sepia is the most commonly used toner, and is capable of producing colours from a sandy shade, right through ginger, brown, dark brown (which I prefer to describe as Bournville), and a cold brown which verges on violet.

The colour variations are the result of several factors, such as toner type, paper type, developer time/concentration, paper contrast, fixing, wash time, bleach time/concentration, toner time/concentration etc. So don't get frustrated if the shade of brown is different each time a print is toned. The biggest influence

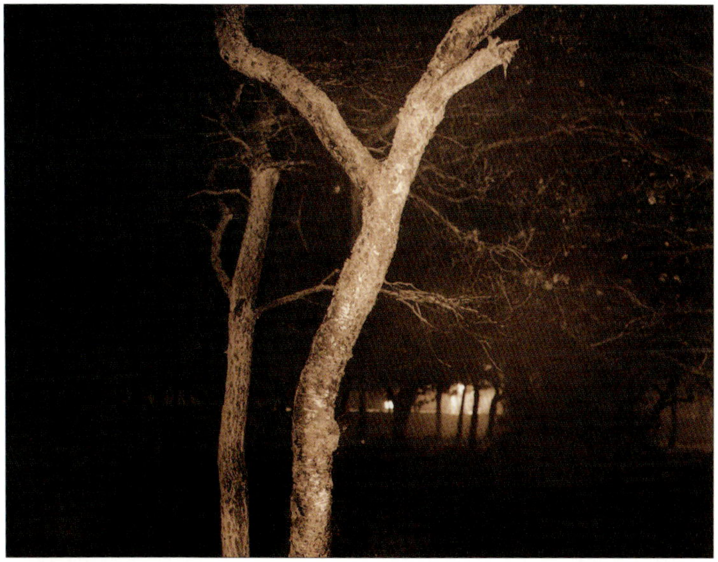

Red toned print

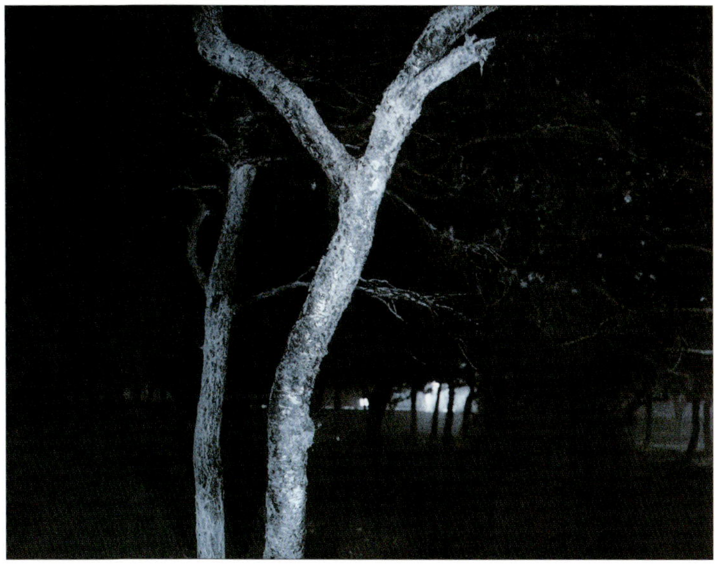

Blue toned print

Lith prints respond well to toners and, in the case of gold toner, better than conventional prints.

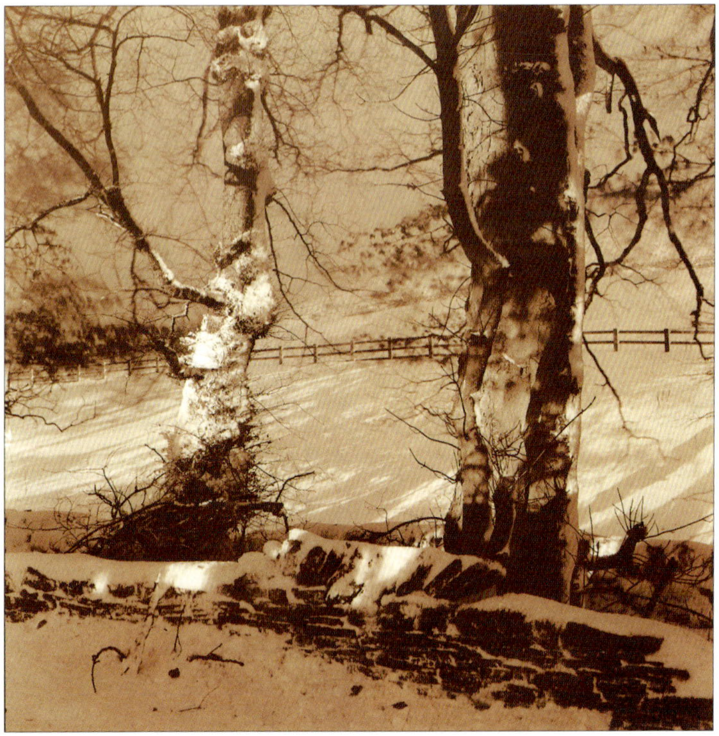

Red toned print

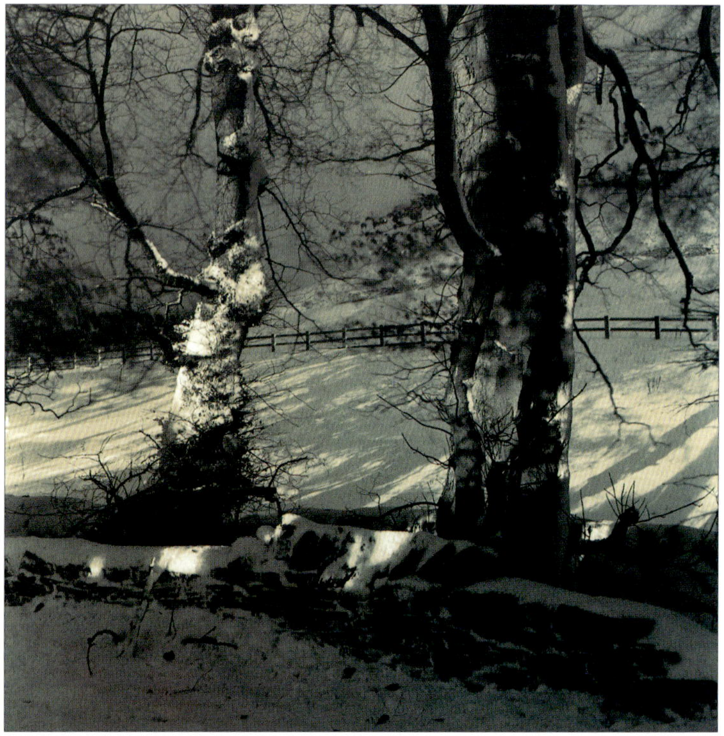

Sepia/blue split toned print

Although the red toner does a very good job of lifting the lower tones making the print brighter, the blue and sepia split tone more accurately represents the scene as I saw it.

on the finished effect is the strength/duration of the bleach, this determines the proportion of brown to black in the print.

Two types of sepia toner are available, the 'bad egg' smelly stuff, which is known as sulphide toner, and the type referred to as either odourless or thiocarbamide, (sometimes called thiourea).

Both types produce good sepia tones, but odourless is probably the most popular, as many find the smell of sulphide toner objectionable.

Method

The print is soaked for a few minutes in water, then immersed in the bleach solution, and gently agitated. The image will appear to begin bleaching in the highlights first, when in fact it is being removed from all areas equally. The highlights, being made up of very little tone, disappear first, but the shadows having much more tone take much longer to be removed. This is not a problem, as it is often not desirable to bleach completely.

The instructions provided with commercially produced sepia toners usually instruct the user to bleach to completion, but this removes all traces of black from the image and imparts a flat, uninteresting coloured look to the finished print.

Best results are created by removing the paper from the bleach much earlier, the amount of bleaching being directly related to the proportion of brown in the finished photograph.

The print, having been taken from the bleach, is washed well until the yellow stain is removed completely. Failure to wash properly will gradually contaminate the toner solution and produce inconsistent results.

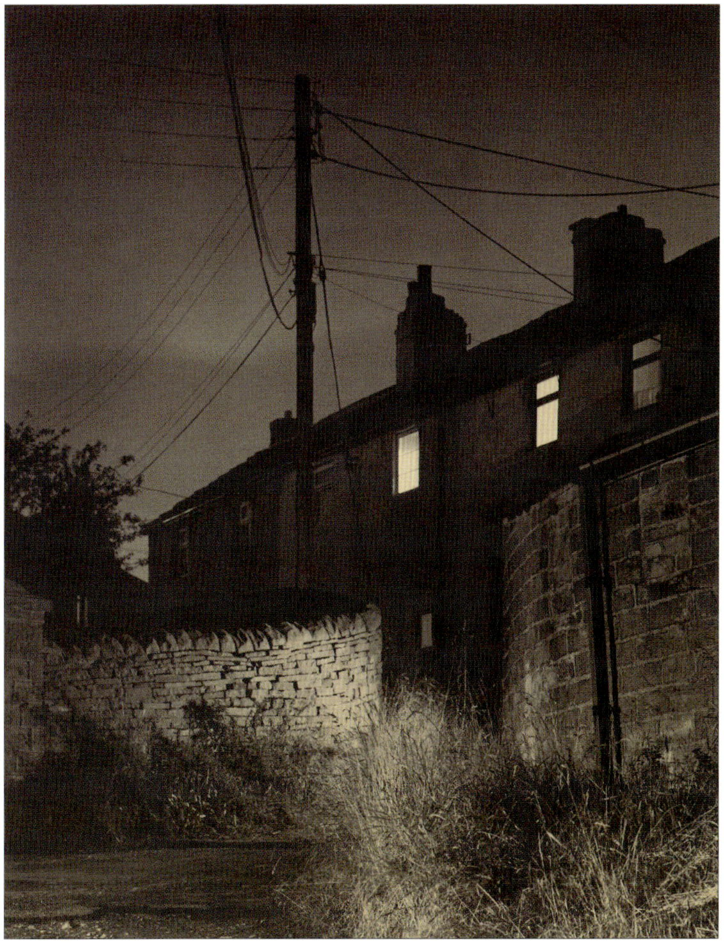

Image title

A heavier print and a longer stain bath combine to give a different mood to an image. Compare it with the full frame version in the section on 5x4 cameras.

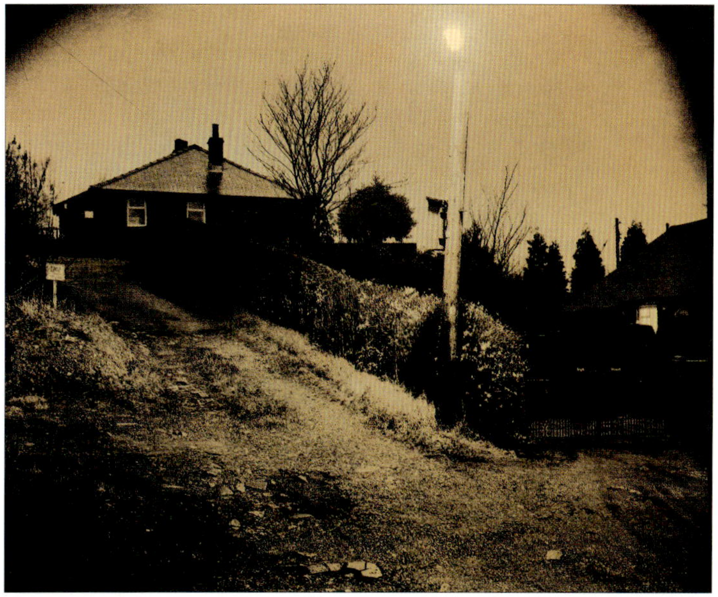

Image title

A combination of selenium and heavy tea stain. For lighter subjects a shorter tea bath would produce a more subtle effect.

The print is then placed into the toning solution, and again agitated gently. The colour will appear quite quickly, unless the solution is exhausted or over diluted.

The print is kept in the solution until the full tone is produced – the print will not be altered by being left in the toner too long, the image will only return to something like its original density, never any further.

Toner which is almost exhausted will not return the highlights. As always, with special work, try the toner out on an unimportant print first. The fully toned print is then well washed and dried. This will be in the region of twenty minutes for working prints and one hour for archival prints.

Blue toner

Blue is a simple and straightforward toner to use, and many commercial brands are commonly available. Unlike sepia, this toner is a one bath solution and requires no preliminary bleaching.

The range of colour with this toner can vary from a subtle gunmetal grey/blue, through to a piercing cyan, depending on how long the print remains in the solution.

Method

The print is soaked for a few minutes, then immersed in the toner and agitated gently until the required depth of colour is achieved, at which point the print is removed and washed for five or ten minutes, then immersed in a solution of common salt to remove

Sepia toner

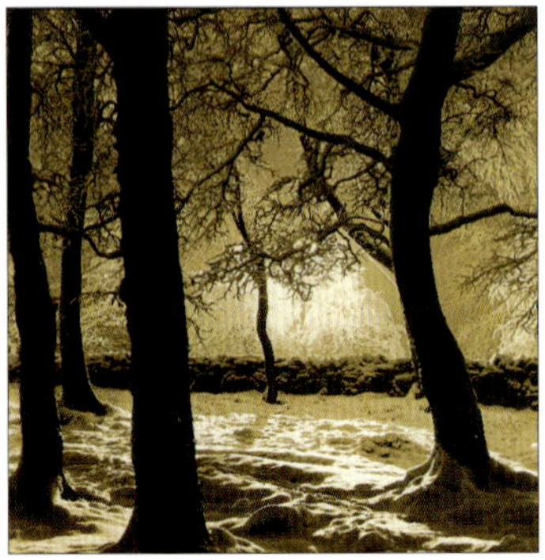

Blue toner

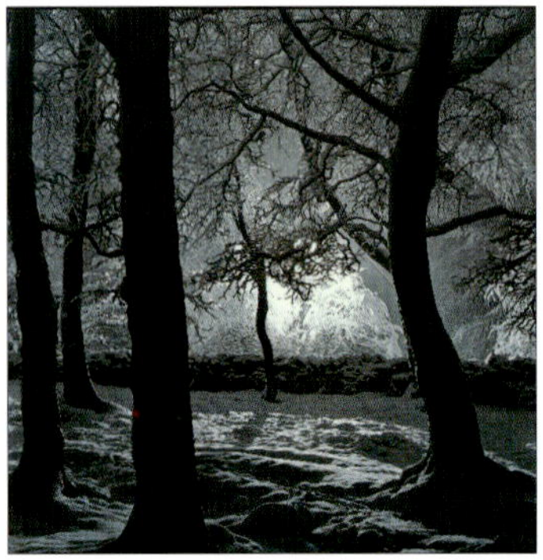

Selenium toner

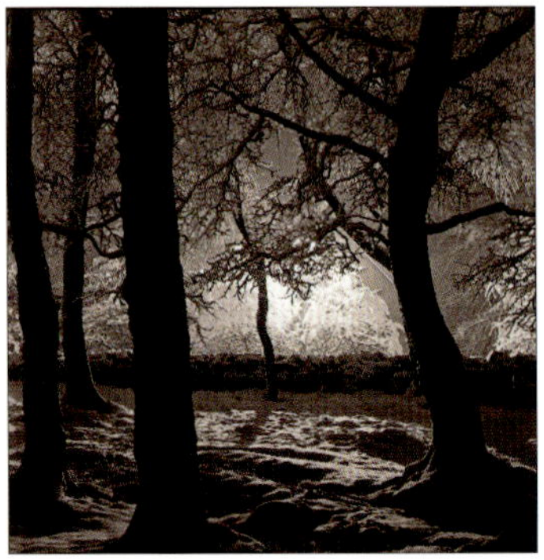

Red toner

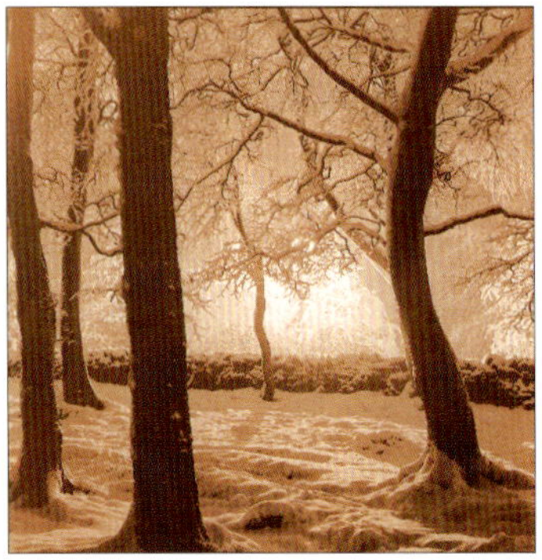

Colour choice is a very personal decision. Toners can be used to invoke mood or simply to help separate the tones in the image.

the yellow staining and clean up the print.

(The salt solution can be made up with a tablespoon of salt in one litre of water, and will need to be replaced after treating the equivalent area of four 10 x 8 prints.) The print is then washed for a further five to ten minutes, and dried.

In practice this toner can sometimes be a little fast acting, and the print may be over toned the first time you use it. Try the toner on a spare print before risking an important photograph. If the colour is being produced too fast, then double the amount of water in the solution, this will give more manageable toning times.

It is worth remembering that toning is still taking place until the chemicals are washed from the paper, so the depth of blue needs to be anticipated somewhat and the print removed from the solution before the required colour is arrived at.

The colour also alters slightly in the salt bath as the yellow stain fades. This too needs to be anticipated. Put spare, or test prints through first, to get familiar with this aspect of blue toning before risking a special picture.

I believe the extreme cyan colour that is produced by excessive toning is too strong for the kind of night prints that I want to produce, and I prefer to remove the print from the solution just after the first sign of blue. By the time the print has been salted and washed, the colour is just right

Wrongly blue toned prints can be 'un-toned' by immersion in normal paper developer. This will return the image to its original colour. After redevelopment, return the print to the stop bath and wash, before attempting to re-tone.

When the blue toner solution starts to precipitate (spontaneously produce floating bits in the solution), it should be discarded.

TONING TIPS

- Make sure that all prints intended for toning are fully washed.
- Make sure that all equipment, tongs, trays, measuring jugs etc, are clean.
- Test the strength of the solution with a scrap print before risking an important picture.
- Soak dry prints for a few minutes before placing into the toner.
- Agitate gently throughout the toning.
- Try not to touch the surface of the print with the tongs when toning.
- Follow the correct sequence when using more than one toner, and wash thoroughly in between
- Keep notes of when things go right and when they go wrong.

See the formulae section for mixing toners from raw chemicals.

Red

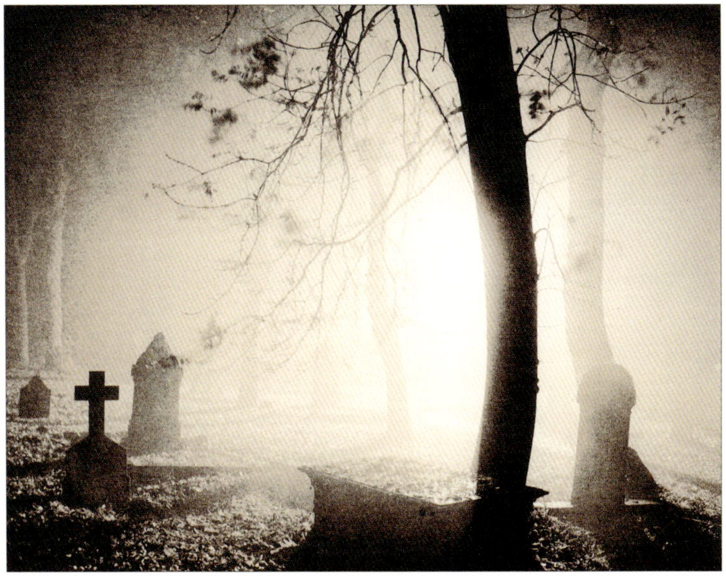

Sepia/blue split

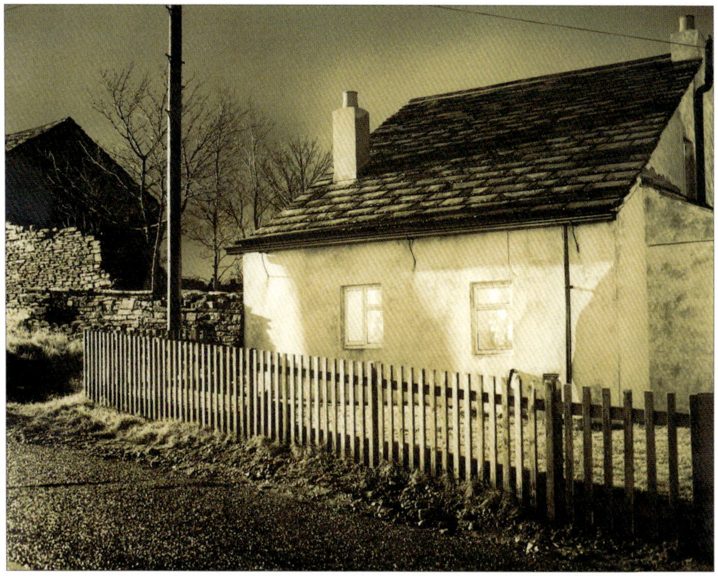

Your choice of toner can determine more than just colour. Very often a toner will change the relationship of the shadows and midtones, either lightening or intensifying them.

Selenium toner

This is a direct, one solution toner which gives a rich plummy brown to warmtone, chlorobromide papers. Selenium toner affects the deepest tones of a print first, and is sometimes used to intensify the shadows of an image. If allowed to go to completion it can create a violet-brown colour throughout, although this is dependent on paper type.

Best results are produced by taking the tone up through the deepest shadows to the dark mid tones, and removing from the solution before the middle tones are affected.

The print may be taken further by the use of other toners, a blue toner will affect the lighter tones of the print, giving a plummy-to-blue split tone.

Sepia bleach will remove the blacks, leaving a redder print, and a red/copper toner will also lighten and give a redder print.

A part selenium toned print can be combined with a slight tea stain to produce a very pleasing effect. This is a very nice combination for night photographs. It does not matter in which sequence the tea or selenium are applied.

Method

Any prints that require toning must have had a sufficiently long and even wash to ensure that all possible traces of fix have been removed, insufficient washing will result in an uneven response to the toner.

Selenium can be used at different dilutions, from 1-3 up to 1-40 depending on the result required.

A dilution of 1-9 is generally used for most toning applications, though a stronger solution of 1-6 may give a more marked effect and shorter working times.

The greater dilutions are used for archivalling where a colour change is not desirable.

Soak the print for a few minutes before placing into the toning solution to ensure that the solution is taken up quickly and evenly by the paper. Agitate gently until the desired colour change has taken place, but bear in mind that the toner will continue to affect the print whilst in the wash to a small degree – enough to be noticeable. Removing the print as it approaches the desired colour should be enough to compensate for this.

The print is then washed for ten minutes or so, and immersed in a solution of hypo clearing agent for the time indicated for that brand. It is then washed again for ten to twenty minutes for working prints and thirty to sixty minutes for archival prints, then dried.

Red toner

Red toner, Copper toner as it is sometimes called, does not really produce a red print. The colour produced by this toner is more like a brick red.

This is a single bath toner like blue, and can also be 'un-toned' afterwards by immersion in developer, as blue can, although it is unlikely that this would be necessary as it can not really be over toned. The red colour is made stronger when the print is given an extended time in the solution. Be aware though, that longer toning will also reduce density. (red toner contains Potassium ferricyanide which is the main constituent in sepia bleach), so prints that are intended for a full red tone may need to be slightly overprinted.

Pulling the print out before it reaches red will give a brown-red, which can, on occasions, look very similar to sepia.

Method

The print is soaked for a few minutes, then immersed in the toner and agitated gently until the required depth of colour is arrived at – this can be in the region of ten minutes, at which point the print is removed and washed for five or ten minutes, and dried

Gold toner

Gold toner does not, as its name suggests, produce a golden yellow tone. In fact, it produces quite the opposite – blue. If gold is used on a print which has previously been sepia toned, then an orange-yellow colour is the result. This is as gold as it gets.

The toner is also capable of a range of other colours, depending on paper type, development, post toning bleaches, and if the print has been sepia toned beforehand.

It is a one solution toner, and is used undiluted. The reason why it is not produced as a stronger solution for dilution is cost. The gold gold chloride in the solution is very expensive. A good reason to ensure that only well washed prints are used.

Split toning

Split toning is the name given to the technique whereby prints are treated in two or more toners, producing interesting combinations of colour. This technique can produce very interesting and dramatic results. For instance, when sepia and blue are used in sucession, and each is allowed to overtone, the result is a vivid green.

When these two toners are used with restraint, an interesting blue shadow/sepia highlight colour is achieved.

For best results with split toning, it is important to use the toners in the correct sequence, and to ensure (as with all toning processes) that prints, trays, tongs, and measuring jugs are all well washed, before, and during the toning sequence.

Failure to observe this rule will result in streaky or patchy results, and in some cases contamination will prevent the toner from working at all.

The following diagram gives the correct sequence for combining toners and the colours that can be expected.

Examples of night photography and an explanation of how they were made

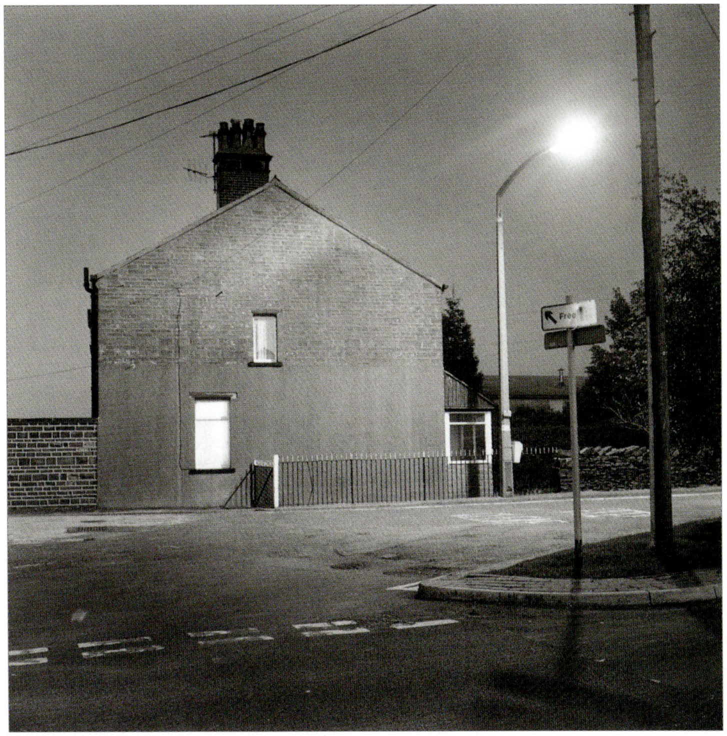

House end and white tipped railings

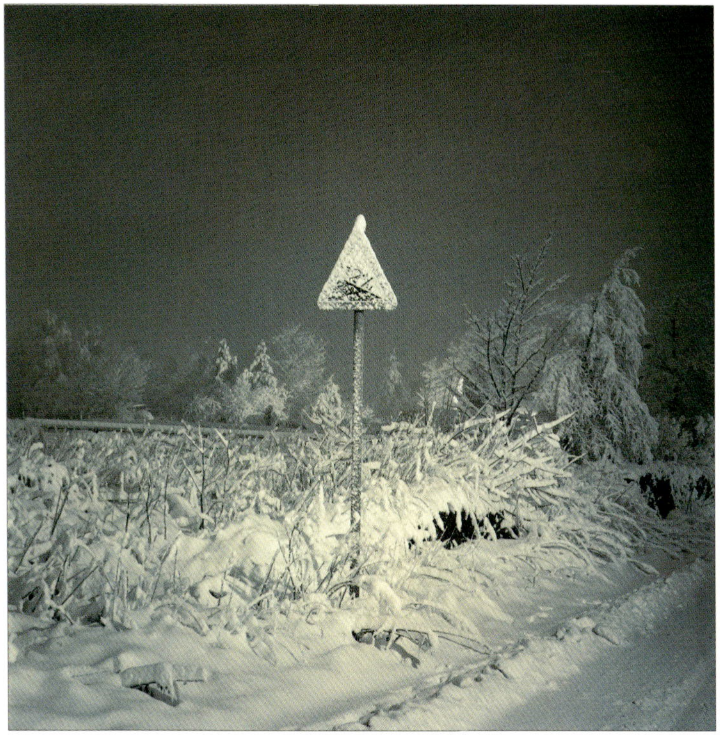

12% incline

House end and white tipped railings

This was taken using a simple folding 6x6 roll film camera,

The negative was exposed for 36 seconds at f8/11 and is more or less printed straight.

There is extra grade 00 exposure in the region of the lamp, but otherwise this shot illustrates that night scenes are not always excessively contrasty, and in some cases can have a complete range of tones that print with ease.

The bright area of the lamp could have been reduced by employing a contrast compensating development, such as pyro, but this was the only night shot on the film and pyro can sometimes be too flat for ordinary subjects, so I decided to process normally in Ilford ID11 and print in the highlight afterwards.

12% incline

A night shot in the snow from a very successful evening's shooting. This kind of situation can cause problems when metering with the camera, as the snow 'fools' the light meter into thinking that the scene is brighter than it actually is.

I used the incident method of metering here to get the most accurate reading, and for all the reflection of light from the snow. I was surprised that the light meter indicated only one stop correction from the normal exposure for this type of lighting.

The usual setting would have been 36 seconds at f8/11, but the extra light allowed me a bit more depth of field, and I decided on the same exposure (time) with an aperture of f11/16.

Printing was easily achieved with one grade of paper (grade 2) and looked acceptable with one exposure. I chose to add an extra

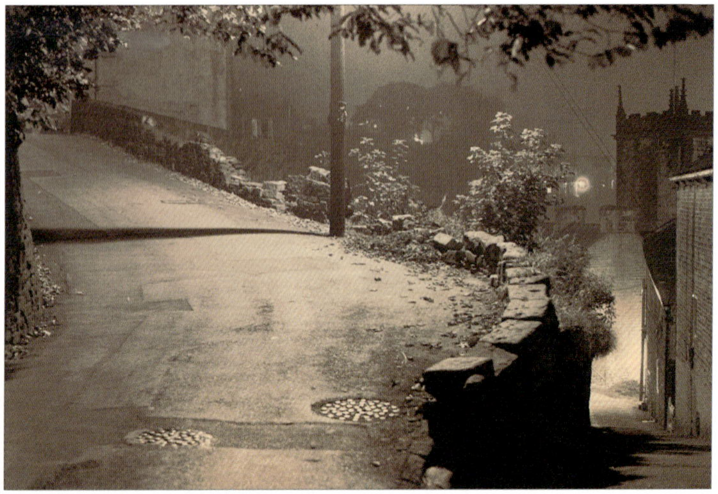

Back lane and church

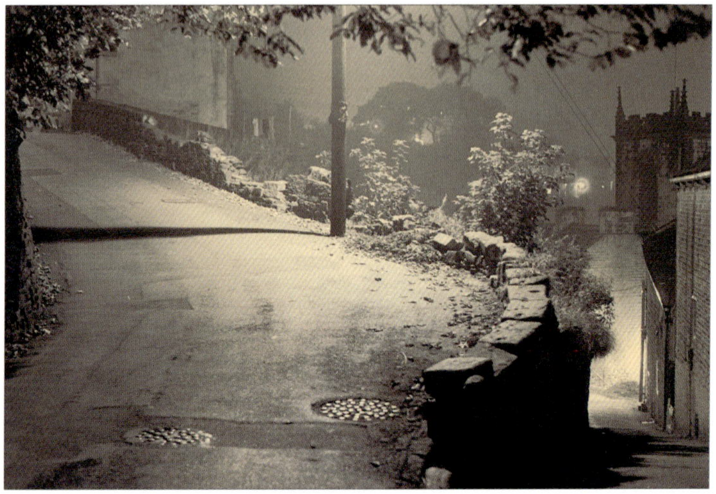

Two versions of 'Back lane and church': one tea stained, the other selenium toned and tea stained.

half a stop of burning in, around the sky behind the sign, to draw the eye in a little – too much would have created a halo effect, and a full stop extra for the foreground/right which was nearer to the light. This also helped to draw the eye in to the sign.

Finally, the print was toned in sepia but with a short bleaching time. This had the effect of warming up the highlights a little, followed by a blue toner to properly convey the feel of a cold scene.

I find that a blue toner used alone can look rather harsh, and a little sepia in the highlights can offset this. But if you wish to recreate this, beware of leaving the print in the bleach too long or having your solution mixed too strong, as this will give a much stronger sepia, which produces a green in combination with a blue toner.

Back lane and church

This was my first successful night photograph, and was produced with very basic equipment. I had no light meter, and no idea what sort of exposure to give, but I remember thinking that it would be hard to overexpose, so I made up the exposure time and hoped for the best. (A real shot in the dark.)

I must have been wearing my lucky underpants that day, because all of the six pictures that I took were exposed correctly. The film was Ilford FP4, and the exposure was not recorded, although I do remember that the film was given dilute/static development in Ilford ID11.

The print was a single exposure on grade 2 with no dodging or burning. The photograph was then toned in selenium and stained with tea.

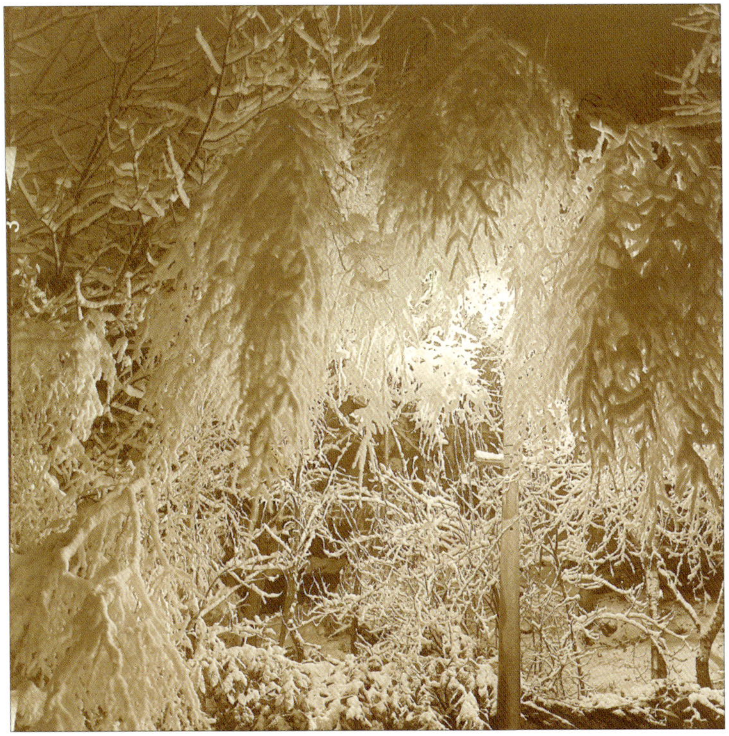

Heavy, snowy branches

Heavy, snowy branches

This was a very difficult photograph to produce, the scene presented an extreme contrast made up of a lot of small areas. The first difficulty was what exposure to give. I wanted to ensure detail from the dark sky through to the snow near the lamp, and couldn't get near enough to meter anything properly. I had to use a combination of technical know-how and guess work.

I took an incident reading from between the camera and the scene, but with the meter pointing towards the light. I stood about ten feet away from the lamp, figuring that the light falling towards me was going to be the same as that falling to the left and right, and would produce a negative that was correct for anything that was that distance from the lamp.

The snowy branches close to the lamp were obviously going to receive an excess of exposure, but I believed that the tones could be rescued by a combination of flashing and Lith masking. (This was before I had discovered pyro.) I allowed this amount of overexposure in the highlights because I wanted to bring out what detail I could in the dark wall and also at the top left, where the branches can be seen against the sky.

For a description of the methods used to print this image, see the section on lith masking.

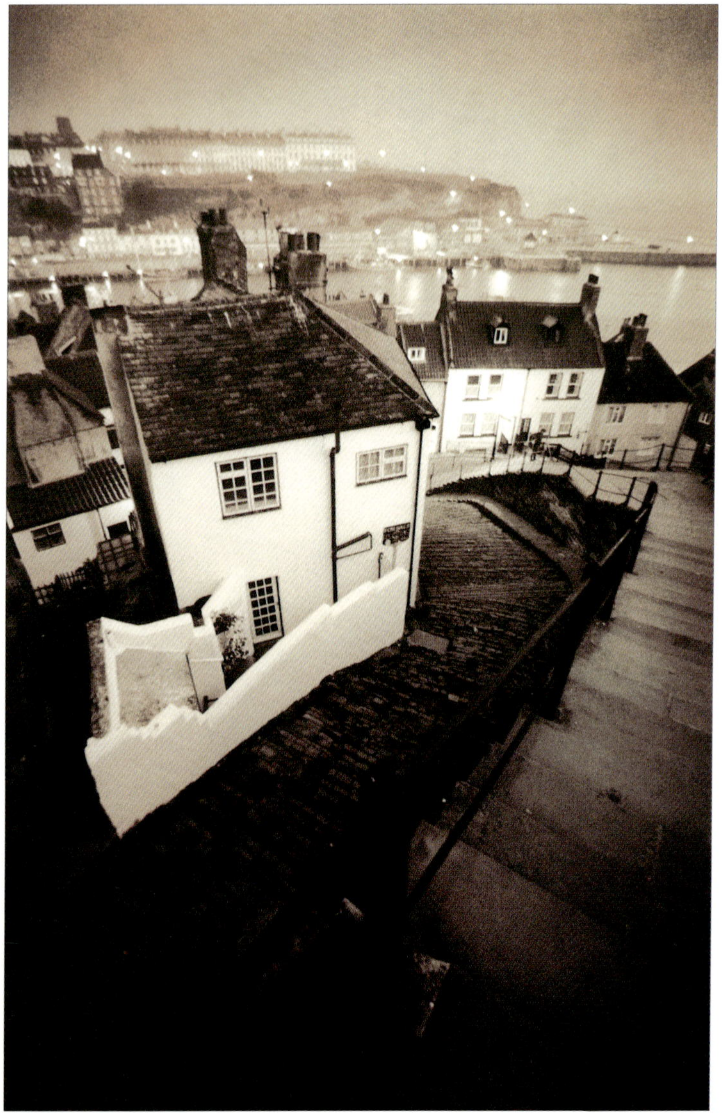

Whitby steps

Whitby steps

An improvised night shot in the sense that I had not intended to take any night photographs, so I was carrying the equipment for something else at the time. The light was beginning to go, and as I packed up the gear and made my way up the steps back to the car, I turned to see the view. The camera was fitted with a super wide lens so I just lifted it to my eye out of interest to see how much of the scene could be captured, and as I looked through the viewfinder I thought – WOW! – toytown at night. I leant against a post for stability, took one shot for fun and walked back to the car.

Because the light was low and I had no tripod, the lens could not be stopped down. The exposure had to be a compromise between lack of sharpness in the corners due to insufficient depth of field, and lack of sharpness all over due to a long hand held exposure. I would have preferred a sharp image, but this was the only possibility, and I believe that I would rather have a slightly soft picture than none at all.

The picture was printed with the minimum of manipulation, jut a little darkening of the sky, and toned with sepia bleach and re development in old paper developer.

Terrace end in snow

With this picture, I did without a meter reading and estimated the exposure to be 36seconds at f11/16. I knew that at that setting, I would have all the highlights and mid tones correct, because I had exposed quite a few other images in this kind of lighting.

What I was a little unsure about, was how the heavy branches in the foreground would appear in the final print. In a situation like this, a spot meter is useless, because it can't read such low exposure values. The best technique for judging tonal similarity in low light is the highly technical practice known as squinting.

When you squint, it has the effect of 'stopping down' your eyes to a smaller aperture, giving you the impression of more depth of field, and darkening the image on your retina, utilising less of the cones. This gives a more monochrome image.

Looking at the scene through squinted eyes therefore, gave me a darker more monochrome view of the picture. If I could see a similarity of tone between the foreground and background, then I had a pretty good idea that it would record on film.

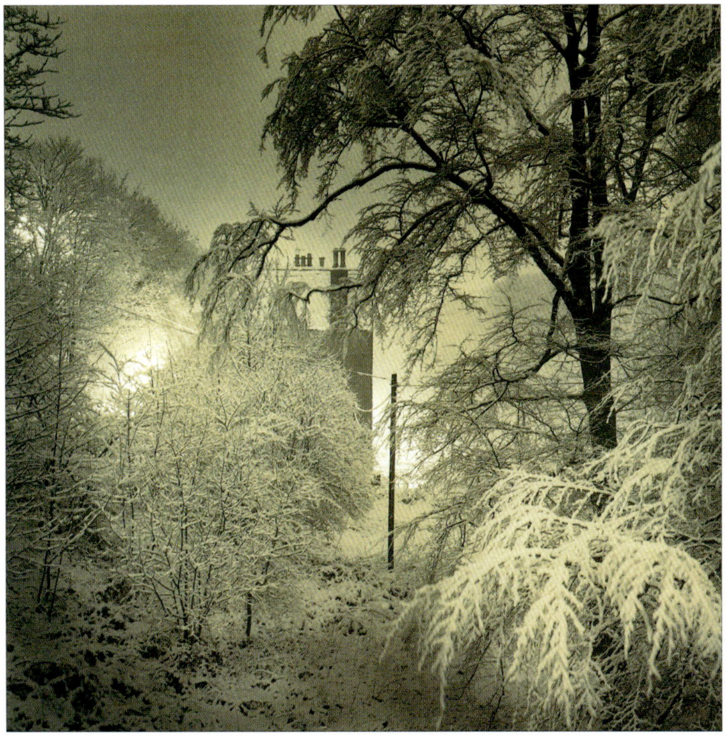

Terrace end in snow

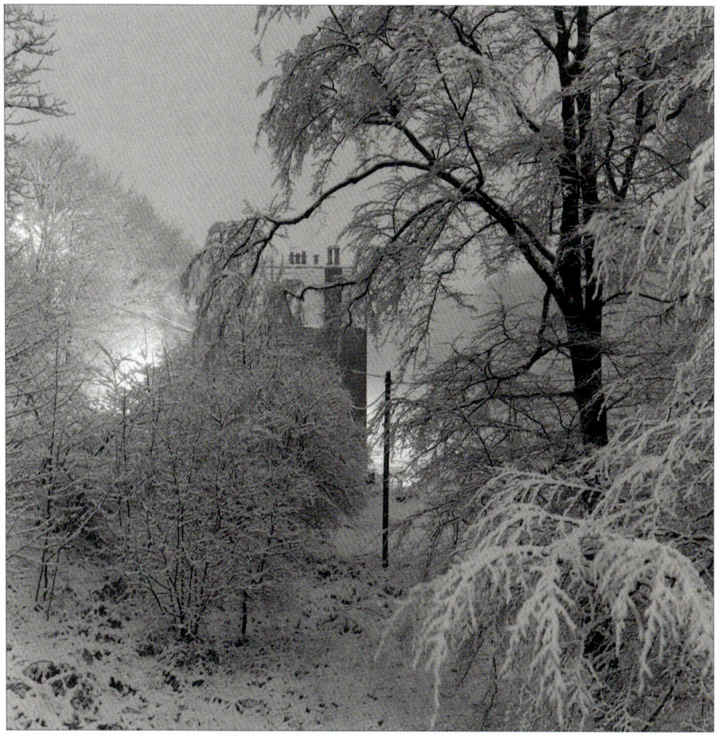

Unmanipulated print

The snowy branches in the lower right of the picture looked to be similar in tone to the roof and sky, so I exposed the frame as I had intended, exposing only one frame.

My confidence was rewarded with a full negative that can be printed, without any additional work, on a grade 2. After printing an unmanipulated version, I decided to give it a little attention anyway, to see if I could improve on it.

The sequence was as follows;

1. The base exposure was eleven seconds, and during this I dodged out two small areas for two seconds each.

2. The sky was exposed in three stages, giving half a stop extra for each, to draw the eye down.

3. I gave another half stop to the centre left and the same to the centre right, where I felt that a slightly darker area would draw the attention toward the more important parts of the print.

4. I could see that there were areas in the lower left that did little for the composition, and were even a little distracting, so I toned these down with an extra half stop.

5. Finally I gave an extra two thirds of a stop for the extreme bottom left.

All of the exposures were done at grade 2. The print was then lightly toned in sepia to warm up the highlights, followed by a blue toner for the shadows and mid tones.

The combination of these two toners works very well for this picture, the slight blue imparting a coldness to the scene, and the small areas of sepia corresponding to the warmer orange lights.

traffic problems/unwanted attentions

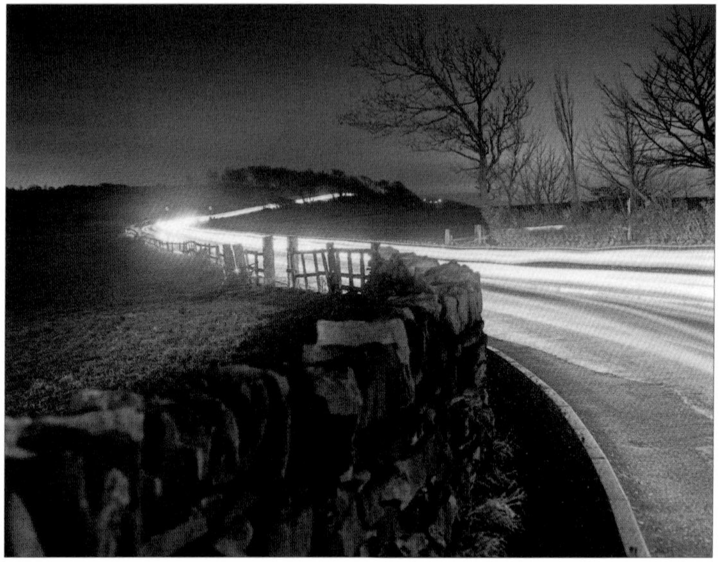

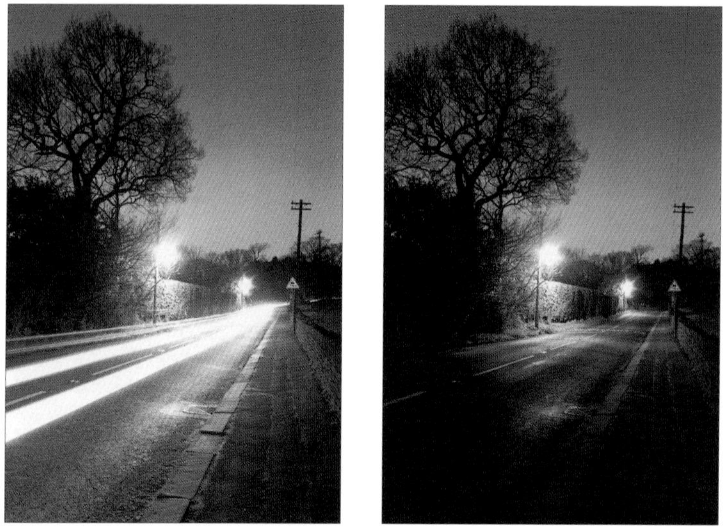

Two pictures that illustrate how car headlights can be avoided in a situation with intermittent traffic. A piece of card was held over the lens whenever a car appeared and the amount of time that the lens was covered was noted and added to the exposure.

Traffic problems

Apart from the technical obstacles to successful photography at night, such as focussing, exposure, reciprocity failure, contrast and colour casts, the night photographer must also cope with the inconvenience of traffic.

Often, a scene is selected, the camera mounted on the tripod, an exposure is decided on, and everything is ready.

Just at that point the previously tranquil scene becomes busy with traffic and continues unabated until one minute after the gear has been dismantled and packed away. At which point, the scene reverts back to its previously tranquil state.

Obviously this is an exaggeration, but it is quite close to the truth, and anyone who has experience of night photography will enjoy a wry smile of recognition.

Sods law will provide you with plenty of traffic when you wish to have none of it and will remove all cars for miles around when your intention is to make a feature of it!

As always in photography, the standard of your work is directly related to the amount of patience you are willing to apply.

Light trails or no light trails?

Sometimes the light trails left by cars can introduce a sense of movement, but this is not always desirable. The bright lines that headlights leave through the image can dominate the composition and destroy a subtle photograph.

In situations where traffic is intermittent or occasional, if a traffic free shot is your intention, it can be frustrating to try to time the exposure between cars. A simple method that will help in these situations is to have a piece of black card that can be held in front of the lens for the duration of the offending vehicle.

To ensure that the length of exposure is not affected, count how long the card is held over the lens and add this to the exposure.

People

Less common, but equally inconvenient, are people who approach you to ask what you are doing. Your response is of

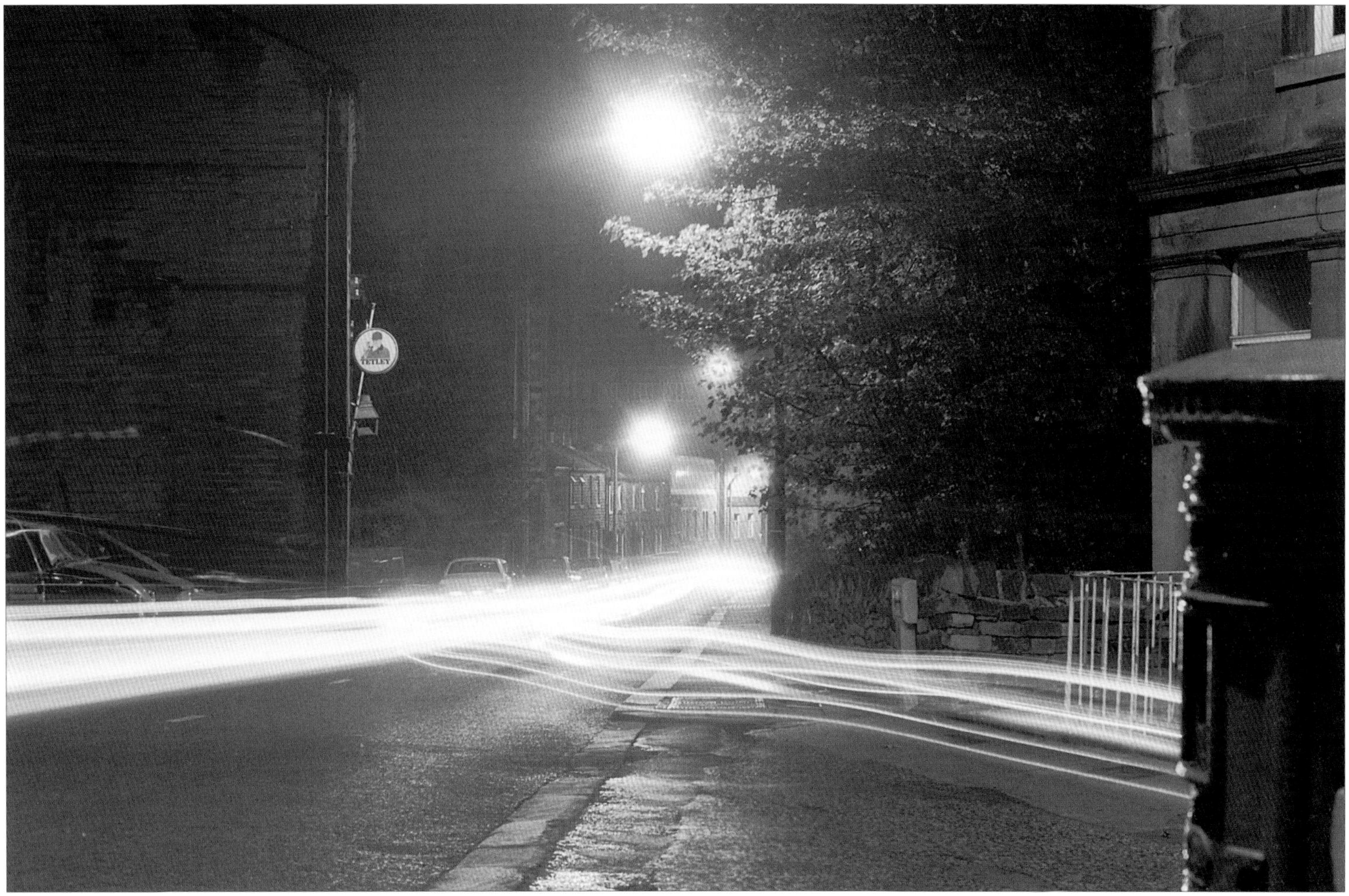

Car headlights can add movement to a picture or totally ruin a good nightscape. If you wish to prevent light trails from recording on the film, simply cover the lens until the vehicle has passed.

course, "taking photographs", which usually prompts the reply "but you haven't got a flash" - don't bother with detailed explanations of the finer points of night photography – just smile, and show them this book. If the person who approaches you is inebriated, and you believe that the situation could become difficult should you insist on working without their help, you may like to adopt my own method; ask them to stand in the scene whilst you take a picture of them (it's a good idea to carry a flash for this eventuality), take their name and address so that you may send them a print when the film is processed (whether you do or not is entirely up to you), thank them for their co-operation, and proceed on your way. This will usually resolve the situation, it is very unlikely that anyone is going to cause you any trouble after your kind offer, and especially when you have their address.

Formulae and calculations

Safety

- Never smoke in the darkroom.
- Never take food or drink into the darkroom.
- Always keep chemicals clearly labled and out of the reach of children.
- Add chemicals in correct order.
- Clean up spillages immediately.
- Wear rubber gloves whenever practical, avoid skin contact.
- Use clean vessels.
- Don't identify chemicals by smell or taste.
- Mix in a well ventilated place.
- Be clear about which chemicals you are using.
- Don't confuse these; Sulphate, sulphite, sulphide, bisulphate, bisulphite.
- Don't confuse these; Chlorate, chloride. Ferric, Ferrous.
- Always dispose of waste chemicals by washing away with plenty of water.

Developers

Standard film developer (similar to ID11 and D76)

Metol, 2g
Sodium sulphite, 100g
Hydroquinone, 5g
Borax, 2g
Water, 1 litre

Development times at 20 deg celsius

Ilford HP5, 7min30s
Ilford FP4, 6min
Ilford Delta 3200 11 min
Ilford Delta 400, 7min
Ilford Delta 100, 8min30s
Kodak Tri-x, 7min30s
Kodak Plus-x, 7min
Kodak T.max 3200, 11min
Kodak T.max 400, 7min
Kodak T.max 100, 8min
Agfapan 400, 10min
Fuji neopan 400 7½ min

Two bath

This is the original stockler formula, and the one I have found produces good results.

bath 1

Metol, 5g
Sodium sulphite, anhyd, 100g
Water to make, 1 litre

bath 2

Borax, 10g
Water to make, 1 litre

Pyro

This is made up as two stock solutions and diluted for use.

stock solution 1

Metol, 10g
Sodium bisulphite, 20g
Pyrogallol, 100g
Distilled/de-ionised water, 1 litre

Mixing;

Make up at 20 deg celsius.
Measure the quantity of sodium bisulphite, and add a pinch to the water. Save the rest until after the metol has been mixed.
Add the metol and stir until completely dissolved.
Add the rest of the bisulphite, and stir until completely dissolved.
Carefully add the pyrogallol (this chemical must not be inhaled), and stir until completely dissolved (remember, this chemical is extremely toxic).
Label the bottle clearly.

stock solution 2

Distilled water, 1400ml
Sodium metaborate, 600g
Water to make up to 2 litres

Mixing

It is important to use distilled or de-ionised water for stock solution 2.

Dissolve the sodium metaborate at 20 deg celsius. Do not worry if it will not dissolve completely. The last bits will go after 24 hours and it is still usable at this stage.

Water is then added to make up the full quantity.

Label the bottle clearly.

These solutions will last for a very long time if stored properly. Gordon Hutchings, who wrote the difinitive book on pyro, claims over ten years. This is probably just as well, because only a very small amount of the stock solution is used at any one time.

Take one part of solution 1, two parts of solution 2, and mix with 100 parts of water.

This translates as; 1ml of No 1, 2ml of No 2, and 100ml of water.

When these are mixed the colour will change, from a greeny colour, to a pale orange.

This shows that everything is ok.

If there is no colour change, or the colours are different, then check you have the correct bottles and have mixed to the correct strength.

Development

Pre soak the film for two minutes at 20 deg celsius.

Pour in the solution and agitate continously for the first 30 seconds.

The agitation for the rest of the process is important – more so than with conventional processing.

The recommended sequence is; invert and twist at the same time – quite vigourously. Give two of these, every 15 seconds. This is to prevent oxidised products in the solution from causing uneven streaking. The tank must be left alone – unagitated in between each inversion cycle. Keep the used developer, it is needed again at the end of the process.

The processing times, and recommended speeds for a number of fast and medium speed films are as follows;
Ilford FP4, 80 ISO, 10 min
Ilford HP5, 320 ISO, 13 min
Ilford Delta 100, 80 ISO, 11 min
Ilford Delta 400, 320 ISO, 12 min
Kodak Tri-x, 260 ISO, 14 min
Kodak T-max 100, 80 ISO, 12 min - ensure full fixing
Kodak T max 400, 400 ISO, 15 min
Agfapan 100, 80 ISO, 13 min
Agfapan 400, 200 ISO, 16 min

Some of the films have slight differences in speed rating, and processing times between roll and 35mm. Test to determine what is correct for your own way of working.

For processing details for slow films (and much more), refer to the pyro book by Gordon Hutchings, published by Bitter dog press, California.

The process does not end with the special development, the stop bath needs to be mixed weaker than normal, about a tenth of its normal strength. A plain water rinse can be substituted.

Fixing is carried out using a plain hypo solution, the Kodak F-24 formula is recommended.

Kodak F-24 fix

Water at 50deg celsius, 600ml
Sodium Thiosulphate, cryst (hypo), 240g
Sodium Sulphite, anhyd, 10g
Sodium Metabisulphite, 25g
Water to make, 1 litre

Immediately after fixing, the used developer is returned to the tank for two minutes, and agitated every 30 seconds. This is an important part of the staining process.

Wash for 30 minutes. Give a final rinse in distilled or de-ionised water, with a drop of wetting agent added.

Don't be alarmed if the negative looks thin. This is normal. Judge density by printing.

Toners

Bleach for sepia

Potassium ferricyanide, 100g
Potassium bromide, 100g
Water, 1 litre

This is quite a strong solution and will bleach very quickly, for more control and longer bleaching times dilute with an equal part of water.

Sepia-thiocarbamide

Thiocarbamide, 50g
Sodium hydroxide, 50g
Water, 1 litre

Sepia-sulphide

Sodium sulphide flake, 35g
Water, 1 litre

Blue

Solution A - Potassium ferricyanide, 3g
Sulphuric acid (10%), 50ml
Water, 1 litre
Solution B - Ferric ammonium citrate, 3g
Sulphuric acid (10%), 50ml
Water, 1 litre
Mix equal parts of each and use immediately.

Red

Solution A - Copper sulphate, 15g
Potassium citrate, 100g
Water, 1 litre
Solution B - Potassium ferricyanide, 10g
Water, 1 litre
Mix equal parts of each and use immediately.

CHART FOR DETERMINING DEVELOPMENT TIME WHEN DOWNRATING FILMS

To determine the adjustment, choose the number down the left hand side of the chart that corresponds with the correct time for your film. Read across the line to the position for a 20% reduction, or a 30% reduction, and read off the new time.

Indicated time	20% reduction	30% reduction
20m 1200s	16m	14min
19.30m 1170s	15m 36s	13m 40s
19m 1140s	15m 12s	13m 20s
18.30m 1110s	14m 48s	12m 55s
18m 1080s	14m 24s	12m 35s
17.30m 1050s	14m	12m 15s
17m 1020s	13m 36s	11m 55s
16.30m 990s	13m 12s	11m 30s
16m 960s	12m 48s	11m 12s
15.30m 930s	12m 24s	10m 50s
15m 900s	12m	10m 30s
14.30m 870s	11m 36s	10m 9s
14m 840s	11m 12s	9m 53s
13.30m 810s	10m 48s	9m 27s
13m 780s	10m 24s	9m 6s
12.30m 750s	10m	8m 45s
12m 720s	9m 36s	8m 24s
11.30m 690s	9m 12s	8m 3s
11m 660s	8m 48s	7m 42s
10.30m 630s	8m 24s	7m 21s
10m 600s	8m	7m
9.30m 570s	7m 36s	6m 39s
9m 540s	7m 12s	6m 18s
8.30m 510s	6m 48s	5m 57s
8m 480s	6m 24s	5 36s
7.30m 450s	6m	5m 15s
7m 420s	5m 36s	4m 54s
6.30m 390s	5m 12s	4m 30s
6m 360s	4m 48s	4m 12s
5.30m 330s	4m 24s	3m 51s
5m 300s	4m	3m 30s
4.30m 270s	3m 36s	3m 9s
4m 240s	3m 12s	2m 48s

ten key steps to good night photography

1. Load your film and set the camera to 'B' before leaving the house.

2. Take along a stopwatch or timer.

3. Carry a torch.

4. Always use a cable release.

5. Use a tripod that is steady.

6. Use a reliable meter and an exposure reference chart.

7. Try to exclude lights from your viewfinder wherever possible.

8. Keep notes of your exposures.

9. Employ a contrast control process.

10. Return to the scene on another occasion if your exposure is incorrect.

end piece

There may seem to be rather a lot to take in within this book. Don't be put off attempting to try your own night photography, it can be rewarding at any level. To begin with, you may like to shoot a 24 exposure roll of Ilford XP2 Super and drop it in at the chemist or a one hour photo-shop. If you follow the exposure guides, you should have some very interesting (and exciting?) pictures. Don't forget that photography is about making pictures and it is all too easy to get wrapped up in the technical side and lose the pleasure aspect.

All that is necessary is patience, good luck with your pictures and don't try too hard, just enjoy the experience.

glossary

A

Acetate mask - A clear film that can be marked with felt pens or opaque paint to mask out areas during printing

Archival - Processing and washing in such a way that all traces of chemicals are removed from the print to ensure that the photograph may last as long as possible.

Automatic exposure - The ability of some cameras to set the shutter speed and/or the aperture to ensure the correct exposure. – sometimes inaccurate for night photography.

Automatic focus - A facility of some modern cameras to set the focus automatically, sometimes inaccurate for night photography.

B

Back lighting - When the predominant light source is coming from behind the subject or scene.

Bracketing - Taking more than one shot of the chosen subject, varying exposure of each frame to ensure one correct exposure.

Burning in - Giving selected areas of a print more exposure.

C

Cable release - A device for firing the shutter remotely

Cast - An overall colour or tint on a colour photograph.

Chlorobromide - Black and white photographic paper with a higher proportion of chloride than bromide, giving a print with a slight colour which can vary from brown to olive.

Chromogenic film - Black and white film which utilises colour technology. The silver image is converted to a dye image during processing.

Contrast control - Any method which can aid in keeping the scene brightness within the tonal range of the photographic paper.

Cyanotype - A process from the early days of photography which produces a blue image.

D

Density - The depth of black in a negative.

Depth of field - The amount in focus, in front of and behind whatever is focussed upon, dependent upon the aperture.

Developer - Chemical solution used for converting the exposed image on paper into shades of grey or black.

Direct flash - Flash fired from the camera position

Dodger - A device to prevent light from reaching the photographic paper for part of the exposure, used to lighten an area.

Double exposure - Combining two images on one frame of film.

Down rating - Exposing a film at less than the manufacturer's recommended rating (overexposing) and reducing development times.

Dry down - The slight darkening of a print as it dries.

E

Emulsion - Light sensitive coating on films and photographic paper.

Exposure - When light reaches the film, usually understood to mean the moment a picture is taken.

F

Fill in - Using a separate light source to illuminate areas that would otherwise be underexposed.

Flare - Stray light scattering inside the lens causing a degrading of the image.

Flashing - Exposing the photographic paper to diffused white light for a short time prior to making the main print exposure. Used to reduce the contrast of the paper.

f-stop - The term for any aperture setting or difference between apertures

Format - The size and shape of a negative.

G

Gold - Chemical solution used to change the colour of a black and white print.

Grain - The light sensitive 'dots' that make up the image on a negative. Grain as we see it on the print, is actually light that has passed between the grains of the film to reach the paper.

Granularity - A description of the visibility of the grain on a photograph

H

Halation - An increase in density around an area of film, which has received an excessive amount of exposure, giving a halo effect. This is due to light scattering and spreading into the surrounding areas, and also because of what is known as 'Infectious development'.

High pressure sodium lamps - The most recently introduced form of street lighting, characterised by the bright, pale pink/orange colour of its illumination. These lamps usually have taller columns.

Hypo eliminator/ hypo clearing agent - A chemical used as part of the wash sequence to speed up removal of fix from the paper fibres.

I

Infectious development - Vigorous development action which spreads to adjacent areas when the image darkens rapidly after a long period of relative inactivity. It causes areas of increased density around bright lights on night negatives.

L

Light meter - A device for measuring the brightness of a scene, and converting this information to camera settings.

Lith film - A high contrast film which can be processed under red safelight.

Lith masking - Exposing onto high contrast Lith film to make a mask. After processing, the Lith is used to prevent light from reaching the photographic paper for part of the printing exposure. Many small areas can be burned in with one exposure using this technique.

Lith printing - Overexposing paper and processing in a vigorous high contrast developer, greatly diluted. This produces a unique type of print giving a contrasty image and a soft one, within the same print. Also gives a colour change without toning, the colour varies with paper type.

M

Mask - A sheet of clear film or glass, with areas of tone, ink or paint upon it, which is used to prevent light from reaching the paper for part of the exposure. Can also be made from black card with cut out shapes.

Medium format - A term used to describe a film size, or camera which is larger than 35mm, but smaller than 5x4 inches. Also known as roll film.

Mercury vapour - An older, less common type of street light, with distinctive white illumination. Produces a greenish colour on colour film.

O

Overexposure - Too much light has reached the film.

P

Painting with light - Using a separate, portable light, usually a torch, to increase the exposure in one or more areas during a long exposure.

Plate camera - A camera from the early days of photography which used light sensitive glass 'plates' instead of film.

Previsualising - Seeing the finished image in your mind before exposure.

Printing map - A number of sketches used to illustrate the sequence of exposures and dodgings/burnings-in for a particular print.

Processing - Chemical solution used for converting the exposed image on film into shades of grey.

Pyro - A film processing solution or technique, which produces negatives with greatly reduced contrast. A very toxic developer.

R

Reciprocity failure - The breakdown in the relationship between exposure times and apertures which occurs with exposures of more than one second.

Roll film - Film with a paper backing, used in medium format cameras.

S

Selenium - Single solution toner producing reddish brown tones.

Sepia - Two bath toner for producing brown tones.

Sheet film - Individual pieces of film for large format cameras.

Sodium lamps - Common orange streetlights.

Split grade printing - Exposing paper to more than one grade of paper to achieve maximum control.

Split toning - Combining two or more toners to get a combination of colours.

Stopping down - Closing the aperture of the lens down to a smaller 'hole', reducing the exposure and increasing depth of field and depth of focus.

Stops - Apertures, or the difference between them

T

Toning - Using chemicals to alter the colour of a print.

Tungsten halogen - Type of lamp usually used in security lighting.

Two bath process - Contrast reducing development technique.

U

Underexposure - Not enough light has reached the film.

V

Variable contrast - Photographic papers which have two light sensitive layers, one which responds to green light, and gives a very low contrast image, and one which responds to blue light, and gives a very high contrast image. The print exposure is made through one or more 'subtractive' filters, which remove the unwanted colour to differing degrees, according to which filter is chosen, producing a range of contrasts.

W

Warm tone papers - Photographic papers containing a large proportion of chloride, which imparts a 'warmth' to the overall colour of the print. Also referred to as chlorobromide papers.

Index

5x4 camera 28

Accelerators 78
Adding light 40
Alfred Steiglitz 8
Alvin Langdon 8
Ansel Adams 90
Aperture bracketing 69
Archivalling 101
Assessing the scene 90
Automatic camera 14

Balance 14
Base exposure 113
Basic equipment 110
Bleach 104
Blue toner 72, 105, 106, 107, 110, 118
Bracketing 30, 32, 33
Brassai 8
Burning in 82, 89, 90

Cable release 18
Calculations 116
Camera shake 16
Cameras 14
Card masks 90
Chloro-bromide 107
Chromogenic films 24, 80
Cityscapes 20
Coburn 8
Colour casts 60
Colour change 101
Colour film 58, 69
Coloured gels 61
Combining negatives 70
Combining toners 113
Compressing highlights 80
Computer manipulation 70
Contact sheet 63
Contrast control 61, 82
Contrast problems 24
Contrast range 64, 92
Contrast reduction 33
Controlling verticals 28
Coping with contrast 76
Correct exposure 6, 20, 26, 40
Creating a moon 75
Creative photographer 45, 61, 63
Cross processing 61

Deciding on exposure 69
Determining exposure 8, 30
Developer activity 35
Developer tanks 78
Developers 116
Developing agents 78
Development 117
Development by inspection 76
Development times 79, 116
Dilute development 79
Disciplines 8
Dodger 85
Dodging 82
Down rating 33, 37, 61, 77
Down-rating chart 119
Dry down 89

Effective film speed 64
Equipment 14
Experimenting 6, 30
Exposure by moonlight 64, 66, 67, 69
Exposure increase chart 29
Exposure inertia 86
Exposure times 86

Fill in flash 40, 43, 61
Film speed 20
Film speed reduction 37
Film types 24
Filtering 58
Filtration 80
Final aperture 30
Fixed grade paper 80
Flagging 35, 37
Flare 16, 34, 35, 39, 80
Flash gun 18, 40
Flashing 87, 111
Flat bed field camera 29
Fluorescent tubes 60
Fog 45
Fogging 34, 87
Foliage 13
Format 27
Formulae 116

Glass plates 76
Gloves 18
Gold toner 101, 108
Good light 13
Good night photography 120
Gordon Hutchins 117
Grain doubling 70

Halation 34, 35, 80
Halo 37, 110

Hand-held photographs 63
Hand meter 30
Headlights 114
High contrast 33
History of photography 8

Ideal conditions 13
Improving the print 101
Improvised night shot 112
Incident reading 111
Infectious development 35, 97
Infra red 25
Intensity 20

Karl Struss 8
Kodak F-24 117

Learning curve 11
Lens aperture 34
Lenses 14
Light reading 80
Lighting range 11
Lighting techniques 41
Lighting types 20
Lith film 89, 90, 93, 94
Lith masking 90, 92, 95, 96, 111
Lith printing 97, 98
Local reduction 82
Long exposures 40
Long lens 16
Lowering contrast 86

Manual camera 14
Margaret Bourke White 8
Mask alignment 92, 93
Masking frames 93
Medium format 28
Mercury vapour 20
Metering 29, 30, 109
Mixed lighting 60
Modern films 76
Moon brightness 64
Moon negatives 70
Moonlight 67
Moonlit landscape 72

Negative contraction 33
Negative detail 67
New possibilities 8
Night exposures 20
Notebook 18

O. Winston Link 8
Older lenses 34
Opaque masking 94
Overexposure 80, 111

Painting with light 42
Paper developer 94
Paper type 103
Paul Diamond 8
People 114
Permanence 103
Personal preferences 23
Perspective control 28
Pictorial possibilities 42
Pin register 93, 94
Polaroid film 25, 26
Potassium ferricyanide 108
Pre flash 86, 87, 88, 89, 90
Print exposure 85
Printing 76
Printing maps 85
Printing style 11
Processing 76
Pyro 64, 80, 81, 109, 116
Pyro development 79
Pyrogallol 79

Quality prints 82

Radio 18
Range of colour 105
Reading an exposure 33
Reciprocity correction 27
Reciprocity failure 25, 29, 32
Red filter 75, 93
Red toner 106, 107, 108, 118
Reducing flare 45
Reflected flash 40
Registration 88
Relative exposure times 23
Richard Misrach 8
Rising front 28
Robert Adams 8
Roll film camera 28, 109

Safelight 92
Seeing in colour 69
Selective flashing 90
Selenium toner 72, 106, 107, 108, 110
Sepia toner 101, 103, 106, 107, 110
Sepia bleach 117
Sepia sulphide 118
Sepia thiocarbamide 118
Serious work 27
SFX 25
Sharpness 112
Shielding the lens 34, 35
Shift 28
Shooting in fog 45, 54
Shooting in snow 42
Simulating night sky 75
Sodium light 6, 20, 34, 58
Spectral bandwidth 34
Speed loss 80
Split grade printing 82, 84
Split printing 99
Split toning 108
Stain 79
Static development 79

Stock solutions 116
Stopping down 112
Stopwatch 18
Stray light 34
Streaky negatives 78
Street lighting 6, 60, 103
Styles 101
Supplementary lighting 40
Swing 28

Tea staining 103, 107, 110
Technical obstacles 114
Test exposure 81
Test strips 86
Testing 99
Thermos 18
Thiocarbamide 104
Threshold exposure 87
Tilt 28
Time chart 119
Tonal range 90, 97
Toner type 103
Toners 117
Toning 101
Toning for permanency 101
Toning tips 106
Torch 18
Tracing paper 88
Traffic problems 114
Transparency film 58
Tripod 112
Tripod 16
Two bath developer 116
Two bath development 77, 78

Underexposed negative 81
Underexposing in sunlight 75
Uprating films 79
Using a torch 42
Using colour film 58

Variable contrast paper 89
Vibration 16
Viewfinder 34
Viewing a scene 90
Visualisation 112

Washing 104
Which grade 85
William Fraser 8
William Mortensen 79
Wooden plate camera 9

Zone system 33
Zoom lenses 29